Anthony S. Rudd

Implementing Practical DB2 Applications

With 69 Figures

 Springer

Anthony S. Rudd, MS(Hons)
Datev eG
Paumgartnerstrasse 6-14
D-90426 Nuremberg, GERMANY

ISBN-13: 978-3-540-19953-3   e-ISBN-13: 978-1-4471-1035-4
DOI: 10.1007/978-1-4471-1035-4

British Library Cataloguing in Publication Data
Rudd, Anthony S.
  Implementing practical DB2 applications. - 2nd ed.
  1.DB2 (Computer program) 2.Database management - Computer programs
  I.Title
  005.7'56'5
ISBN-13: 978-3-540-19953-3

Library of Congress Cataloging-in-Publication Data
A catalog record for this book is available from the Library of Congress

The use of registered names, trademarks etc. in this publication does not imply, even in the absence of a specific statement, that such names are exempt from the relevant laws and regulations and therefore free for general use.

The publisher makes no representation, express or implied, with regard to the accuracy of the information contained in this book and cannot accept any legal responsibility or liability for any errors or omissions that may be made.

Typesetting: camera ready by author

34/3830-543210 Printed on acid-free paper

Preface

The title of this book "IMPLEMENTING DB2 APPLICATIONS" reveals the purpose I had in writing it: a concise, complete, source of information necessary for the development and implication of applications using IBM's DB2 relational database package in the MVS environment. When I started writing DB2 applications I was quite literally overwhelmed by the physical amount of literature available. And usually all of this literature was necessary as reference for the writing of an application, because the required information was distributed amongst the manuals. With this book I have tried to separate out that information necessary to put an application together. This book is hopefully more than a mere reference; it contains tips and notes I and my colleagues found out the hard way. I have tried to present this practical information in such a form that it is easy to find and use. I hope this will enable readers to spend more productive time developing applications, rather than trying to find out why something works in a particular way.

Good though the IBM manuals are, they suffer from two drawbacks:
·   they have now attained a size (and weight) that they are unwieldy to use;
·   reference manuals offer limited scope to explain background information or critique, where it might be required.

And who should read this book? Both beginners and experts. Beginners are lead through the steps required to put DB2 applications together; complete worked examples, large enough to be practical but devoid of superfluous detail, enable the DB2 novice to see what is necessary to implement a simple application. Experts have a compact reference for those features necessary to write a DB2 application. In particular, the mechanics of preparing and testing a DB2 application program.

What this book is not? This is not a book about SQL; there have been enough books published already on this subject. This book does not go into the details of writing SQL statements, although it is sufficiently detailed to serve as a basic reference, rather it describes how the various components fit together. Similarly, it does not treat the subjects of distributed applications and optimisation. Also, it does not discuss the internal processing and optimisation aspects of DB2 systems. These are all specialised topics, a discussion of which would conflict with the aim of having a compact book.

At this point I would like to thank Elke Berger for her help and suggestions for improvements.

Table of Contents

1

Introduction

A hard beginning maketh a good ending

Proverbs

John Heywood

1.1 DATABASE2 (DB2) ENVIRONMENT

DB2 is IBM's relational database system in the MVS operating system environment. DB2 operates with the MVS transaction processing subsystems: CICS, IMS and TSO, and in batch using CAF (or batch TSO). Figure 1.1 shows the DB2 operating environment.

DB2 offers connection support to both local and remote data stored in other DB2 subsystems and to other databases that support DRDA (Distributed Relational Database Architecture), for example, DB2/2.

The common interface to the DB2 data means that the same DB2 tables can be used by all three subsystems. This book only covers the TSO (Time Sharing Option) subsystem, as TSO, the name notwithstanding, is now a standard MVS component. However, the features discussed are generally applicable (provided the requirements for the particular subsystem are observed).

Although TSO is principally an on-line transaction processing system, it can also be invoked from batch. By this means, DB2, with certain restrictions, can also be used in the batch environment. Furthermore, application programs can use the CAF (Call Attachment Facility) interface to access DB2 tables without having to be in the DB2 environment. CAF itself makes the connection from the application program (typically in batch) to DB2. CAF is a specialised interface and should only be used by experienced database programmers, although a generalised CAF user interface may well be made available to application programmers.

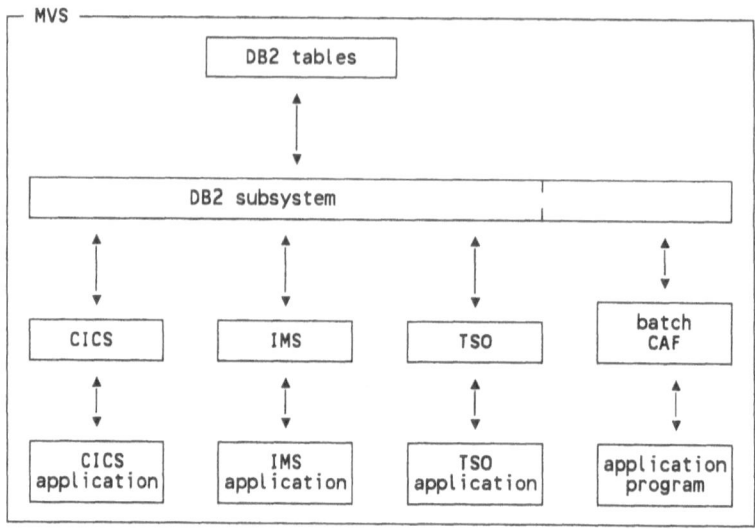

Figure 1.1 - DB2 operating environment

1.2 DB2 DATA OBJECTS

The DB2 data objects form a hierarchy:

- Databases   A database is a set of DB2 data objects.
- Table space   A table space is one or more data sets (files) that contains one or more tables. There are three forms of table space: simple, partitioned, and segmented.
- Table   A table is a named data collection of rows and columns. Any one table has the same columns.
- View   A view is an alternative representation of the data from one or more tables or views.
- Index   An index is a set of pointers to the data in a table. Indexes are optional, but can significantly improve performance.

1.3 ACCESS TO DB2 TABLES

Operations on data stored in DB2 tables are made using Structured Query Language (SQL). The name SQL is misnomer, as it is not restricted to processing queries, indeed it has three sub-languages:

· Data Definition Language (DDL).
· Data Manipulation Language (DML).
· Data Control Language (DCL).

DDL is used for the definition and modification of tables, indexes, etc. DCL is used for the definition and modification of authorisations, etc. (e.g. to grant access to a user table). DML is used to access and change data stored in DB2 tables. This book is principally concerned with DML.

1.4 USE OF SQL

SQL statements can be used in the following ways:
· embedded in an application program;
· as input to one of the subsystems or products which interface to DB2.

IBM provides three standard products to process SQL statements from the TSO environment:

· Query Management Facility (QMF).
· SQL Processor Using File Input (SPUFI).
· Cross System Product (CSP).

SPUFI is an integral part of the DB2 Interactive (DB2I) interface provided with DB2. QMF is a separately licensed product. CSP is an application generator, sometimes termed IBM's fourth generation language. QMF and SPUFI require the Interactive System Productivity Facility (ISPF). Figure 1.2 shows the SQL operating environment (the CAF interface, being essentially functionally equivalent to a TSO application, is not shown to avoid introducing unnecessary complexity into the diagram).

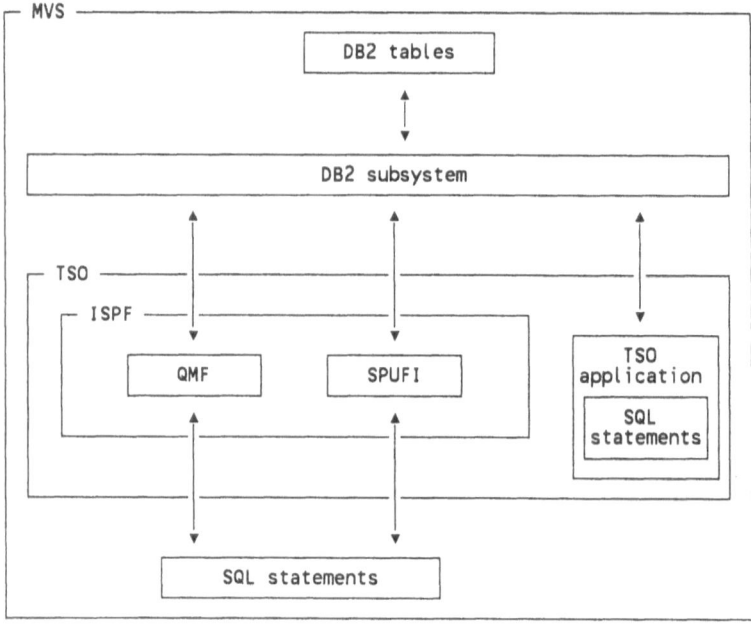

Figure 1.2 - SQL operating environment

1.5 USE OF SQL FROM APPLICATIONS

This book uses the following pragmatic definition of an application: An application is an interrelated sequence of operations to perform some function without requiring a knowledge of the underlying data base from the user of the application (data base here is used in its general sense).

Section 1.4 briefly discussed how SQL can be used. The two standard IBM products, QMF and SPUFI, are suitable for the direct processing of DB2 data. However, they do not satisfy my definition of an application. An application will usually require a more comprehensive operational interface which leads the user through the various steps. This is especially true for applications for end-users. An end-user is not restricted to being a person having limited data processing experience, rather it is someone who lacks knowledge of the underlying data base. A "professional" is also an end-user for applications other than his own. A well implemented application should remove unnecessary complexity from the user interface.
    The isolation of the user from the data base will normally require a dialogue, for which the IBM licensed product ISPF is ideally suited. ISPF is a dialogue management system operating in the TSO environment, and has the advantage of having interfaces to both QMF and SPUFI. SPUFI is primarily designed as an aid for the system developer and administration, and will not be further discussed concerning its use in applications. CSP has not yet reached such a wide acceptance

to be of general interest. This leaves two practical methods of using SQL for applications:

·   QMF via ISPF and Command Procedure (REXX exec or CLIST);
·   as embedded statements in a program (**embedded SQL**).

These two methods will be further described in the following chapters.

An increasing number of third-party products that are becoming available as front-ends to DB2 accept SQL input. Similarly, DB2 interfaces for REXX allow REXX to be used as a script language for DB2 applications. This book restricts itself to standard IBM products, and so does not discuss these topics.

2

Application Design

The bearings of this application lays in the application on it.

Dombey and Son
Charles Dickens

2.1 INTRODUCTION

Application design as used in this book does not take into consideration the administrative functions, such as: data modelling, performance, etc. These important aspects are so complex as to warrant a specialised book.

Figure 2.1 shows the simplified schematic flow for a "typical" application, based on the definition of an application from Section 1.4. The figure depicts that the original "query" by itself is not sufficient to produce the required results, rather the returned results are reformatted to produce the next "query". The worked example in Chapter 11 illustrates this technique.

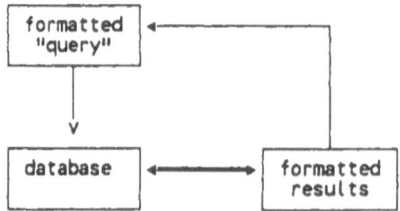

Figure 2.1 - "Typical" application flow

The form and complexity of the "query" may well depend on the class of user, for example, a DB2 expert may be capable of formulating SQL queries, whereas other users are limited to supplying values in predefined panels.

2.2 APPLICATION CONSIDERATIONS

The design of applications using the DB2 database is based on a number of criteria, some of which are:

·   Is the application to run as a dialogue or as batch?
·   Are the queries (database accesses) static or dynamic; i.e. can the structure of the queries be predefined?
·   May database values be altered and, if so, are the changes to be made only in a controlled manner?
·   What rights (authorisations) must the end-user have?

The answers to these questions significantly influence the design of the database application.

2.2.1 Dialogue or Batch?

Chapter 1 showed that DB2 primarily operates in dialogue environments (TSO or CICS). Although TSO was designed as a time sharing (dialogue) system, the TSO program can also run as a batch job. Batch TSO is subject to the usual restrictions of a batch job; the input must be predefined, as no dialogue with the user can take place, etc. Similarly, the components which operate in the TSO environment (DB2, ISPF, QMF, etc.) can also be invoked from batch TSO to run as batch applications. Naturally, such batch applications are subject to the same constraints as batch TSO. There are, however, many practical uses for such non-dialogue applications, e.g. long-running queries, large reports.

Batch programs that use CAF to build the connection to the DB2 subsystem do not need to operate from batch TSO.

2.2.1.1 Batch TSO. Figure 2.2 shows typical JCL required to invoke batch TSO.

```
//stepname EXEC PGM=IKJEFT01,DYNAMNBR=20
//SYSTSPRT DD    SYSOUT=*
//SYSTSIN  DD    *
```

Figure 2.2 - Sample JCL statements to invoke batch TSO

Batch TSO requires the following JCL statements.

stepname
> The name to be given to the step. This entry is optional, but is useful for monitoring purposes if the job has more than one step.

PGM = IKJEFT01
> IKJEFT01 is the TSO terminal monitor program, i.e. what is generally referred to as TSO.

DYNAMNBR

The number of dynamic allocations which can be active at any one time. The number specified will depend on the number of ALLOC statements (implicit and explicit) used in the application; 20 usually will be sufficient.

SYSTSPRT

The file to contain the TSO list output.

SYSTSIN

The file containing the TSO input. The TSO input includes the TSO commands and subcommands, etc.

In addition to the job control statements required by TSO, the commands and programs invoked from the TSO batch job will normally require their own file allocations (DD statements) to be made. Refer to the command or program description for the required JCL statements.

2.2.2 Command Procedure

An application rarely consists of a single program call, rather it will usually involve one or more program calls with the associated services (file allocations, etc.). A script language or **command procedure** automates such application control processing.

TSO has two command procedure languages: CLISTs (command lists) and REXX execs. The CLIST language was the original TSO command procedure language, but has been largely superseded by REXX. Compared with CLISTs, REXX is a more powerful language with a large repertoire of built-in functions that can be extended with user-written interfaces.

2.2.3 Static or Dynamic SQL?

The use of static or dynamic SQL directly influences the application in the following manner:

· flexibility;
· performance.

Static SQL statements have a fixed form, although values may be specified as parameters. Dynamic SQL statements are created at run-time and so need not be hard-coded in the program; this **flexibility** means that the processing which the DB2 precompiler performs (authorisations, path analysis, etc.) for each statement must also be performed at run-time, this processing can be time consuming and so adversely affect the **performance**.

Indirectly, this flexibility can also have an effect on the overall security. With static SQL the allowed queries are predefined; with dynamic SQL those queries created must be validated by the program. A program using static SQL can itself be assigned authorisation, i.e. the user need only have authorisation to execute the program and not authorisation to perform the underlying functions (only the person binding the program must have these authorisations). For a program using dynamic SQL, the end-user must have the required authority for the created query. Section 2.2.4 contains a more detailed description of authorisations.

Flexibility is usually confined to the selection criteria. Although static SQL requires that the hard-coded SQL queries have a fixed structure, there are ways of creating a generalised criterion having a fixed structure. This can be done by defining a selection skeleton having all those allowed columns.

A selection criterion has the following general form:
column condition value
e.g. PNO = 2222

The **column** specifies the database (table or view) attribute. The **condition** and **value** will usually be variable. It is possible to generalise a selection criterion so that it can be parameterized in such a way that it always yields the required result. This can be achieved by introduced dummy values, based on the known range of values, when no specific value is supplied.

Example:
Assume that the database table has two columns: PNO (numeric) and PNAME (alphabetic); it is possible to construct a generalised static selection criterion of the form:
    PNO cond1 value1 logop PNAME cond2 value2
where the parameters are written in lowercase.

The selection criteria can be defined by assigning the required values to the two conditions: cond1 and cond2, the logical operator (AND or OR): logop, and the two values: value1 and value2. Table 2.1 shows those parameters required for generalised selection criteria. This table satisfies the 4 possible combinations of simple selection; the same logic could be used to extend the table to cater for selection ranges.

Table 2.1 - Generalised selection criteria

selection criterion	COND1	VALUE1	LOGOP	COND2	VALUE2
PNO = 11 AND PNAME = 'A'	=	11	AND	=	'A'
PNO = 11 OR PNAME = 'A'	=	11	OR	=	'A'
PNO = 11	=	11	AND	>=	' '
PNAME = 'A'	>=	0	AND	=	'A'

The logic shown in Table 2.1 is not suitable for columns which can contain null values and where a parameter for such columns is optional. Here a more comprehensive selection must be performed. For example: PNO >= 0 OR PNO IS NULL.

A simpler, although less transparent, method involves passing the search condition as parameter. The search condition must be specified within doubled-paired parentheses, with a null condition being simply a set of doubled-paired parentheses "(())". This method is restricted to being used with a procedure invoked externally, and is not officially described. The advantage of this method compared with that shown in Table 2.1 is that the number of parameters is reduced by a factor of three (or more). Table 2.2 shows the equivalent parameters for the same selection criteria shown in Table 2.1.

2.2.3.1 Example.

The CLIST statements:

```
SET &P1 = &STR(((PNO > 2222)))
SET &P2 = &STR(((OR PNAME = 'BETA')))
ISPEXEC SELECT PGM(DSQCCI) +
 PARM(RUN PROC (&&&&PP1 = &P1  &&&&PP2 = &P2)
```

invoke the procedure (PE1):

```
RUN QE1 (&&PQ1=&PP1 &&PQ2=&PP2
```

which invokes the query (QE1):

```
SELECT * FROM PERS WHERE &PQ1 &PQ2
```

which in turn generates the following query after substitution:

```
SELECT * FROM PERS WHERE PNO > 2222 OR PNAME = 'BETA'
```

The following REXX statements are equivalent to the above CLIST statements:

```
p1 = '((PNO > 2222))'
p2 = '((OR PNAME = 'BETA'))'
ADDRESS ISPEXEC 'SELECT PGM(DSQCCI)',
 'PARM(RUN PROC (&&&PP1 = 'p1 '&&&PP2 = 'p2')'
```

Note: The null string (()) is used to indicate that no selection condition applies for the parameter.

Table 2.2 - Parametric selection criteria

selection criterion	P1	P2
PNO = 11 AND PNAME = 'A'	((PNO = 11))	((AND PNAME = 'A'))
PNO = 11 OR PNAME = 'A'	((PNO = 11))	((OR PNAME = 'A'))
PNO = 11	((PNO = 11))	(())
PNAME = 'A'	(())	((OR PNAME = 'A'))

2.2.4 Changes to the Database

Any changes (insertions, deletions, updates, etc.) made to the database can affect its integrity. This was especially true of the earlier versions of DB2. However, there are few applications that can allow uncontrolled changes to be made to the database. This means that changes to the database will usually be made by special programs having update authorisation. Such programs should use static SQL, and the user need only be authorised to execute them. If the user also had update authorisation he could use other programs or QMF to make changes to the database.

2.2.5 Authorisation Considerations

SQL authorisations are made using the GRANT command; authorisations previously made are revoked using the REVOKE command. Because GRANT and REVOKE are not directly concerned with application development, they are not discussed in detail in this book, although some general aspects are described here.

The following use authorisations can be granted:
·   delete
·   insert
·   select
·   update.

The following plan (package = program) authorisations can be granted:
·   bind
·   execution.

2.3 WHICH PRODUCT TO USE

At the present time there are only two IBM products suited to be used to implement
DB2 applications in the TSO environment:
·   QMF (with ISPF and REXX (or CLIST));
·   application programs using embedded SQL (ESQL).

ESQL itself has two variants:
·   static;
·   dynamic.
Note: QMF uses dynamic SQL.

Table 2.3 summarises the principal aspects concerning the selection of the products
to be used.

Table 2.3 - Suggested product usage

operation	QMF	ESQL
fixed retrieval	x	static
variable retrieval	x	dynamic
update	x	static

update = change to database

3

QMF Facilities

The fatal facility of octosyllabic verse

The Corsair
Lord Byron

3.1 INTRODUCTION

QMF is the acronym for Query Management Facility. As in many cases, this product name is a misnomer. QMF is more concerned with the management of **objects**, one class of which are queries. This management takes the form of a dialogue application which enables the user to easily access the DB2 database and to have the results presented in a formatted manner. QMF facilities can also be used from application programs and command procedures, for example to access DB2 databases.

3.2 QMF OBJECTS

QMF manages the following objects:

· queries
· data
· reports
· forms
· procedures
· profile
· charts (indirectly).

The management of these objects is performed using QMF **commands**. The objects are processed in the corresponding internal **work area** (also known as **temporary storage area**), and may be stored (**exported** or **printed**) and retrieved (**imported**) from either the database or external datasets. Whereas QMF queries are SQL statements, the other objects are exclusive to QMF. Figure 3.1 shows the interaction of the QMF objects.

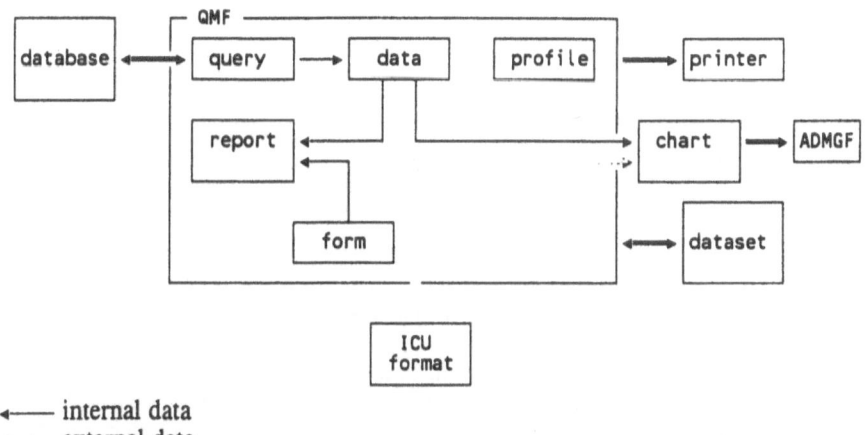

←——— internal data
←——— external data

Figure 3.1 Interaction of QMF objects

3.2.1 QMF Query

A QMF query is a statement and initiates an access, possibly complex, to the database; there are three forms of queries: SQL (Structured Query Language), QBE (Query by Example) or prompted query. Notwithstanding the name, a query can not only read but also update a database, etc. In most general terms, a query produces **data**. The size of such data can range from being extensive to non-existent. A query may have either a constant form or be parameterized, the current values for the parameters are either specified when the query is invoked or obtained from the user by prompting.

3.2.2 QMF Data

QMF data are produced in the **data work area** as a result of running a query. Data are formatted and displayed as a **report**. Exported QMF data have the same form as a DB2 table.

3.2.3 QMF Form

A QMF form defines the report format. Either default forms or user-defined forms may be specified. QMF forms offer a powerful report generation facility, which enables complex report formatting (such as subtotals) to be easily defined.

3.2.4 QMF Report

A QMF report is the formatted data produced as a result of running a query.

3.2.5 QMF Procedure

A QMF procedure is an aggregate of QMF commands, i.e. rather than invoking various QMF commands individually, the predefined invocation of these commands can be defined as a procedure. As for a query, a procedure can have either a constant form or be parameterized. Furthermore, the name of the procedure to be invoked can be specified as parameter when QMF is initiated from a command procedure.

3.2.6 QMF Profile

Each QMF user has his own QMF profile. The profile contains the standard options to be used during the QMF session, e.g. is a confirmation panel to be displayed before changes are made to an external object (database, dataset). The user can change certain defaults.

3.2.7 QMF Chart

Suitable results in the QMF data area can be presented graphically. The graphic presentation is known as a **chart**. QMF interfaces with ICU (Interactive Chart Utility, a part of the IBM GDDM/PGF product) to produce the chart. The chart may be either displayed or printed on suitable devices (graphics display terminal, e.g. 3129G, 3279G; graphics printer, e.g. 3287, 3268). QMF provides standard formatting options for charts, however, the experienced ICU user can use its full facilities.

3.3 QMF INVOCATION

QMF can be invoked in one of two ways:
·   as a DB2 application;
·   from a command procedure (REXX exec or CLIST) or application program.
CICS also supports a subset of QMF.

QMF can be invoked as a DB2 application from either TSO or CICS. QMF procedures can be used to automate the QMF processing. Although the direct invocation of QMF as a DB2 application is simpler than the second method, it is often less appropriate for practical applications, because for such applications the use of QMF should be largely transparent to the user. Transparency can be achieved by using an application-oriented dialogue interface, for which IBM's Dialog Manager (ISPF, Interactive System Productivity Facility) is ideally suited. Dialog Manager, as the name implies, is a system for the management of dialogue components (panels, that is, screen display definitions, etc.) and may be directly called from command procedures. The interaction of these various components is illustrated in Figure 3.2.

Two QMF interfaces are available:

·   the **Callable Interface**
·   the **Command Interface**

Whereas the Callable Interface can be used by both application programs and command procedures, the Command Interface can be used only by command procedures.

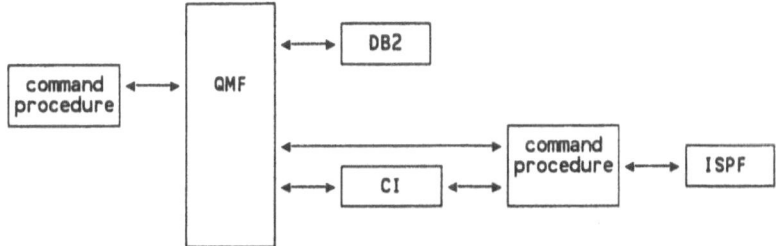

Figure 3.2 - Command procedure access to DB2 using QMF

As depicted in Figure 3.2, QMF is the central component in the dialogue application management. Thus, the facilities offered by QMF to a large extent determine the overall capabilities of the application.

3.4 QMF COMMAND FACILITIES

The command facilities offered by QMF can be broadly classified into the following groups:
- Transfer queries, forms, procedures or reports to/from the host system.
- Administer QMF objects;
- Invoke host system component (command procedure, etc.).

3.4.1 Transfer of QMF Objects to/from Host System

Import and export facilities to transfer QMF objects from, respectively to, the host system (MVS environment) are available. For example, QMF reports could be processed (formatted) using host system facilities.

3.4.2 Administration of QMF Objects

Administration of QMF objects involves such activities as displaying their contents, changing (editing) their contents, etc.

3.4.3 Invoke Host System Component

From an application point of view, one of the most useful QMF facilities (excluding QMF queries) is the ability to be able to pass control temporarily to a host system (TSO) component. Such a component can be a command procedure, which in turn can invoke ISPF facilities.

3.5 DIRECT INVOCATION OF QMF

QMF is a program (DSQQMFE) which executes in the ISPF environment. As such, it can be invoked from a command procedure in one of two ways, dependent on whether ISPF is currently active. In this method of invocation, QMF retains the control.

Syntax:

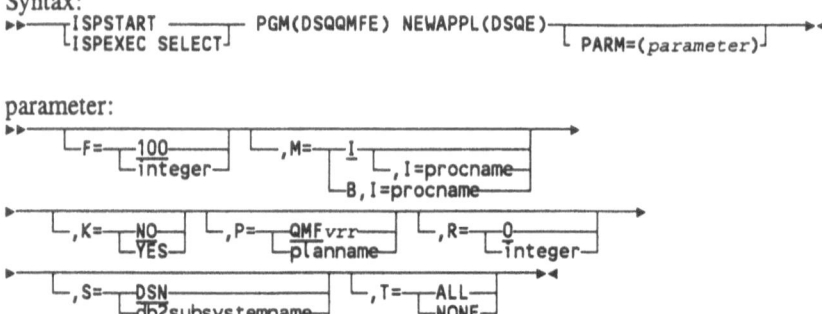

ISPSTART
Invoke the ISPF environment and select (execute) the specified component, in this case the DSQQMFE program.

ISPEXEC SELECT
Invoke the specified component from within the ISPF environment.

F=maxrows
Specify the maximum number of fetched rows; maximum 99,999,999. Default: 100.

M=mode
Specify the mode in which QMF is to operate:
B = batch
I = interactive (dialogue). This is the default.

I=procname
Specify the name of the QMF procedure which is to be invoked on initiation of QMF. This parameter is mandatory for batch operation (M=B). If this parameter is omitted, the QMF home panel is displayed on initiation of QMF.

K=DBCSsupport
Specify whether the terminal supports DBCS (Double-Byte Character Set) operation. This parameter may be specified as either:
YES
NO (default).

P=planname
Specify the name of the QMF application plan.

Default (QMF *vrr* — *v* = version, *rr* = release).

R = TSOsize

Specify the amount (in bytes) of virtual storage to be reserved by QMF in its work-areas for TSO commands; maximum 99,999,999 bytes. Default: 0.

S = subsystem

Specify the name of the DB2 sub-system. Default: DSN

T = traceoption

Specify the default QMF trace options. This option may be later overridden by the value from the user's QMF profile.

ALL   QMF tracing at its most detailed level.

NONE   (M-parameter = B) QMF tracing of messages and commands.

NONE   (M-parameter = I) no QMF tracing.

If a QMF procedure (**procname**) is specified, it is initiated and the display of the QMF home panel is suppressed.

Most dialogue applications require that the invoked QMF procedure returns control to the TSO/ISPF environment. This QMF procedure must be present in the database before QMF is invoked. Remember, QMF facilities can only be used in the QMF environment.

The name of a QMF procedure has the following general form:

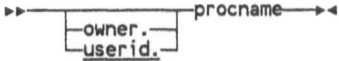

Tip

If a general application is being written, the initial QMF procedure should be made available as a public procedure. This obviates every user having to define the initiation procedure.

Example:

```
ISPEXEC SELECT PGM(DSQQMFE) NEWAPPL(DSQE) PARM=(M=I,I=ARAB000.ALPHA)
```

Initiate QMF and invoke the procedure ALPHA owned by ARAB000.

If the procedure ARAB000.ALPHA is defined as TSO %BETA, the TSO command procedure BETA is invoked. This TSO procedure could, for example, display an ISPF panel.

3.5.1 QMF Files

Table 3.1 lists the standard files required by QMF.

Table 3.1 - Primary QMF files (DD-names)

DSQDEBUG	M	user-specified trace information (may be set to DUMMY).
DSQUDUMP	O	QMF SNAP-dump if QMF terminates abnormally.
DSQPRINT	O	output from the QMF PRINT command.
DSQSPILL	O	auxiliary storage for report data which does not fit into available main-storage.
DSQEDIT	O	used by QMF EDIT command.
DSQUCFRM	O	library containing chart format members.
ADMGDF	O	used by QMF EXPORT CHART command.
ADMGGMAP	M	GDDM panel library.

M = mandatory, O = optional.

Note on Table 3.1: Other files may be required for supplementary products (e.g. ICU).

3.5.2 Sample CLIST for the Invocation of QMF

The sample procedure shows a sample CLIST for the invocation of QMF; in this example QMF is invoked with initial procedure ARAB123.PEX1.

```
PROC 0
CONTROL NOMSG
ALLOC F(ADMGGMAP) DSN('QMF.TEST.DSQMAPE') SHR REUS
ALLOC F(DSQDEBUG) DUMMY REUS
ISPEXEC SELECT PGM(DSQQMFE) NEWAPPL(DSQE) +
  PARM(S=DB2,M=I,I=ARAB123.PEX1)
FREE F(DSQDEBUG ADMGGMAP)
```

3.6 QMF CALLABLE INTERFACE

Application programs and REXX execs can use the QMF Callable Interface to pass commands to QMF and to receive returned data.

The communications area (the DSQCOMM) and a command are passed to the Callable Interface (the calling sequence is programming-language dependent).

The START command initiates the Callable Interface for the processing of QMF commands. The QMF EXIT command terminates the Callable Interface.

3.6.1 The DSQCOMM Communications Area

QMF uses the DSQCOMM to communicate with the application. For compiled programming languages (e.g. COBOL), the DSQCOMM is a data area defined in the invoking program. For REXX, the DSQCOMM fields are REXX variables.

The following DSQCOMM field names are shown in their COBOL form, the other languages (e.g. Assembler, REXX) substitute an underscore for the dash (e.g. DSQ_RETURN_CODE rather than DSQ-RETURN-CODE).

The DSQCOMM definitions are supplied as part of the QMF sample library. Application programs must include the appropriate definition with the source code

(COPY statement in COBOL, macro call in Assembler, #include directive in C/370, %INCLUDE directive in PL/I). The DSQCOMM definitions for COBOL and PL/I are actually declarations. The application needs to set only one field, the DSQ-COMM-LEVEL variable to the contents of DSQ-CURRENT-COMM-LEVEL that is contained in the DSQCOMM definition.

DSQ-RETURN-CODE
The QMF command status.

DSQ-SUCCESS   command successfully processed (0)

DSQ-WARNING   command successfully processed but with warnings (4)

DSQ-FAILURE   command not successfully processed (8)

DSQ-SEVERE   severe error; QMF session terminated (16).

DSQ-INSTANCE-ID
The identifier set by the QMF START command.

DSQ-COMM-LEVEL
The DSQCOMM level. The application should set DSQ-CURRENT-COMM-LEVEL from the DSQCOMM definition into this field.

DSQ-PRODUCT
The query manager product identifier.

DSQ-PRODUCT-RELEASE
The query manager release number.

DSQ-RESERVE1
A reserved field.

DSQ-MESSAGE-ID
The message identifier for the completed command.

DSQ-Q-MESSAGE-ID
The message identifier for the completed query.

DSQ-START-PARM-ERROR
The erroneous parameter, if the START command fails because of a parameter error.

DSQ-CANCEL-IND
The status of the QMF command as to whether it has been cancelled by the user: DSQ-CANCEL-YES or DSQ-CANCEL-NO.

DSQ-RESERVE2
A reserved field.

DSQ-RESERVE3
A reserved field.

DSQ-MESSAGE-TEXT
>   Command message text.

DSQ-Q-MESSAGE-TEXT
>   Query message text.

3.6.2 Callable Interface Invocation Syntax

The Callable Interface is language specific and is invoked with a language-specific function call; Table 3.1 lists the appropriate function names. The extended form is used for those commands that require parameters (START, SET GLOBAL, GET GLOBAL).

Note: The Callable Interface is very sensitive to the parameter format; invalid parameter formats can cause unexpected (and undocumented) errors (e.g. endless processing loops, addressing exceptions, etc.).

	Assembler	COBOL	C	PL/I	REXX
normal form	DSQCIA	DSQCIB	dsqcic	DSQCIPL	DSQCIX
extended form	DSQCIA	DSQCIB	dsqcice	DSQCIPX	DSQCIX
include file	DSQCOMMA	DSQCOMMB	DSQCOMMC	DSQCOMMP	-

3.6.2.1 Parameter List Format. The compiled languages (i.e. all languages except REXX) require the following parameters.

Number of variables
>   The number of keywords specified (fullword).

Keyword lengths
>   An array of fullwords that contains the length of the corresponding keyword.

Keywords
>   The list of the keywords that are to be passed to the interface.

Value lengths
>   An array of fullwords that contains the length of the corresponding value.

Values
>   The list of the values that are to be passed to the interface. Each value is assigned to the corresponding keyword.

Value type
>   The data type of the specified values. All the values for a call must have the same type, either character or fullword integer. Two calls must be made if the values are of different types. The DSQCOMM include file contains the definitions for the value type: DSQ-VARIABLE-CHAR (DSQ_VARIABLE_CHAR) or DSQ-VARIABLE-FINT (DSQ_VARIABLE_FINT) for character or fullword integer, respectively.

3.6.3 START Command

The START command initiates the Callable Interface, which completes the DSQCOMM. Only one entry in the DSQCOMM needs to be set; DSQ-COMM-LEVEL should be set to DSQ-CURRENT-COMM-LEVEL from the DSQCOMM definition. A list of the START parameters follows. All the parameters have default values. The START parameters are all character values.

DSQALANG
> The language to be used for messages, etc. Default: E (English).

DSQSBSTG
> The amount of storage (in bytes) that QMF is to use for report generation. Default: 0 (TSO, no limit) or 500000 (CICS). If a value is specified, it should be at least 15000 bytes. The DSQSRSTG value, if specified, takes precedence.

DSQSCMD
> The REXX exec that QMF invokes when receives control from the START command. The default exec DSQSCMDE initialises QMF-dependent information.

DSQSDBCS
> The DBCS support to be provided from SBCS terminals. The keyword value may be either YES or NO (default).

DSQSDBUG
> The debug option for tracing during the QMF initialisation. The keyword value may be either ALL or NONE (default).

DSQSIROW
> The number of result lines QMF will fetch prior to them being displayed. Default: 100.

DSQSMODE
> The QMF processing mode option. The keyword value may be either I (interactive) or B (batch, default).

DSQSPILL
> The option for the spill file availability. The keyword value may be either YES (TSO default) or NO (CICS default).

DSQSPLAN
> The DB2 application plan for QMF. Default: QMFVVRr (v = version, r = release). This option is available only for TSO.

DSQSPRID
> This option specifies which identifier is to be used to select from Q.PROFILES and to qualify the Q.ERROR_LOG entries. The keyword value may be either

PRIMEID (the primary authorisation identifier, default) or TSOID (the TSO login userid). This option is available only for TSO.

DSQSRSTG

The amount of storage (in bytes) that is available for QMF use. Default: 0 (no limit).

DSQSRUN

The name of the QMF procedure that is to be executed at the completion of the QMF initialisation phase. Default: NULL (no procedure).

DSQSSUBS

The name of the DB2 subsystem in which the QMF commands are to run. Default: DSN. This option is available only for TSO.

3.6.4 Examples

The following examples illustrate the use of the Callable Interface from the most commonly used programming languages (Assembler, COBOL, C/370, PL/I and REXX).

In all cases the processing is identical:

· Initialise the QMF Callable Interface to execute in the DSNT subsystem with the debugging mode set to ALL (START command).
· Set the two symbolic global parameters &PROG and &QNO to 'DEMO' and 5, respectively (two SET GLOBAL command calls with character and numeric parameters are required).
· Execute the QMF query SELECT * FROM PLAN_TABLE WHERE QUERYID > &QNO AND PROGNAME = &PROG. This query must have been made available as the QMF QPLAN query; i.e. the query has been stored in the QMF database with this name. Note: The two QMF commands IMPORT QUERY and SAVE QUERY can be used to automate the creation of a QMF query.
· Export the resulting QMF report to the RFILE report file (EXPORT REPORT command; the (CONFIRM=NO option allows the exported report to overwrite a currently existing file with this name, should it exist - QMF in batch mode terminates if a confirmation panel needs to displayed).
· Terminate the Callable Interface (EXIT command).

3.6.4.1 Assembler Interface. For simplicity, the sample Assembler program uses the TPUT service for message display. The TPUT service has two drawbacks: it can process only 24-bit addresses, and it operates only in the TSO environment.

```
QMFCIAO  CSECT
QMFCIAO  AMODE 31 required for Callable Interface
QMFCIAO  RMODE 24 required for TPUT
         BAKR  14,0    save registers and return address
         BALR  12,0    set base address
         USING *,12
         LA    13,SA   user save-area
         LOAD  EP=DSQCIA load Callable Interface
```

```
            ST      0,ADSQCIA store entry-point address
            LA      9,CICOMM  set user Communications Area
            USING DSQCOMM,9
            MVC     DSQ_COMM_LEVEL,DSQ_CURRENT_COMM_LEVEL
            MVC     VTYPE,DSQ_VARIABLE_CHAR
            MVC     CMDSTR,=C'START'
            MVC     CMDLEN,=F'5'
            MVC     KYWDNUM,=F'2' NUMBER OF KEYWORDS
            MVC     KYWD(8),=C'DSQSSUBS'
            MVC     KYWDLEN(4),=F'8'
            MVC     VALCHAR(4),=C'DB2T'
            MVC     VALLEN(4),=F'4'
            MVC     KYWD+8(8),=C'DSQSMODE'
            MVC     KYWDLEN+4(4),=F'8'
            MVC     VALCHAR+4(1),=C'B'
            MVC     VALLEN+4(4),=F'1'
            L       15,ADSQCIA
            CALL    (15),(CICOMM,CMDLEN,CMDSTR,KYWDNUM,                 X
                    KYWDLEN,KYWD,VALLEN,VALCHAR,VTYPE),VL
            BAL     2,LISTMSGS
* SET GLOBAL (PROG='DEMO'
            MVC     CMDSTR,=C'SET GLOBAL'
            MVC     CMDLEN,=F'10'
            MVC     KYWDNUM,=F'1'
            MVC     KYWD(4),=C'PROG'
            MVC     KYWDLEN(4),=F'4'
            MVC     VALCHAR(6),=C'''DEMO'''
            MVC     VALLEN(4),=F'6'
            L       15,ADSQCIA
            CALL    (15),(CICOMM,CMDLEN,CMDSTR,KYWDNUM,                 X
                    KYWDLEN,KYWD,VALLEN,VALCHAR,VTYPE),VL
            BAL     2,LISTMSGS
* SET GLOBAL (QUERYID=5
            MVC     CMDSTR,=C'SET GLOBAL'
            MVC     CMDLEN,=F'10'
            MVC     KYWDNUM,=F'1'
            MVC     KYWD(4),=C'QNO'
            MVC     KYWDLEN(4),=F'3'
            MVC     VALNUM(4),=F'5'
            MVC     VALLEN(4),=F'4'
            MVC     VTYPE,DSQ_VARIABLE_FINT
            L       15,ADSQCIA
            CALL    (15),(CICOMM,CMDLEN,CMDSTR,KYWDNUM,                 X
                    KYWDLEN,KYWD,VALLEN,VALNUM,VTYPE),VL
            BAL     2,LISTMSGS
* RUN QUERY
            MVC     CMDSTR,=CL16'RUN QUERY QPLAN'
            MVC     CMDLEN,=F'16'
            L       15,ADSQCIA
            CALL    (15),(CICOMM,CMDLEN,CMDSTR),VL
            BAL     2,LISTMSGS
* RUN QUERY
            MVC     CMDSTR,=CL34'EXPORT REPORT TO RFILE (CONFIRM=NO'
            MVC     CMDLEN,=F'34'
            L       15,ADSQCIA
            CALL    (15),(CICOMM,CMDLEN,CMDSTR),VL
            BAL     2,LISTMSGS
* EXIT
            MVC     CMDSTR,=CL4'EXIT'
```

```
              MVC    CMDLEN,=F'4'
              L      15,ADSQCIA
              CALL   (15),(CICOMM,CMDLEN,CMDSTR),VL
              LA     15,0  set program return code
              PR     , terminate program
LISTMSGS DS          OH list messages (if error condition)
              CLC    DSQ_RETURN_CODE,=A(DSQ_FAILURE)
              BLR    2 ok
              TPUT   DSQ_MESSAGE_ID,8
              TPUT   DSQ_MESSAGE_TEXT,64
              BR     2
CMDSTR   DS    CL36
CMDLEN   DS    F
KYWDNUM  DS    F
KYWDLEN  DS    10F
KYWD     DS    CL256
VALLEN   DS    10F
VALCHAR  DS    CL256
VALNUM   DS    10F
VTYPE    DS    CL4
ADSQCIA  DS    A
*
SA       DS    18F user save-area
CICOMM   DS    CL(DSQCOMM_LEN) user Communications Area
              DSQCOMMA Communications Area definitions
              END
```

3.6.4.2 COBOL Interface.

```
         IDENTIFICATION DIVISION.
         PROGRAM-ID. QMFCIBO.
         ENVIRONMENT DIVISION.
         DATA DIVISION.
         WORKING-STORAGE SECTION.
             COPY DSQCOMMB.
        * CALLABLE INTERFACE COMMANDS
         01  CMDSTR PIC X(36).
         01  CMDLEN PIC 9(9) BINARY.
         01  KYWDNUM PIC 9(9) BINARY.
         01  KYWDLEN-ARRAY.
          02  KYWDLEN PIC 9(9) OCCURS 10 BINARY.
         01  KYWD-ARRAY.
          02  KYWD PIC X(8) OCCURS 10.
         01  VALLEN-ARRAY.
          02  VALLEN PIC 9(9) OCCURS 10 BINARY.
         01  VALCHAR-ARRAY.
          02  VALCHAR PIC X(16) OCCURS 10.
         01  VALNUM-ARRAY.
          02  VALNUM PIC S9(9) OCCURS 10 BINARY.
         01  VALTYPE PIC X(8).
         PROCEDURE DIVISION.
        * START
             MOVE DSQ-CURRENT-COMM-LEVEL TO DSQ-COMM-LEVEL
             MOVE "START" TO CMDSTR
             MOVE 5 TO CMDLEN
             MOVE 3 TO KYWDNUM
             MOVE "DSQSDBUG" TO KYWD(1)
             MOVE 8 TO KYWDLEN(1)
             MOVE "ALL" TO VALCHAR(1)
```

```
              MOVE 16 TO VALLEN(1)
              MOVE "DSQSMODE" TO KYWD(2)
              MOVE 8 TO KYWDLEN(2)
              MOVE "B" TO VALCHAR(2)
              MOVE 16 TO VALLEN(2)
              MOVE "DSQSSUBS" TO KYWD(3)
              MOVE 8 TO KYWDLEN(3)
              MOVE "DB2T" TO VALCHAR(3)
              MOVE 16 TO VALLEN(3)
              CALL "DSQCIB"
               USING DSQCOMM, CMDLEN, CMDSTR, KYWDNUM,
                     KYWDLEN-ARRAY, KYWD-ARRAY,
                     VALLEN-ARRAY, VALCHAR-ARRAY,
                     DSQ-VARIABLE-CHAR.
       * SET GLOBAL
              MOVE "SET GLOBAL" TO CMDSTR
              MOVE 10 TO CMDLEN
              MOVE 1 TO KYWDNUM
              MOVE "PROG" TO KYWD(1)
              MOVE 4 TO KYWDLEN(1)
              MOVE "'DEMO'" TO VALCHAR(1)
              MOVE 6 TO VALLEN(1)
              CALL "DSQCIB"
               USING DSQCOMM, CMDLEN, CMDSTR, KYWDNUM,
                     KYWDLEN-ARRAY, KYWD-ARRAY,
                     VALLEN-ARRAY, VALCHAR-ARRAY,
                     DSQ-VARIABLE-CHAR.
              PERFORM LIST-MSGS.
       * SET GLOBAL
              MOVE "SET GLOBAL" TO CMDSTR
              MOVE 10 TO CMDLEN
              MOVE 1 TO KYWDNUM
              MOVE "QNO" TO KYWD(1)
              MOVE 3 TO KYWDLEN(1)
              MOVE 5 TO VALNUM(1)
              MOVE 4 TO VALLEN(1)
              CALL "DSQCIB"
               USING DSQCOMM, CMDLEN, CMDSTR, KYWDNUM,
                     KYWDLEN-ARRAY, KYWD-ARRAY,
                     VALLEN-ARRAY, VALNUM-ARRAY,
                     DSQ-VARIABLE-FINT.
              PERFORM LIST-MSGS.
       * RUN QUERY
              MOVE "RUN QUERY QPLAN" TO CMDSTR
              MOVE 15 TO CMDLEN
              CALL "DSQCIB"
               USING DSQCOMM, CMDLEN, CMDSTR.
              PERFORM LIST-MSGS.
       * EXPORT REPORT
              MOVE "EXPORT REPORT TO RFILE (CONFIRM=NO" TO CMDSTR
              MOVE 34 TO CMDLEN
              CALL "DSQCIB"
               USING DSQCOMM, CMDLEN, CMDSTR.
              PERFORM LIST-MSGS.
       * EXIT
              MOVE "EXIT" TO CMDSTR
              MOVE 4 TO CMDLEN
              CALL "DSQCIB"
               USING DSQCOMM, CMDLEN, CMDSTR.
```

```
         GOBACK.
    LIST-MSGS.
        IF DSQ-RETURN-CODE > DSQ-WARNING THEN
           DISPLAY "DSQ-RETURN-CODE:" DSQ-RETURN-CODE
           DISPLAY "DSQ-MESSAGE-ID:" DSQ-MESSAGE-ID
           DISPLAY "DSQ-Q-MESSAGE-ID:" DSQ-Q-MESSAGE-ID
           DISPLAY "DSQ-MESSAGE-TEXT:" DSQ-MESSAGE-TEXT
           DISPLAY "DSQ-Q-MESSAGE-TEXT:" DSQ-Q-MESSAGE-TEXT
        END-IF.
```

3.6.4.3 C Interface. Although C programs use a language-specific
Communications Area (DSQCOMMC), the character fields in the Communications Area
are not true C-strings (i.e. they do not have a terminating null character).

```
#include "DSQCOMMC.H"
#include <string.h>
#include <stdio.h>

/* function prototypes */
void list_msgs();

/* common variables */
static int rc;
static struct dsqcomm cicomm;

main()
{
  #define MAXKYWDS 10
  #define MAXLEN 9
  #define MAXVALLEN 9
  #define BUFSIZE 256

  long cmdlen;
  long kywdnum;
  long kywdlen[MAXKYWDS];
  char kywd[BUFSIZE];
  long vallen[MAXKYWDS];
  char valchar[BUFSIZE];
  long valnum[MAXKYWDS];
  char vtype[4];
  int i, j;

  char cmd_start[] = "START";
  char cmd_set[] = "SET GLOBAL";
  char cmd_query[] = "RUN QUERY QPLAN";
  char cmd_export[] = "EXPORT REPORT TO RFILE (CONFIRM=NO";
  char cmd_exit[] = "EXIT";

  /* start QMF */
  cmdlen = sizeof(cmd_start);
  i = j = 0;
  strcpy(&kywd[i],"DSQSSUBS");
  i = strlen(&kywd[i])+1;
  kywdlen[0] = i;
  strcpy(&valchar[j],"DB2T");
  j = strlen(&valchar[j])+1;
  vallen[0] = j;
```

```
        strcpy(&kywd[i],"DSQSMODE");
        i = strlen(&kywd[i])+1;
        kywdlen[1] = i;
        strcpy(&valchar[j],"I"); /* I (=interactive) for test */
        j = strlen(&valchar[j])+1;
        vallen[1] = j;
        kywdnum = 2;
        strcpy(vtype,DSQ_VARIABLE_CHAR);
        rc = dsqcice(&cicomm,&cmdlen,cmd_start,
                     &kywdnum,kywdlen,kywd,
                     vallen,valchar,
                     vtype);
        list_msgs();

        /* run query */
        cmdlen = sizeof(cmd_query);
        rc = dsqcic(&cicomm,&cmdlen,cmd_query);
        list_msgs();

        /* export report */
        cmdlen = sizeof(cmd_export);
        rc = dsqcic(&cicomm,&cmdlen,cmd_export);
        list_msgs();

        /* terminate QMF */
        cmdlen = sizeof(cmd_exit);
        rc = dsqcic(&cicomm,&cmdlen,cmd_exit);
        list_msgs();
    }

    void list_msgs() {
      /* list return codes and message ids (if error) */
      char str[256]; /* work field */
      if (cicomm.dsq_return_code > DSQ_WARNING) {
        printf("DSQRC:%ld\n",cicomm.dsq_return_code);
        /* create C-processable strings */
        memcpy(str,cicomm.dsq_message_id,sizeof(cicomm.dsq_message_id));
        str[sizeof(cicomm.dsq_message_id)] = 0x00;
        printf("DSQMSG:%s\n",str);
        memcpy(str,cicomm.dsq_q_message_id,sizeof(cicomm.dsq_q_message_id));
        str[sizeof(cicomm.dsq_q_message_id)] = 0x00;
        printf("DSQQMSG:%s\n",str);
      }
      return;
    }
```

3.6.4.4 PL/I Interface.

```
        QMFCIPO: PROC OPTIONS(MAIN);
        %INCLUDE SYSLIB(DSQCOMML);

        /* declarations */
        DCL CMD_START CHAR(5) INIT('START');
        DCL CMD_QUERY CHAR(16) INIT('RUN QUERY QPLAN');
        DCL CMD_SET CHAR(10) INIT('SET GLOBAL');
        DCL CMD_EXPORT CHAR(34) INIT('EXPORT REPORT TO RFILE (CONFIRM=NO)');
        DCL CMD_EXIT CHAR(4) INIT('EXIT');
```

```
DCL CMDLEN FIXED BIN(31);
DCL KYWDNUM FIXED BIN(31);
DCL 1 KYWDLEN(10) FIXED BIN(31);
DCL 1 KYWD,
    2 KYWD1 CHAR(8),
    2 KYWD2 CHAR(8);
DCL 1 VALLEN(10) FIXED BIN(31);
DCL 1 VALCHAR,
    2 VALCHAR1 CHAR(8),
    2 VALCHAR2 CHAR(8);
DCL 1 VALNUM,
    2 VALNUM1 FIXED BIN(31),
    2 VALNUM2 FIXED BIN(31);

/* execution code */
/* START QMF Callable Interface */
CMDLEN = LENGTH(CMD_START);
KYWDNUM = 2;
KYWD1 = 'DSQSSUBS';
KYWDLEN(1) = LENGTH(KYWD1);
VALCHAR1 = 'DB2T';
VALLEN(1) = LENGTH(VALCHAR1);
KYWD2 = 'DSQSMODE';
KYWDLEN(2) = LENGTH(KYWD2);
VALCHAR2 = 'B';
VALLEN(2) = LENGTH(VALCHAR2);
DSQCOMM = '';
DSQ_COMM_LEVEL = DSQ_CURRENT_COMM_LEVEL;
FETCH DSQCIPX;
CALL DSQCIPX(DSQCOMM,CMDLEN,CMD_START,
             KYWDNUM,KYWDLEN,KYWD,
             VALLEN,VALCHAR,
             DSQ_VARIABLE_CHAR);
CALL LIST_MSGS(CMD_START);
/* SET GLOBAL (PROG='DEMO' */
CMDLEN = LENGTH(CMD_SET);
KYWDNUM = 1;
KYWD1 = 'PROG';
KYWDLEN(1) = 4;
VALCHAR1 = '''DEMO''';
VALLEN(1) = 6;
FETCH DSQCIPX;
CALL DSQCIPX(DSQCOMM,CMDLEN,CMD_SET,
             KYWDNUM,KYWDLEN,KYWD,
             VALLEN,VALCHAR,
             DSQ_VARIABLE_CHAR);
CALL LIST_MSGS(CMD_SET);
/* SET GLOBAL (QNO=5 */
CMDLEN = LENGTH(CMD_SET);
KYWDNUM = 1;
KYWD1 = 'QNO';
KYWDLEN(1) = 3;
VALNUM1 = 5;
VALLEN(1) = 4;
FETCH DSQCIPX;
CALL DSQCIPX(DSQCOMM,CMDLEN,CMD_SET,
             KYWDNUM,KYWDLEN,KYWD,
             VALLEN,VALNUM,
             DSQ_VARIABLE_FINT);
```

```
    CALL LIST_MSGS(CMD_SET);
    /* RUN QUERY */
    CMDLEN = LENGTH(CMD_QUERY);
    FETCH DSQCIPL;
    CALL DSQCIPL(DSQCOMM,CMDLEN,CMD_QUERY);
    CALL LIST_MSGS(CMD_QUERY);
    /* EXPORT REPORT */
    CMDLEN = LENGTH(CMD_EXPORT);
    FETCH DSQCIPL;
    CALL DSQCIPL(DSQCOMM,CMDLEN,CMD_EXPORT);
    CALL LIST_MSGS(CMD_EXPORT);
    /* EXIT - terminate Callable Interface */
    CMDLEN = LENGTH(CMD_EXIT);
    FETCH DSQCIPL;
    CALL DSQCIPL(DSQCOMM,CMDLEN,CMD_EXIT);
    CALL LIST_MSGS(CMD_EXIT);

    RETURN;

      LIST_MSGS: PROCEDURE(CMD);
        DCL CMD CHAR(3);
        IF DSQ_RETURN_CODE < DSQ_FAILURE THEN RETURN;
        PUT SKIP LIST('CMD:',CMD);
        PUT SKIP LIST('DSQRC:',DSQ_RETURN_CODE,DSQ_MESSAGE_ID,
                      DSQ_Q_MESSAGE_ID, DSQ_Q_MESSAGE_TEXT);
        RETURN;
      END;
    END;
```

3.6.4.5 REXX Interface.

```
/* REXX */
ADDRESS TSO
"ALLOC F(DSQDEBUG) DUMMY REUS" /* required for error processing */
"ALLOC F(DSQPNLE) DSN('QMF.TEST.DSQPNLE') SHR REUS" /* DSQSMODE I */
"ALLOC F(ADMGGMAP) DSN('QMF.TEST.DSQMAPE') SHR REUS"
cmd = "START (DSQSMODE=I,DSQSSUBS=DB2T"
CALL DSQCIX cmd
IF dsq_return_code > DSQ_WARNING THEN CALL ListMsgs
cmd = "SET GLOBAL (PROG='''RUDD''', QNO=5"
CALL DSQCIX cmd
IF dsq_return_code > DSQ_WARNING THEN CALL ListMsgs
cmd = "RUN QUERY QPLAN"
CALL DSQCIX cmd
IF dsq_return_code > DSQ_WARNING THEN CALL ListMsgs
cmd = "EXPORT REPORT TO RFILE (CONFIRM=NO"
CALL DSQCIX cmd
IF dsq_return_code > DSQ_WARNING THEN CALL ListMsgs
CALL DSQCIX "EXIT"
EXIT
ListMsgs:
  SAY 'DSQCIX error:' cmd
  SAY dsq_return_code dsq_message_id dsq_q_message_id,
    dsq_q_message_text
  CALL DSQCIX "EXIT"
  EXIT
```

3.7 QMF COMMAND INTERFACE

The QMF Command Interface (CI) is a largely obsolete interface that command procedures (CLISTs or REXX execs) can use to perform QMF processing. With the exception of invocation from CLISTs, the simpler Callable Interface has replaced the CI.

With the CI, once the QMF environment has been initiated, individual QMF commands can be invoked from a command procedure or program, using the CI. The CI is the QMF program DSQCCI. The parameter specified to CI is executed as a QMF command. Figure 3.3 illustrates a typical use of QMF to retrieve data from the database.

Syntax:
```
►►──ISPEXEC SELECT PGM(DSQCCI) PARM(qmfcommand)──►◄
```

qmfcommand
>   The QMF command to be invoked.

Example:
```
    ISPEXEC SELECT PGM(DSQCCI) PARM(RUN QUERY Q1)
```
Use the CI to invoke the QMF command RUN QUERY Q1.

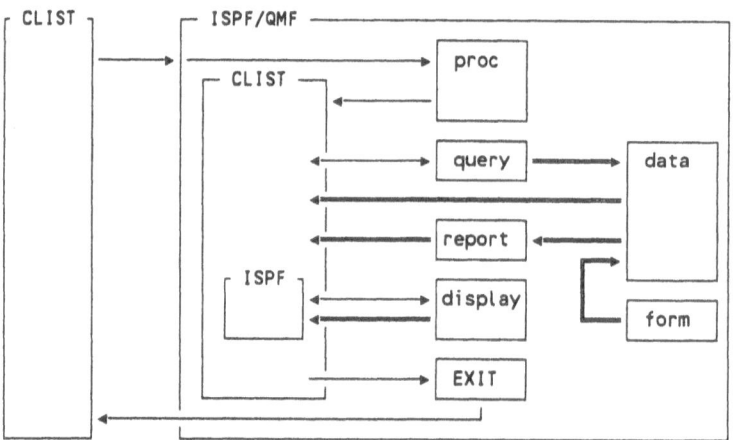

Figure 3.3 - Typical use of QMF to pass data to ISPF

3.7.1 QMF Status

The CI sets the return code (LASTCC variable in a CLIST, RC variable in a REXX procedure) and certain ISPF variables. The QMF STATE command returns the current QMF select status in ISPF variables; select status is the status after having run a query. Table 3.2 lists ISPF shared pool variables containing important status information.

One of the following return codes is set:

      0   Successful completion of command.
      4   QMF session terminated with END or EXIT command.
      8   Unsuccessful completion of command.
    16   Severe error.

Table 3.2 - Useful QMF status variables

DSQAROWS	s	number of data rows retrieved; 0 = none.
DSQCIQMG	q	query message after variables have been substituted.
DSQCIMSG	c	command message after variables have been substituted.
DSQCIQ09	q	SQL error code.

c = command, q = query, s = state (the QMF STATE command must have been issued).

CLIST example:
```
    PROC 0
    ISPEXEC SELECT PGM(DSQCCI) PARM(RUN QUERY Q1)
    IF &LASTCC NE 0 THEN DO
      ISPEXEC VGET (DSQCIQMG DSQCIMSG DSQCIQ09) SHARED
      ISPEXEC SELECT PGM(DSQCCI) PARM(STATE)
      ISPEXEC VGET (DSQAROWS) SHARED
      WRITE SQLCODE: &DSQCIQ09
      WRITE CMD-MSG: &DSQCIMSG
      WRITE QUERY-MSG: &DSQCIQMG
      WRITE ROWS RETRIEVED: &DSQAROWS
    END
```
This CLIST invokes CI to run query Q1 and displays error messages associated with this query, if an error is signalled.

3.7.2 Passing Parameters to a QMF Command

The PARM keyword for the CI is used to specify which QMF command is to be executed. Most QMF commands themselves have parameters, which are passed as sub-parameters. Unfortunately, CLISTs, ISPF and QMF adopt the same conventions for naming variables, namely by prefixing the variable name with "&" (ampersand). The following method is compatible with both CLISTs and QMF, and may be used to pass parameters from a CLIST to a QMF command: the name of the QMF variable is prefixed with four ampersands when passed from a CLIST, see Figure 3.5.

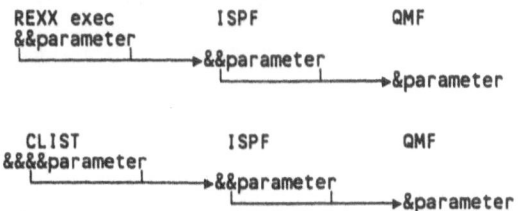

Figure 3.5 - Passing command procedure variables to QMF

The QMF restrictions for using parameters with queries (a maximum of 10 variables may be set, and the length of the value for a variable after substitution may not exceed 55 characters) also apply to this method of passing variables.

Example 1:
```
ISPEXEC SELECT PGM(DSQCCI) PARM(RUN QUERY Q2 (&&&&ALPHA=27)
```
Invoke the QMF query Q2 giving its variable ALPHA the value 27. This is equivalent to the QMF query: RUN QUERY Q2 (&ALPHA=27

Example 2:
```
SET &BETA = 27
ISPEXEC SELECT PGM(DSQCCI) PARM(RUN QUERY Q2 (&&&&ALPHA=&BETA)
```
This code uses the CLIST substitution facility to assign the value of 27 to the CLIST variable BETA before it is passed to QMF; these two statements have the same effect as in Example 1.

4

QMF Commands

Those he commands move only in command

Macbeth
William Shakespeare

4.1 INTRODUCTION

QMF commands may be issued as follows:
·   direct in QMF command line;
·   from a QMF procedure;
·   passed from the Command Interface (DSQCCI program).

4.2 COMMANDS

QMF offers a large number of commands, many of which, however, are only of
interest for users of the QMF dialogue (e.g. BACKWARD - scroll panel back towards
start of display). This book describes only those commands which are of use in
applications using QMF as an interface to the database:

·   DISPLAY   Display an object.
·   END   End current operation.
·   ERASE   Remove object from database.
·   EXIT   Terminate QMF session.
·   EXPORT   Transfer object to external dataset.
·   HELP   Display help information.

·	IMPORT	Import object into the QMF environment.
·	INTERACT	Provide interactive support.
·	ISPF	Invoke ISPF/PDF panel.
·	LIST	Display list of QMF objects.
·	MESSAGE	Display message.
·	PRINT	Print content of object.
·	QMF	Execute explicit QMF command.
·	RESET	Clear object.
·	RESET QUERY	Clear query object.
·	RESET GLOBAL	Clear global variable.
·	RUN	Execute object.
·	SAVE	Save contents of work area.
·	SAVE DATA	Save contents of data area.
·	SAVE PROFILE	Save profile.
·	SET (PROFILE)	Set profile.
·	SET GLOBAL	Set global variable.
·	STATE	Return QMF status.
·	TSO	Invoke TSO command.

Although some of these commands are available in CICS, they are used only interactively and not in applications.

Note 1): Those operands which cannot be replaced by user values may in general be abbreviated, provided the abbreviation is non-ambiguous, e.g. DISPLAY PROFILE may be abbreviated to DI PROF.

Note 2): If QMF commands are invoked from a REXX exec, QMF commands that have the same name as REXX statements (END, EXIT) must be written in quotes to distinguish them.

4.2.1 DISPLAY - Display an Object

The DISPLAY command displays an object which may be in either work area or the database.

Syntax (object in work area):

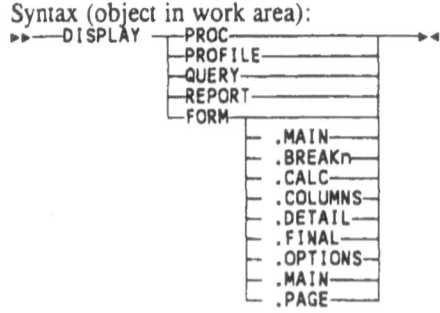

Syntax (for graphic display):

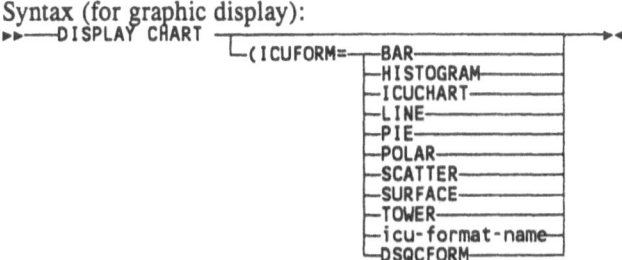

ICUFORM
The graphic form of the display; this may be either the chart type (e.g. BAR, PIE) or the member name of a chart format previously stored in the DSQUCFRM file. A chart format file must always be defined, even if no explicit member is specified.
Default: DSQCFORM (predefined as bar chart).

Syntax (object in the database):

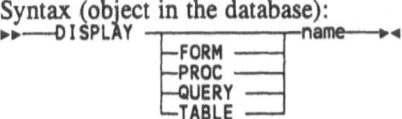

name
The database object to be displayed.

Example:
    DISPLAY TABLE PERS
Display the contents of the PERS table.

4.2.2 END - End Current Operation

The END command terminates the current operation, i.e. returns to the QMF home panel.

Syntax:

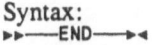

4.2.3 ERASE - Remove Object from Database

The ERASE command removes (deletes) the specified object from the database.

Syntax:

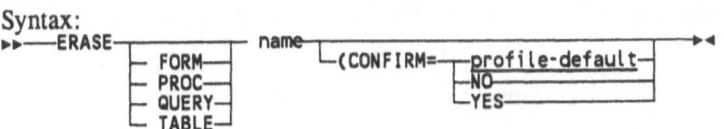

name
>   The database object to be deleted.

CONFIRM
>   Keyword to indicate whether the confirmation panel is to be displayed. This
>   panel is used to confirm, or otherwise, that the object is to be deleted.
>   NO - the confirmation panel is not to be displayed.
>   YES - the confirmation panel is to be displayed.
>   Default: The confirm option specified in the QMF profile.

Example:
```
ERASE TABLE PERS (CONFIRM=NO
```
Delete the PERS table; no confirmation panel is to be displayed.

4.2.4 EXIT - Terminate QMF Session

The EXIT command terminates the current QMF session.

Syntax:
```
►►──EXIT──►◄
```

4.2.5 EXPORT - Transfer Object to External Dataset

The EXPORT command is used to transfer the specified object (QMF or database) to
an external (TSO) dataset. The name of the target dataset conforms to TSO naming
conventions and will be created if it does not exist.

The EXPORT command has three forms:
·   object (form, procedure, query or report);
·   data;
·   chart (graphic data).

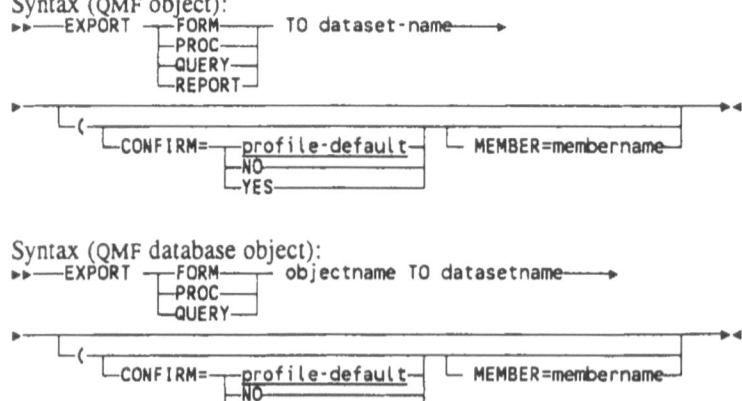

Syntax (QMF object):
```
►►──EXPORT ──┬─FORM────┬── TO dataset-name──►
             ├─PROC────┤
             ├─QUERY───┤
             └─REPORT──┘

►──────────────────────────────────────────────────────────────►◄
    └─(─┬────────────────────────────────┬──────────────────────┘
        └─CONFIRM=─┬─profile-default─┬─┘  └─ MEMBER=membername─┘
                   ├─NO──────────────┤
                   └─YES─────────────┘
```

Syntax (QMF database object):
```
►►──EXPORT ──┬─FORM───┬── objectname TO datasetname──►
             ├─PROC───┤
             └─QUERY──┘

►──────────────────────────────────────────────────────────────►◄
    └─(─┬────────────────────────────────┬──────────────────────┘
        └─CONFIRM=─┬─profile-default─┬─┘  └─ MEMBER=membername─┘
                   ├─NO──────────────┤
                   └─YES─────────────┘
```

Syntax (database object):

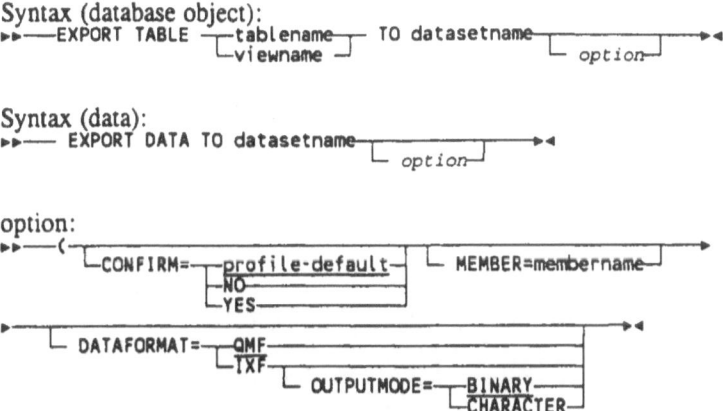

Syntax (data):

option:

datasetname
>   The name of the TSO dataset to receive the exported object. This dataset is
>   allocated if it does not exist. The **dataset-name** conforms to the TSO
>   naming conventions. For a dataset name which is not fully qualified, the
>   following dataset name is generated:
>   'user-prefix.**dataset-name.object-type**'
>   **object-type** is the object type (i.e. DATA, FORM, PROC, QUERY, REPORT).

CONFIRM
>   Keyword to indicate whether the confirmation panel is to be displayed. This
>   panel is used to confirm, or otherwise, that the target dataset is to be
>   overwritten.
>   NO - the confirmation panel is not to be displayed.
>   YES - the confirmation panel is to be displayed.
>   Default: the confirm option specified in the QMF profile.

MEMBER=member-name
>   **Membername** specifies the name of the member to be created in a
>   partitioned dataset. **Membername** must be specified for a partitioned
>   dataset and may not be specified for a sequential dataset.

DATAFORMAT
>   The DATAFORMAT keyword introduces the parameters defining the form of the
>   data to be exported:
>   QMF - data is to be exported in QMF external data format.
>   IXF - data is to be exported in Integration Exchange Format.
>
>   OUTPUTMODE introduces the parameter specifying the form of the IXF data:
>   BINARY - binary format
>   CHARACTER - character format.
>
>   Section 4.6 provides a detailed description of IXF data. Section 4.8 provides
>   a detailed description of QMF external data.

objectname
> The name of the object in the database.

Example:
```
EXPORT DATA TO ALPHA (DATAFORMAT=IXF OUTPUTMODE=BINARY
```
Export the current contents of the QMF data area to the dataset userid.ALPHA.DATA in
IXF binary format.

Syntax (chart data):
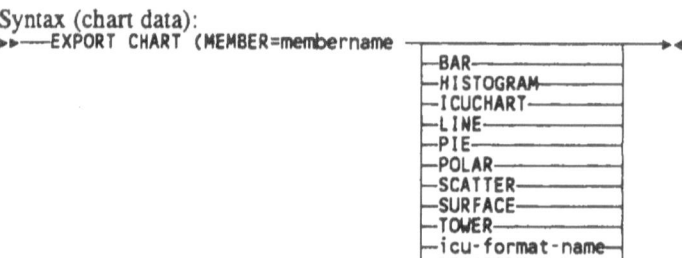

MEMBER=membername
> **Membername** specifies the name of the member to be created in the
> partitioned dataset assigned to the ADMGDF file.

icu-format-name
> The name of the format previously saved in PGF which is to be used to
> format the chart to be exported. The chart format file DSQUCFRM must always
> be defined, even if no explicit member is specified.
> Default: DSQCFORM (predefined as bar chart).

4.2.6 HELP - Display Help Information

The HELP command displays help information concerning either the current panel
or the message which has just been displayed.

Syntax:

4.2.7 IMPORT - Import Object into the QMF Environment

The IMPORT command imports data from a dataset into either a QMF work area or
the database.

Syntax (import dataset into a QMF work area):
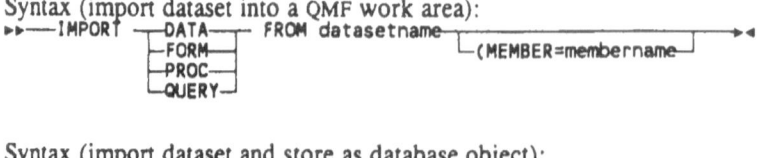

Syntax (import dataset and store as database object):
```
▶▶──IMPORT ──┬─FORM──┬─ objectname FROM datasetname─┬──────────┬──▶◀
             ├─PROC──┤                              └─(option─┘
             └─QUERY─┘
```

Syntax (import dataset and store as database table):

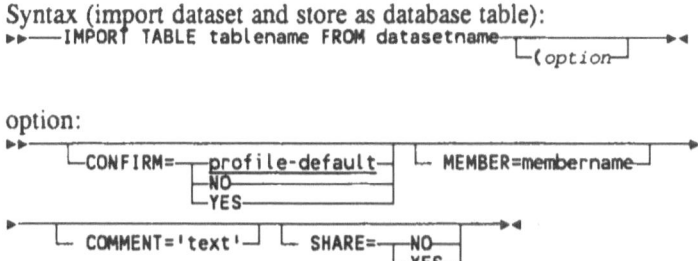

DATA, FORM, PROC, QUERY
The type of object to be imported.

FROM datasetname
The name of the dataset containing the object to be imported. For a dataset name which is not fully qualified, the following dataset name is generated: 'userprefix.**datasetname.objecttype**'
Objecttype is the object type (i.e. DATA, FORM, PROC, QUERY, REPORT).

MEMBER=membername
The name of the member of a partitioned dataset (library).

objectname
The name with which the object is to be stored in the database.

CONFIRM
Keyword to indicate whether a confirmation prompt to overwrite an object having the same name is to be made.
NO - the confirmation panel is not to be displayed.
YES - the confirmation panel is to be displayed.
Default: the confirm option specified in the QMF profile.

COMMENT='text'
Text is a comment which is to be stored with the database object. The maximum length of a comment is 57 characters.

SHARE
YES - all QMF users may use the imported object.
NO - only the current QMF users may use the imported object.
Default: NO for an object being imported for the first time; in other cases the current share option is retained.

4.2.8 INTERACT - Provide Interactive Support

The INTERACT command is used make the following commands be executed interactively. Interactive execution means that prompting is done where necessary.

Syntax:
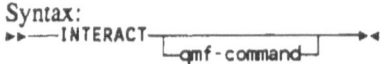

qmf-command
>   The QMF command which is to be interactively invoked.

Example:
>   INTERACT RUN QUERY
executes the current query interactively.

4.2.9 ISPF - Invoke ISPF/PDF Panel

The ISPF command displays the ISPF/PDF panel associated with the specified parameter. The invoked ISPF/PDF panel must not be currently active, this causes a recursive error. The PF3 key is used to terminate the panel display.

Syntax:
>►►——ISPF———————————————————————►◄
>   └─ ispf/pdf-parameter─┘

ispf/pdf-parameter
>   The panel in the ISPF/PDF hierarchy which is to be displayed. Default: the ISPF/PDF Primary Option Menu

Example:
>   ISPF 3.2
Display the ISPF/PDF Utility selection panel.

4.2.10 LIST - Display List of QMF Objects

The LIST command displays a list of those selected QMF objects which the user is authorised to use. The content of those objects can be subsequently displayed or procedures (and queries) started.

Note: Object type must be specified as plural (unless abbreviated), i.e. QUERY is invalid, QUERIES or Q is valid.

Syntax:
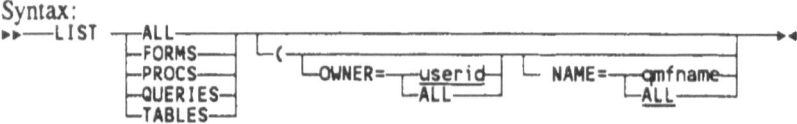

OWNER
>   The owner of the objects to be displayed.
>   **userid** - all objects belonging to **userid**.
>   ALL - all objects which the current user may access.
>   Default: current userid.

NAME

The objects that are to be listed.

qmfname - the objects with this name (a generic name according to the SQL name conventions may be used).

ALL - all objects for the specified owner.

Default: ALL.

Example:

    LIST QUERIES (OWNER=ALL

List all the queries which may be used by the current user.

4.2.11 MESSAGE - Display Message

The MESSAGE command has a number of functions, not all directly connected with message processing:

· display an ISPF message;
· display a QMF message;
· assign a help panel;
· suppress execution of QMF procedures.

Table 4.1 shows the relationship of MESSAGE variables with fields in the ISPF message definition, MESSAGE variables take precedence. Note: QMF does not use the .ALARM field to sound the acoustic signal, rather it is used to stop procedure execution.

Table 4.1 - Relationship of MESSAGE variables to ISPF message fields

ISPMLIB entry	MESSAGE entry
short message	-
.HELP	HELP
.ALARM	STOPPROC
long message	message-text

Syntax:

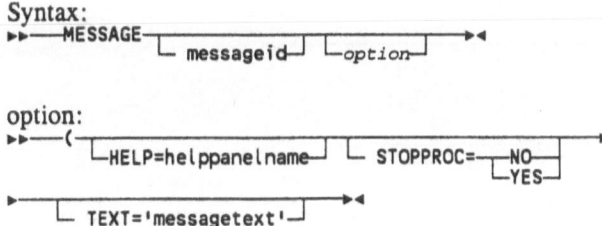

messageid

The message identifier of an ISPF message; the message must have been stored in the ISPMLIB library.

Default: the specified **message-text** is displayed.

helppanelname
>The name of the help panel which will be displayed if help is requested; the help panel must have been stored in the ISPPLIB library.

STOPPROC
>Termination keyword as to whether those QMF procedures in a higher hierarchy are to be terminated.
>
>YES = QMF procedures are terminated.
>
>NO = QMF procedures are not terminated.

TEXT='messagetext'
>**Messagetext** specifies the message text to be displayed.

Example:
```
MESSAGE (TEXT='object not found'
```
Display the message text "object not found".

4.2.12 PRINT - Print contents of object

The PRINT command prints an object stored either in a work area or in the database. Some objects require a GDDM printer.

Syntax:

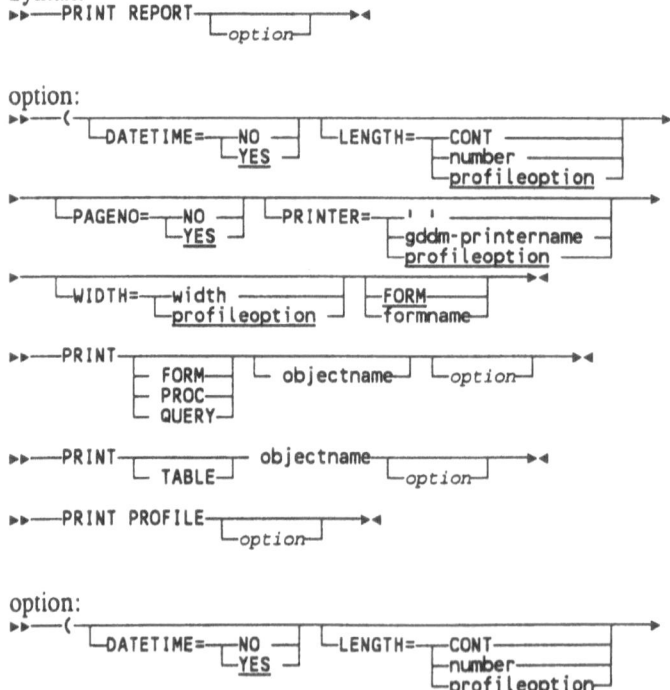

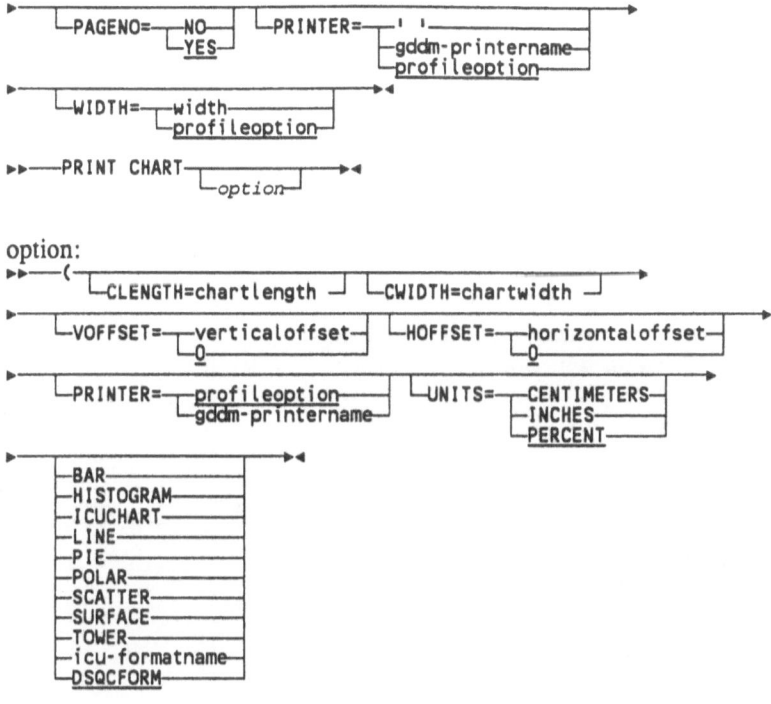

option:

objectname

    The name of the database object to be printed.
    Default: the contents of the specified work area.

DATETIME

    Keyword to specify whether the system date and time are to be printed. The
    &DATE and &TIME variables in the form override the DATETIME entry.
    Default: YES.

LENGTH

    The page length.
    number is the maximum number of lines per page (1,...,999).
    CONT forces continuous printing without page breaks.
    Default: profile option.

PAGENO

    Keyword to specify whether the page number is to be printed. The &PAGE
    variable in the form overrides the PAGENO entry.
    Default: YES.

PRINTER

    The printer to be used for output.
    ' ' routes the print output to the DSQPRINT file.

gddm-printername routes the print output to the specified GDDM graphics printer.
Default: profile option.

WIDTH

The maximum number of characters per line (22,...,999).
Default: profile option.

FORM

The form to be used for report formatting.
formname is the name of a form stored in the database.
FORM the current contents of the form work area.
Default: FORM (formatting defaults are used if no entry has be made in the work area).

CLENGTH

The length (height) of the chart area.
The UNITS parameter specifies the units for **chartlength**.
Default: 95 (if UNITS=PERCENT) or
        6 (if UNITS=INCHES or CENTIMETERS).

CWIDTH

The width of the chart area.
The UNITS parameter specifies the units for **chartwidth**.
Default: 95 (if UNITS=PERCENT) or
        6 (if UNITS=INCHES or CENTIMETERS).

VOFFSET

The vertical offset from the top of the physical page to the top of the chart area. The UNITS parameter specifies the units for **voffset**.
Default: 0

HOFFSET

The horizontal offset to the left hand side of the chart area. The UNITS parameter specifies the units for **hoffset**.
Default: 0

UNITS

The units to be used for chart dimensions (CLENGTH, etc.).
Default: PERCENT.

icu-formatname

The member name of the ICU format previously stored in the DSQUCFRM file which is to be used to format the chart. A chart format file DSQUCFRM must always be defined, even if no explicit member is specified. A chart type (e.g. BAR) may also be used to specify the form of the printed chart.
Default: DSQCFORM (predefined as bar chart).

Example:
```
PRINT QUERY QEX1 (PRINTER=' '
```
Print the database query QEX1 on the printer file defined by DSQPRINT.

4.2.13 QMF - Execute Explicit QMF Command

The QMF command is used to execute a QMF command having the same name as an installation-defined command.

Syntax:
```
»»——QMF qmfcommand——»◄
```

qmfcommand
> The name of the QMF command to be executed.

Example:
```
QMF BATCH
```
Execute the standard BATCH command instead of the installation-defined BATCH command.

4.2.14 RESET - Clear Object

The RESET command resets the specified object space to its original state.

Syntax:
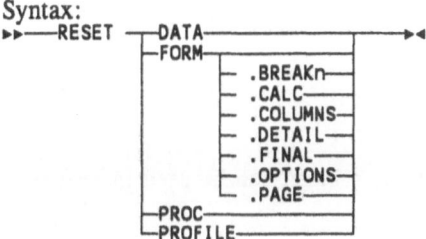

DATA
> Clear the contents of the data work area.

FORM
> Reset the form to those defaults appropriate for the current contents of the data work area. If no specific sub-options are specified, the complete form is reset.

PROC
> Display an empty procedure input panel.

PROFILE
> Reset the profile to those values saved in the database.

Example:
```
RESET FORM .PAGE
```
Reset the form .PAGE options to their defaults.

4.2.15 RESET QUERY - Clear Query Object

The RESET QUERY command displays an empty query input panel, and, if the LANGUAGE option is specified, sets the default language contained in the profile to the given value.

Syntax:

Example:
```
RESET QUERY (LANGUAGE=SQL
```
Display an empty query input panel and set the profile language default to SQL.

4.2.16 RESET GLOBAL - Clear Query Object

The RESET GLOBAL command deletes values previously set with the SET GLOBAL command.

Syntax:

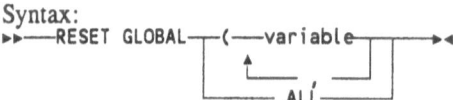

variable
> The name of the variable to be deleted; a blank can be used instead of a comma to separate variable names.

ALL
> All variables are to be deleted.

Example:
```
RESET GLOBAL (ALPHA BETA
```
Delete the two variables ALPHA and BETA.

4.2.17 RUN - Execute Object

The RUN command executes either a named object or the object currently contained in the specified QMF work area.

Syntax (for procedure):

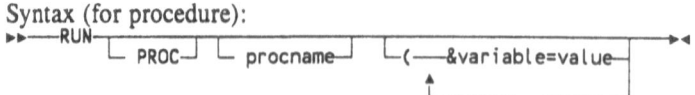

Syntax (for query):

option:

```
►►───────────────────────────────────────────────────────────────────
      └─FORM=──┬─FORM──────┬──    └─CONFIRM=──┬─profiledefault─┐
               └─formname──┘                  ├─NO────────────┤
                                              └─YES───────────┘

►───────────────────────────────────────────────◄
      └────&variable=value─┘
           ▲            │
           └──────, ────┘
```

procname

> The name of the database procedure to be executed.
> Default: the contents of the procedure work area.

queryname

> The name of the database query to be executed.
> Default: the contents of the query work area.

variable

> The name of the variable to be assigned **value**. The RUN command may specify a maximum of 10 variables, the length of any value may not exceed 55 characters. Character values must be specified within quotes. A blank can be used instead of a comma to separate variable-value entries.

FORM

> The form to be used to format the results.
> **formname** - is the name of the form in the database which is to be used.
> FORM - the form (or defaults) currently in the form work area.
> Default: FORM.

CONFIRM

> Keyword to indicate whether the confirmation panel is to be displayed before any changes are made to the database as a result of running the query.
> NO - the confirmation panel is not to be displayed.
> YES - the confirmation panel is to be displayed.
> Default: the confirm option specified in the QMF profile.

Example:
>   RUN PROC PEX1 (&ALPHA=27
> Execute the procedure PEX1 with ALPHA set to 27.

4.2.18 SAVE - Save Contents of Work Area

The SAVE command stores the contents of the specified QMF work area in the database.

Syntax:
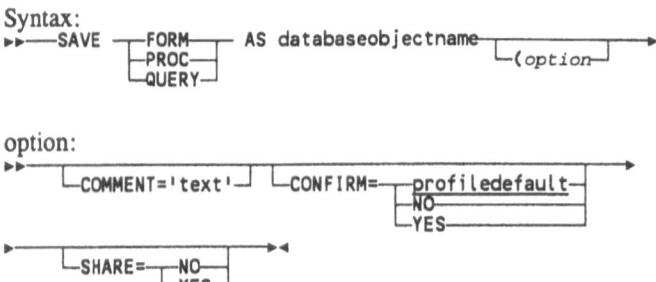

option:

databaseobjectname
    The name with which the object is to be stored in the database.
    databaseobjectname must be unique (across object types) for the user.

COMMENT = 'text'
    Text specifies a comment which is to be stored with the object in the
    database. **Text** may have a maximum of 57 characters.

CONFIRM
    Keyword to indicate whether the confirmation panel is to be displayed.
    NO - the confirmation panel is not to be displayed.
    YES - the confirmation panel is to be displayed.
    Default: the confirm option specified in the QMF profile.

SHARE
    Share option keyword.
    YES - all QMF users may use the saved object.
    NO - only the current QMF user may use the saved object.
    Default: NO for an object being saved for the first time; in other cases the
    current share option is retained.

Example:
    SAVE QUERY AS QEX1
Save the current contents of the query work area with the name QEX1.

4.2.19 SAVE DATA - Save Contents of Data Area

The SAVE DATA command stores the contents of the QMF data area in the database.

Syntax:
▶▶——SAVE DATA AS name—────▶◀
                    └(option─┘

option:
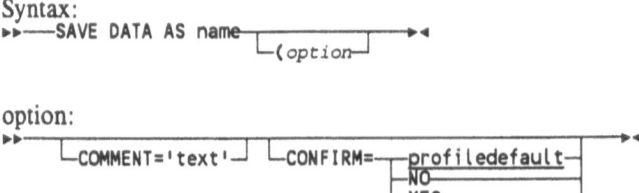

name

The name under which the object is to be stored in the database. **name** must be unique (across object types) for the user.

COMMENT = 'text'

Text specifies a comment which is to be stored with the object in the database. **Text** may have a maximum of 57 characters.

CONFIRM

Keyword to indicate whether the confirmation panel is to be displayed.
NO - the confirmation panel is not to be displayed.
YES - the confirmation panel is to be displayed.
Default: the confirm option specified in the QMF profile.

Example:
SAVE DATA AS ALPHA
Save the current contents of the data area with the name ALPHA.

4.2.20 SAVE PROFILE - Save Profile

The SAVE PROFILE command saves the contents of the user's profile work area in the database.

Syntax:
▶▶──SAVE PROFILE──▶◀

4.2.21 SET (PROFILE) - Set Profile

The SET (or SET PROFILE) command sets the specified values in the user's QMF profile.

Syntax:

option:

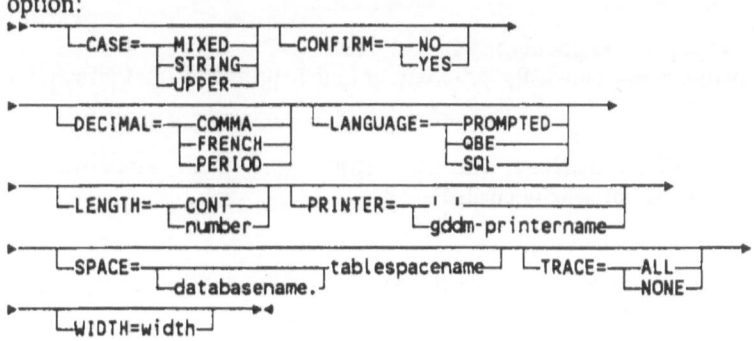

CASE

> The conversion to be made on the input.
> UPPER - input is converted to upper case.
> STRING - all input, except the following, is converted to upper case: data within quotation marks (single or double); comments in queries or procedures; headings and footings.
> MIXED - retain data as entered.

CONFIRM

> Keyword to indicate whether the confirmation panel is to be displayed.
> NO - the confirmation panel is not to be displayed.
> YES - the confirmation panel is to be displayed.
> Default: the confirm option specified in the QMF profile.

DECIMAL

> The number punctuation keyword.
> PERIOD - "," (comma) separates thousands and "." (period) is used as decimal separator, e.g. 123,456.78
> COMMA - "." (period) separates thousands and "," (comma) is used as decimal separator, e.g. 123.456,78
> FRENCH - blank separates thousands and "," (comma) is used as decimal separator, e.g. 123 456,78

LANGUAGE

> The default type of the query panel.
> PROMPTED - prompted query.
> QBE - query-by-example.
> SQL - structured query language.

LENGTH

> The page length.
> **number** is the maximum number of lines per page (1,...,999).
> CONT forces continuous printing without page breaks.

PRINTER

> The printer to be used for output.
> ' ' routes the print output to the DSQPRINT file.
> **gddm-printername** routes the print output to the specified GDDM printer.

SPACE

> The name of the database and table space; this is an administrative parameter and is not usually changed.

TRACE

> The QMF trace options to be used; this is an administrative parameter and is not usually changed.

WIDTH

> The maximum number of characters per line (22,...,999).

Example:
```
SET PROFILE (CASE=MIXED DECIMAL=PERIOD
```
Set the profile default to no data input conversion and use "." as decimal separator.

4.2.22 SET GLOBAL - Set Global Variable

The SET GLOBAL command assigns the specified values to the named variables. A maximum of 10 global variables may be set. The global variables exist only during the current QMF session, or until reset with the RESET GLOBAL command.

Syntax:
```
▶▶──SET GLOBAL(──variable=value──────▶◀
               ▲_____┐
               └─────── , ──────┘
```

variable
>   The name of the variable to be assigned **value**. A maximum of 10 variables may be specified, the length of any value may not exceed 55 characters. Character values must be specified within quotes. A blank may be used instead of a comma to separate variable-value entries.

Example:
```
SET GLOBAL (ALPHA='beta'
```
Set the value of the character variable ALPHA to beta.

4.2.23 STATE - Return QMF Status

The STATE command returns QMF status in the form of variables in the ISPF shared variable pool. Table 3.2 lists the more useful QMF status variables.

Syntax:
```
▶▶──STATE──▶◀
```

4.2.24 TSO - Invoke TSO Command

The TSO command invokes a TSO command or command procedure without leaving the QMF environment. Return is made to the QMF environment when the TSO command or command procedure completes.

Syntax:
```
▶▶──TSO ──┬─tsocommand──────────┬─────────────▶◀
          └─commandprocedurename─┘ ▲
                                   └─ parameter─┘
```

tsocommand
>   The name of the TSO command to be invoked.

commandprocedurename
>   The name of the command procedure to be invoked; commands contained in the command procedure library may be prefixed with the % character.

Example:
```
    TSO LISTC
```
Execute the TSO LISTC command.

4.3 EXAMPLE

A command procedure is to display a report containing all columns and rows from the DB2 table PERS.

There are three general ways of using QMF to solve this exercise:

· static QMF definition;
· parameterized QMF definition;
· import QMF definition.

These solutions are ordered in increasing flexibility. Figure 4.1 shows the function diagram for the first two solutions.

4.3.1 Solution 1 (Using Static QMF Definition)

Five principal operations are required to perform this exercise:

· invoke QMF (using EXQMF CLIST);
· invoke the processing CLIST (using EXQP11 QMF procedure);
· pass control to QMF to perform SQL selection (using EXQP12 QMF procedure);
· copy the QMF report (which contains forms information) into a dataset and display the contents of this dataset using the ISPF BROWSE service;
· terminate QMF.

Notes: It is not strictly necessary to use ISPF services to display the report, but this method is used to show how DB2 data can be passed to ISPF for further processing.
     Error checking has been omitted from this example to avoid overcomplication.

EXQMF CLIST procedure to invoke QMF:
```
    PROC 0
    ISPEXEC SELECT PGM(DSQQMFE) NEWAPPL(DSQE) PARM(S=DB2,I=TSOU001.EXQP11)
```

EXQP11 QMF procedure:
```
    TSO %EXC11
```

EXC11 processing CLIST:
```
    PROC 0
    ISPEXEC SELECT PGM(DSQCCI) PARM(RUN EXQQ11)
    ISPEXEC SELECT PGM(DSQCCI) PARM(EXPORT REPORT TO 'TSOU001.QMF.LIST')
    ISPEXEC BROWSE DATASET('TSOU001.QMF.LIST')
    ISPEXEC SELECT PGM(DSQCCI) PARM(EXIT)
```

EXQQ11 QMF processing query:
```
    SELECT * FROM PERS
```

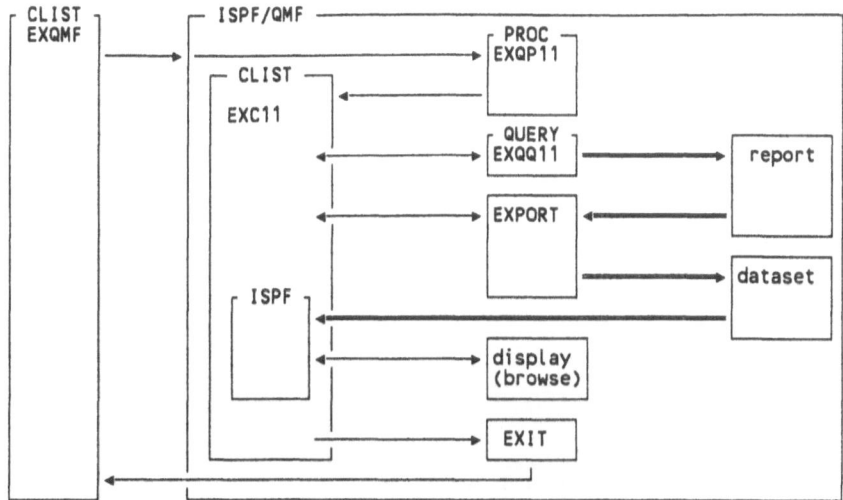

Figure 4.1 - Simple QMF application (solution 1 and 2)

4.3.2 Solution 2 (Using Parameterized QMF Definition)

The method used here is similar to solution 1, however, the names of the columns
to be returned are passed as parameters.

EXQMF CLIST procedure to invoke QMF:

```
PROC 0
ISPEXEC SELECT PGM(DSQQMFE) NEWAPPL(DSQE) PARM(S=DB2,I=TSOU001.EXQP21)
```

EXQP21 QMF procedure:

```
TSO %EXC21
```

EXC21 processing CLIST:

```
PROC 0
ISPEXEC SELECT PGM(DSQCCI) PARM(RUN EXQQ21 (&&&&COLS = PNO,PNAME)
ISPEXEC SELECT PGM(DSQCCI) PARM(EXPORT REPORT TO 'TSOU001.QMF.LIST')
ISPEXEC BROWSE DATASET('TSOU001.QMF.LIST')
ISPEXEC SELECT PGM(DSQCCI) PARM(EXIT)
```

EXQQ21 QMF processing query:

```
SELECT &COLS FROM PERS
```

4.3.3 Solution 3 (Importing Query to QMF)

The query is passed (imported) to QMF; this avoids having to predefine the query
in QMF. Figure 4.1 shows the function diagram for this solution.

EXQMF CLIST procedure to invoke QMF:

```
PROC 0
ISPEXEC SELECT PGM(DSQQMFE) NEWAPPL(DSQE) PARM(S=DB2,I=TSOU001.EXQP31)
```

EXQP31 QMF procedure:
```
TSO %EXC31
```

EXC31 processing CLIST:
```
PROC 0
ISPEXEC SELECT PGM(DSQCCI) PARM(IMPORT QUERY FROM 'TSOU001.DB2.QUERY' +
(MEMBER=Q2)
ISPEXEC SELECT PGM(DSQCCI) PARM(RUN QUERY)
ISPEXEC SELECT PGM(DSQCCI) PARM(EXPORT REPORT TO 'TSOU001.QMF.LIST')
ISPEXEC BROWSE DATASET('TSOU001.QMF.LIST')
ISPEXEC SELECT PGM(DSQCCI) PARM(EXIT)
```

Q2 imported query:
```
SELECT * FROM PERS
```

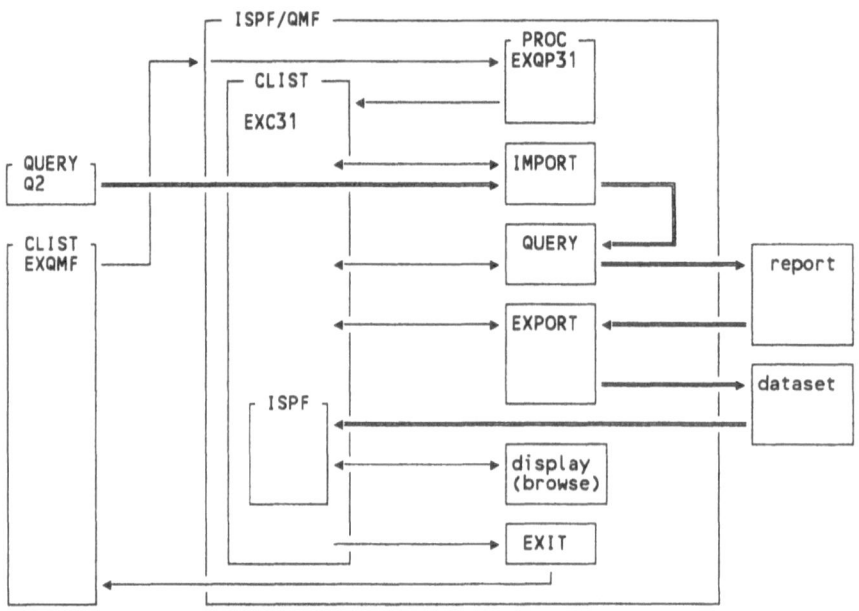

Figure 4.2 - Simple QMF application (solution 3)

4.4 EXTERNAL QMF DATA

QMF objects (i.e. data, forms, procedures, queries and reports) and database objects accessible from QMF (i.e. tables and views) can be transferred to external media.

The following general forms of external QMF data are available:
· data;
· formatted report;
· graphic output.

The external medium can be in the required end form (e.g. a formatted report) or in an intermediate form which needs to be further processed.

Note: The formats may change with future releases. The header record contains the version and release number.

Figure 4.3 depicts how QMF objects may be transferred to or from external datasets. Figure 4.4 shows the printing of QMF objects.

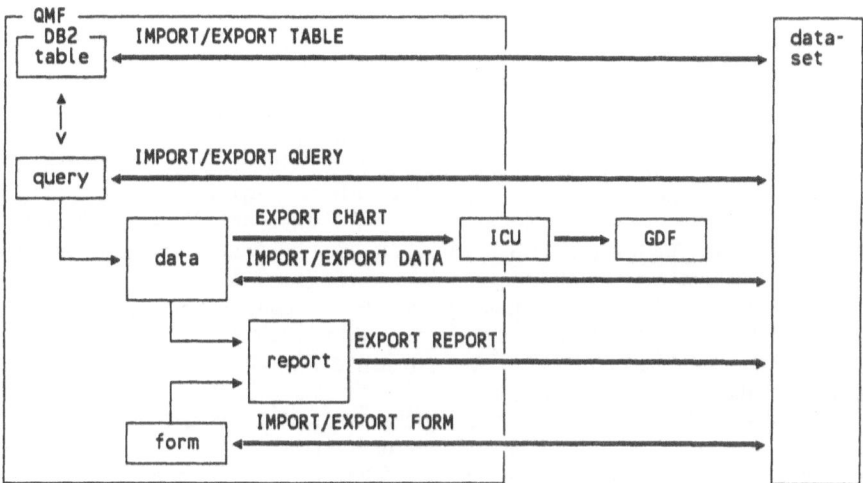

Figure 4.3 - Transfer of QMF object to or from external dataset

Note: Exported DATA can be imported as a DB2 table.

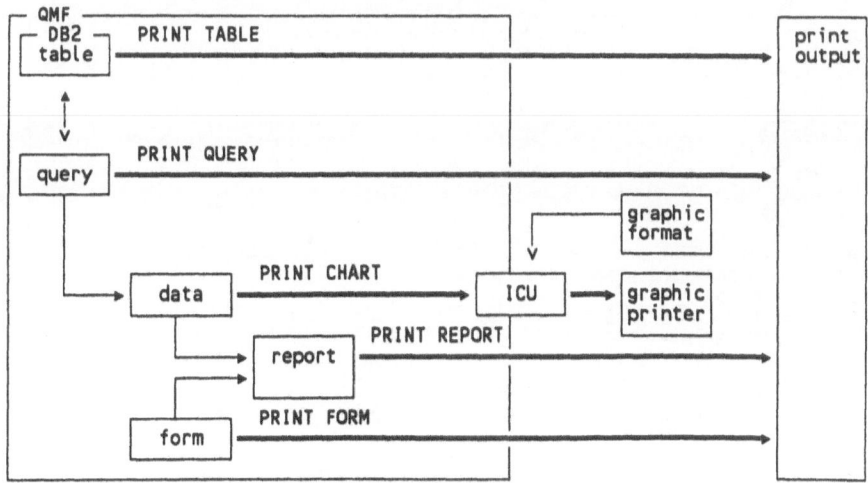

Figure 4.4 - Printing of QMF object

The power of the QMF formatting facilities is best illustrated using an example.
The query

```
SELECT * FROM PERS ORDER BY DEPTNO
```

produces the standard QMF report shown in Figure 4.5 using the default form
shown in Figure 4.6.

```
 PNO   PNAME                           DEPTNO    SALARY
------- ------------------------       ------   ---------
 1111  ALPHA                             D1       10000
 4444  DELTA                             D1       18000
 4555  DDELTA                            D2       16000
 1222  ABETA                             D2       12000
 2333  BBETA                             D2       11500
 2222  BETA                              D2       12500
```

Figure 4.5 - Default report

A few simple modifications to the form produces the comprehensively formatted
report shown in Figure 4.7; the corresponding form is shown in Figure 4.8. This
report replaces the database column names with more meaningful text (e.g.
EMPLOYEE NO rather than PNO), formats the salary as a currency unit (EDIT format
"D"), and produces a subtotal for each department (function BREAK1 on column
DEPTNO causes a control break; function AVERAGE on column SALARY causes the
average in the column to be calculated, the group totals (and overall total) is
produced on each control break). These are just a few of the report generation
facilities available with QMF forms.

For appropriate query data a graphic chart can be produced (and may be
printed on a graphic printer). The previous query must be slightly modified to
produce the equivalent data (the database AVG (average) function and the GROUP BY
clause are used to return the subtotals). The query

```
SELECT DEPTNO,AVG(SALARY) FROM PERS GROUP BY DEPTNO
```

produces a chart. The standard chart format (bar chart) is used, although one of the
other chart formats (line graph, pie chart, histogram, etc.) could have been used.

```
COLUMNS:                    Total Width of Report Columns: 54
  NUM COLUMN HEADING                          USAGE   INDENT WIDTH EDIT  SEQ
  --- -------------------------------------   ------- ------ ----- ----  ---
    1 PNO                                               2      7    L     1
    2 PNAME                                             2     24    C     2
    3 DEPTNO                                            2      6    C     3
    4 SALARY                                            2      9    L     4
      *** END ***

PAGE:     HEADING   ===>
          FOOTING   ===>
FINAL:    TEXT      ===>
BREAK1:   NEW PAGE FOR BREAK? ===> NO
          FOOTING   ===>
BREAK2:   NEW PAGE FOR BREAK? ===> NO
          FOOTING   ===>
OPTIONS: OUTLINE? ===> YES            DEFAULT BREAK TEXT? ===> YES
```

Figure 4.6 - Default form (for report shown in Figure 4.5)

SALARY REPORT

EMPLOYEE NO	EMPLOYEE NAME	DEPT NO	SALARY
1111	ALPHA	D1	$10,000
4444	DELTA		$18,000
		DEPT. AVERAGE	$14,000
4555	DDELTA	D2	$16,000
1222	ABETA		$12,000
2333	BBETA		$11,500
2222	BETA		$12,500
		DEPT. AVERAGE	$13,000
		COMPANY AVERAGE	$13,333

Figure 4.7 - Formatted report

```
COLUMNS:                  Total Width of Report Columns: 55
NUM COLUMN HEADING                              USAGE    INDENT WIDTH EDIT  SEQ
--- -----------------------------------------   -------  ------ ----- ----- ---
  1 EMPLOYEE_NO                                            2      8     L    1
  2 EMPLOYEE_NAME                                          2     24     C    2
  3 DEPT NO                               BREAK1           2      6     C    3
  4 SALARY                                AVERAGE          2      9     D    4
    *** END ***

PAGE:     HEADING  ===> SALARY REPORT
          FOOTING  ===>
FINAL:    TEXT     ===> COMPANY AVERAGE
BREAK1:   NEW PAGE FOR BREAK? ===> NO
          FOOTING  ===> DEPT. AVERAGE
BREAK2:   NEW PAGE FOR BREAK? ===> NO
          FOOTING  ===>
OPTIONS: OUTLINE? ===> YES             DEFAULT BREAK TEXT? ===> YES
```

Figure 4.8 - Form for report shown in Figure 4.7 using subtotalling (average),
SALARY column formatted as currency, and column heading text

4.5 QMF EXTERNAL DATA FORMAT

QMF objects are transferred to external datasets using the QMF command EXPORT.
The QMF command IMPORT is used to transfer an external dataset to QMF.

These external datasets can then be processed using conventional techniques.
The internal QMF object **data**, which contains the results of running a procedure,
query, etc., can also be transferred to external datasets. An external dataset is in
many cases the most suitable format to process.

There a two external data formats available:
· QMF format;
· Integration Exchange Format (IXF).

The required format is specified as parameter for the EXPORT command; the format
is explicitly defined in the data and so is not required for the IMPORT command. The

QMF format can be used for all objects, whereas the IXF format can only be used for tables and data.

Note 1): The field names used in tables and figures are in most cases not standard IBM names, and are used to simplify the showing of interrelationships between fields.

Note 2): The formats may change in future QMF releases. The version number is present in the header record.

4.6 IXF DATA

The external IXF data consist of the following records:

- header record;
- table record;
- column record;
- data record.

Each record is identified by its type. Figure 4.9 shows the form of an external dataset having n columns and m rows. Every data record contains m data values for each row; the corresponding column record points to the location and attributes of the data values.

4.6.1 IXF Header Record

The (one) header record is always the first record in the external dataset and describes the attributes of the dataset. Table 4.1 shows the format of the header record (p = number of records preceding the first data record (= IXFHNREC); m = number of columns (= IXFTNCOL); n = number of data records).

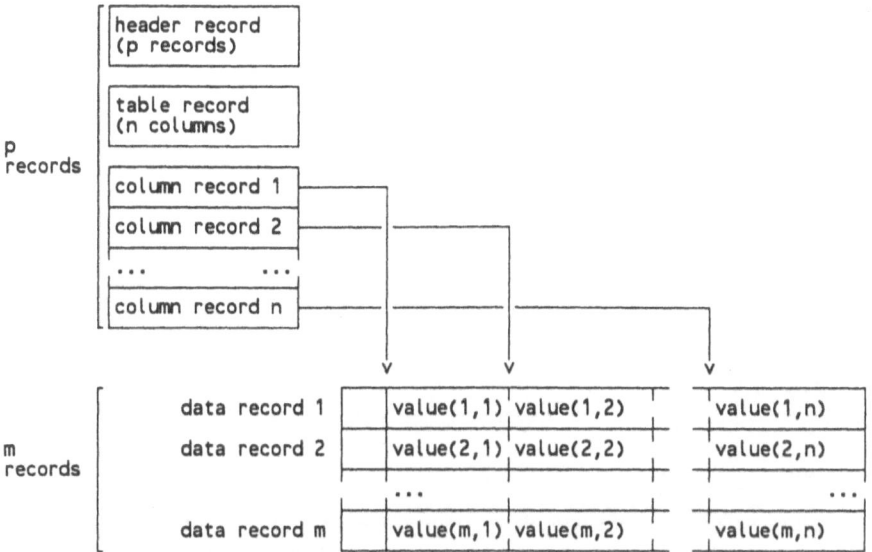

Figure 4.9 - Format of external dataset

Table 4.1 - Format of IXF header record

byte position	field name	content
01	IXFIDENT	record type identifier "H"
02-04	IXFHTYPE	data type identifier "IXF"
05-08	IXFHIXVR	IXF version number
09-14	IXFHPROD	originating product name
15-20	IXFHPVR	originating product release and version number
21-28	IXFHCDAT	creation date of dataset (yyyymmdd)
29-34	IXFHCTIM	creation time of dataset (hhmmss)
35-39	IXFHNREC	number of records preceding the first data record in the dataset
40	IXFHDBCS	DBCS indicator. "Y" = DBCS data may be present
41-		reserved

All data contained in the header record are in character format.

4.6.2 IXF Table Record

The (one) table record describes the table. The table record always follows the header record. Table 4.2 shows the format of the table record.

Table 4.2 - Format of IXF table record

byte position	field name	content
01	IXFIDENT	record type identifier "T"
02-03	IXFTLNM	length of the following name field
04-21*	IXFTNAME	name of table from which the data were retrieved
22-29*	IXFTOWNR	name of the owner of the database table
30-41	IXFTSRC	data source "DB2"
42	IXFTDD	form of data description "C" (by column)
43	IXFTFMT	data format; "C" = character (OUTPUTMODE=CHARACTER) "M" = machine (OUTPUTMODE=BINARY)
44	IXFTLOC	data location "I" (internal)
45-49	IXFTNCOL	number of column records present
50-		reserved

* blank indicates that no entry is present.

All data contained in the table record are in character format.

4.6.3 IXF Column Record

A column record describes each column. One column record exists for each column in the data. The column records are grouped together and follow the table record. Table 4.3 shows the format of a column record.

Table 4.3 - Format of IXF column record

byte position	field name	content
01	IXFIDENT	record type identifier "C"
02-03	IXFCLNM	length of the following column name field
04-21	IXFCNAME	column name
22	IXFCNULL	indicator set to show whether nulls are allowed "Y" = nulls are allowed "N" = nulls are not allowed
23	IXFCSEL	column selected indicator "Y"
24	IXFCKEY	key indicator "K" = key field "N" = non-key field
25	IXFCCL	data class "R"
26-28	IXFCTYPE	data type code, see Appendix E
29-33	IXFCCODE	code page "00000"
34-38		reserved
39-43	IXFCLENG	column data length
44-49	IXFCPOS	starting position of column data
50-79	IXFCLBL	column label information, blank if not present
80-81	IXFCZERO	"00"

All data contained in the column record are in character format.

4.6.4 IXF Data Record

One data record is present for each row. The data record contains the data values for that row; the corresponding column record indicates the position and characteristics of the data value in the record. Table 4.4 shows the format of a data record.

The column record field IXFCPOS points to the starting position in the data record for the value pertaining to that column. This position is relative to IXFDBLNK. Two parameters affect the position of the pointer; are nulls permitted (i.e. NOT NULL has not been specified) and is the field type VARCHAR. The two parameters may be used in combination. Figure 4.10 shows the interrelationship between column record and data record.

Table 4.4 - Format of IXF data record

byte position	field name	content
01 02-04 05 06-	IXFIDENT IXFDBLNK IXFDDATA	record type identifier "D" reserved blank row data in either character or binary form as specified in the table record.

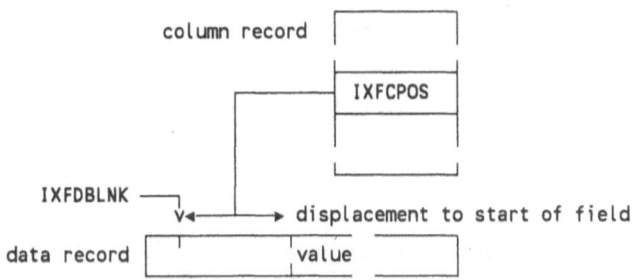

Figure 4.10 - Interrelationship between column record and data record

4.6.4.1 Format of character data (IXFTFMT="C"). The data value for a VARCHAR field is prefixed with a 5-digit field containing the current data length field. A single byte is reserved for the null indicator. Figure 4.11 shows the position of the pointer to the start of data value. An example is shown in Figure 4.13.

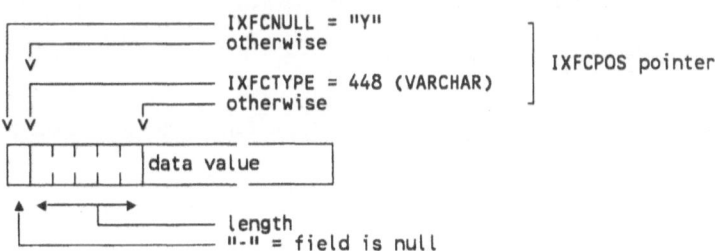

Figure 4.11 - Form of data value (character format)

Format of binary data (IXFTFMT="M"). The data value for a VARCHAR field is prefixed with a half-word containing the current data length field. A half-word is reserved for the null indicator. Figure 4.12 shows the position of the pointer to the start of data value. An example is shown in Figure 4.14.

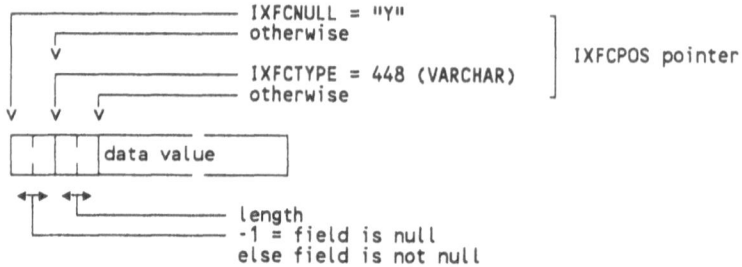

Figure 4.12 - Form of data value (binary format)

4.6.5 Example

Appendix H shows the content of the PERS table from which the external data are to be extracted. Figure 4.13 shows the content of the external dataset exported by the QMF procedure EXPORT DATA TO TEMP (DATAFORMAT=IXF,OUTPUTMODE=CHARACTER after running the QMF query SELECT * FROM PERS. Figure 4.14 shows the content of the binary external data set exported by the QMF procedure EXPORT DATA TO TEMP (DATAFORMAT=IXF,OUTPUTMODE=BINARY after running the QMF query SELECT * FROM PERS. Each record is displayed in character and hexadecimal format.

```
HIXF0000QMF    V2R2M019891013133242000004N
T18                        DB2           CCI00002
C03PNO              NYNR48400000    00400000002
00
C05PNAME            YYNR44800000    00024000007
00
D      1111 00005ALPHA
D      2222 00004BETA
D      3333 00005GAMMA
D      4444-00000
```

Figure 4.13 - External character data format

4.7 QMF EXTERNAL DATA

QMF external data format can be used to export the following QMF objects:

- data;
- form;
- procedure;
- query;
- report;
- table.

QMF external data can be used for the following purposes:

- further processing;
- transfer objects between databases;
- create back-up.

The chart, form and table external data formats are not particularly useful for further processing by an application, and so are not discussed here. Procedures and queries are stored as character data in the same form as in QMF. The data and report formats are described in the following sections of this chapter.

Note: As printed, some of the rows wrap onto a second line.

```
 HIXF0000QMF   V2R2M01989101313330600004N
 CCECFFFFDDC444EFDFDFFFFFFFFFFFFFFFFFFFFD
 8976000084600052924019891013133306000045

 T18                         DB2         CMI00002
 EFF44444444444444444444444444CCF444444444CDCFFFFF
 3180000000000000000000000000042200000000034900002

 C03PNO               NYNR48400000     00400000003
00

CFFDDD444444444444444DEDDFFFFFFFF44444FFFFFFFFFFF444444444444444444444444
4444444FF

303756000000000000000585948400000000000040000000300000000000000000000000
000000000

 C05PNAME             YYNR44800000     00024000006
00

CFFDDCDC4444444444444EEDDFFFFFFFF44444FFFFFFFFFFF444444444444444444444444
4444444FF

305751450000000000000885944800000000000002400000600000000000000000000000
000000000

 D    .........ALPHA...................
 C44440001100000CDDCC0000000000000000000
 400000011C0005137810000000000000000000

 D    .........BETA....................
 C4444000220000CCEC00000000000000000000
 400000022C0004253100000000000000000000

 D    .........GAMMA...................
 C4444000330000CCDDC0000000000000000000
 400000033C0005714410000000000000000000

 D    ....<............................
 C444400044FF00000000000000000000000000
 400000044CFF00000000000000000000000000
```

Figure 4.14 - External binary data format

4.8 QMF DATA FORMAT

The QMF data comprise a logical data stream consisting of physical fixed length records.

There are two types of record:
· header records;
· data records.

The length of a data record determines the logical record length. One data record exists for each data row. Figure 4.15 shows the format of the external QMF data (p = number of physical header records; n = number of columns).

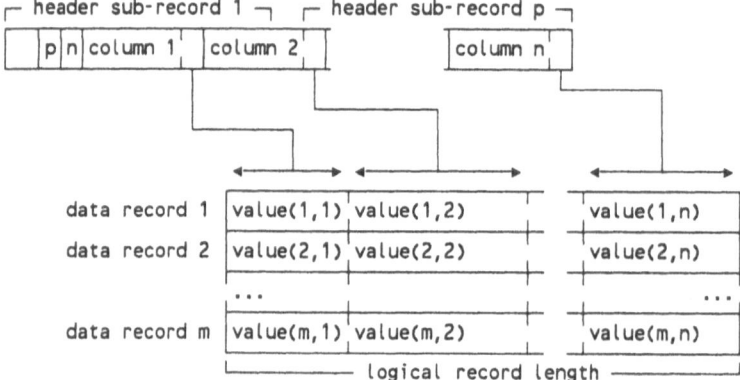

Figure 4.15 - Form of dataset containing external QMF data

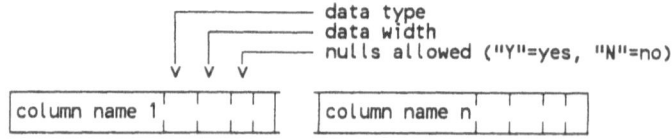

Figure 4.16 - Data header sub-record format

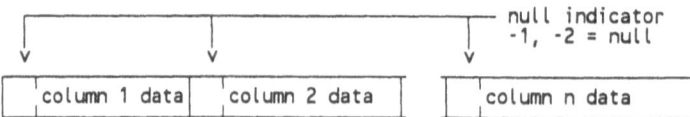

Figure 4.17 - Data value sub-record format

4.8.1 QMF Data Header Record

The data header records describe the characteristics of the stored data. A data header record is comprised of data header sub-records; each data header sub-record describes the corresponding column. The data heading sub-records are present as a stream of data in the physical header records. The data heading sub-records may be split across physical data header records. The length of the data determines the length of a physical data header record. Table 4.5 and Figure 4.16 show the format of a data header sub-record.

Table 4.5 - Format of data header sub-record

byte position	field name	content
01-08	QMFDLVL	QMF format level
09-10	QMFDNREC	number of header records (half-word)
11-12	QMFDNCOL	number of columns (half-word)
13-30	QMFDNAME	column name
31-32	QMFDTYPE	data type code, see Appendix E
33-34	QMFDWID	data width (half-word), see Table 4.7
35	QMFDNULL	indicator set to show whether nulls are allowed "Y" = nulls are allowed "N" = nulls are not allowed
36		reserved

4.8.2 QMF Data Value Record

One data value record is present for each row. The data value record consists of data value sub-records, one sub-record for each column. The data value record contains the data values for that row; the corresponding logical header record describes the characteristics of the data value sub-record. Table 4.6 and Figure 4.17 show the format of a data value sub-record.

Table 4.6 - Format of QMF data value sub-record

byte position	field name	content
01-02	QMFDIND	indicator variable (half-word) -1 or -2 = null value else non-null value
03-	QMFDDATA	row data in the format as stored in the database table, see Table 4.8 for the external length

Table 4.7 - Width of external data

DB2 field type	width
DECIMAL(p,s)	CEIL((p+1)/2)
VARCHAR(n)	n+2; the actual data length is in a half-word preceding the data, QMFDWID is the maximum width
FLOAT	8
other	defined width

Note: CEIL represents the round-up function.

4.8.3 Example

Figure 4.18 shows the content of the external data exported by the QMF procedure EXPORT DATA TO TEMP (DATAFORMAT=QMF after running the QMF query SELECT * FROM PERS.

```
REL 1.0 ....PNO                   .U.
DCD4F4F40000DDD444444444444444440E0
95301B0002027560000000000000000144

.N.PNAME                .(..Y.
0D0DDCDC4444444444444440C01E0444444
0507514500000000000000100880000000

.........ALPHA
000110000CDDCC444444444444444444444
0011C000513781000000000000000000000

.........BETA
000220000CCEC444444444444444444444
0022C000425310000000000000000000000

.........GAMMA
000330000CCDDC44444444444444444444
0033C000571441000000000000000000000

....<....
00044FF004444444444444444444444444
0044CFF0000000000000000000000000000
```

Figure 4.18 - QMF external data format

4.9 QMF REPORT FORMAT

The QMF report data comprise the following record types:

· header record (H-record);
· data value record (V-record);
· data continuation record (C-record);
· data table descriptor record (T-record);
· table row record (R-record);
· report line record (L-record);
· end record (E-record).

The dataset consists of variable length records. The length of the largest record determines the maximum logical record length. Of these seven record formats only the H-, T-, R-, L- and E-records are of interest for general applications. The other records are only required for special applications, and are not described in this book. Figure 4.20 shows an example of the format of a QMF external report.

4.9.1 QMF Report Header Record Format

The report header record (Table 4.8) identifies the exported report.

4.9.2 QMF Report Table Record Format (T-Record)

The report table record (Table 4.9) describes the form of the subsequent row records (R-records).

4.9.3 QMF Report Table Row Record (R-Record)

The report table row record (Table 4.10) describes the form of the data values for a single row. The actual data values are present as report line records (L-records).

Table 4.8 - Format of QMF report header record

byte position	field name	content
01	QMFIDENT	record type identifier "H"
02		blank
03-05	QMFHPROD	product identifier "QMF"
06		blank
07-08	QMFHQVR	QMF version number used for the export
09		blank
10	QMFHTYPE	object type "F" = form "R" = report "T" = prompted query
11		blank
12-13	QMFHOLVL	QMF object level "01" = report "03" = form "01" = prompted query
14		blank
15	QMFHFMT	format "E"
16		blank
17	QMFHSTAT	status "E" = contains errors "W" = contains warnings "V" = valid
18		blank
19	QMFHIND	whole or partial object indicator "W" = whole object
20		blank
21	QMFHLANG	national language in use at time of export "E" = English
22		blank
23	QMFHACT	action to be taken when object imported "R" = replace existing object
24		blank
25-26	QMFHLCA	length of control area at the beginning of each following record "01" for form "02" for report "01" for prompted query
27		blank
28-29	QMFHLIF	length of integer fields in V and T records, "03"
30		blank
31-38	QMFHDATE	date stamp (yy/mm/dd)
39		blank
40-44	QMFHTIME	time stamp (hh:mm)

Table 4.9 - Format of QMF report table record

byte position	field name	content
01	QMFIDENT	record type identifier "T"
02		blank
displacements following the control area (QMFHLCA = length)		
+01		blank
+02-05	QMFTNO	table number (1001-9999)
+06		blank
+07-09	QMFTROWS	number of rows in table (000-999 or "* ") "* " means table consists of all following R-records
+10		blank
+11-13	QMFTCOLS	number of columns in the record (000-999
displacements apply to the following sub-record		
+01		blank
+02-05	QMFTFNO	field number for this column
+06		blank
+07-09	QMFTDLEN	length of data values in this column

Table 4.10 - Format of QMF report data table record

byte position	field name	content
01	QMFIDENT	record type identifier "R"
02-03		blank
04-05	QMFRTYPE	column type "C " = CHAR or VARCHAR "D " = currency notation "E " = FLOAT "K " = decimal notation (thousands separator) "L " = INTEGER, SMALLINT or DECIMAL "P " = percent notation "TD" = DATE "TT" = TIME
06-08		reserved
09		blank
10-15	QMFRDSPP	displacement to previous field
16		blank
17-22	QMFRDSPS	displacement to start of field
23		blank
24-29	QMFRDSPE	displacement to end of field
30		blank
31-36		"000001"

Note: The displacements are relative to QMFLDATA

4.9.4 QMF Report Line Record (L-Record)

An L-record contains the data values for each report line. Table 4.11 shows the format of a report line record. L-records may be continued; the field QMFCONT is set to indicate a continuation. The continuation record (C-record) immediately follows the record being continued.

Table 4.11 - Format of QMF report line record

byte position	field name	content
01	QMFIDENT	record type identifier "L"
02	QMFCONT	continuation indicator " " = not continued "C" = continued "D" = DBCS continuation
03		blank
04-06	QMFLPART	report part "110" = page heading "120" = foot heading "13n" = break heading; n = break number, 1-6 "15n" = break footing; n = break number, 1-6 "170" = column heading "180" = detail line "181" = group summary line "190" = final footing
07		blank
08-15	QMFLATTR	line type attributes
the following displacements are relative to QMFLATTR		
+01		"1"
+02		"1" = data present , "0" = absent
+03		"1" = text present , "0" = absent
+04		"1" = separator present , "0" = absent
+05		"1" = column wrap present , "0" = absent
+06		"1" = line wrap present , "0" = absent
+07		"1" = second data line present , "0" = absent
+08		reserved
16		blank
17-	QMFLDATA	report line

4.9.5 QMF Report Line Continuation Record (C-Record)

A C-record is a continuation of the preceding record and may itself be continued. Table 4.12 shows the format of a report line continuation record.

Table 4.12 - Format of QMF report line record

byte position	field name	content
01	QMFIDENT	record type identifier "C"
02	QMFCONT	continuation indicator " " = not continued "C" = continued "D" = DBCS continuation
03		blank
04-	QMFCDATA	report line continuation

4.9.6 QMF Report End Record (E-Record)

The single E-record is the final record in the external object. Table 4.13 shows the format of the report end record.

Table 4.13 - Format of QMF report end record

byte position	field name	content
01 02	QMFIDENT	record type identifier "E" blank

```
H QMF 05 R 01 E V W E R 02 03 94/10/13 18:49
V  1001 006 PERIOO
V  1002 003 016
T  1010 002 006 1013 005 1014 006 1015 006 1016 006 1017 006 1012 008
R  L      000001 000003 000009 000001
R  C      000010 000012 000035 000001
L  110 10000000
L  110 10000000
L  170 10000000       PNO   PNAME
L  170 10010000       -------  --------------------------
L  180 11000000       1111   ALPHA
L  180 11000000       2222   BETA
L  180 11000000       3333   GAMMA
L  180 11000000       4444   -
L  120 10000000
L  120 10000000
E
```

Figure 4.20 - External QMF report format

5

Program Preparation

All the vital mechanisms, varied as they are, have only one object, that of preserving constant the conditions of life in the internal environment.

Leçons sur les Phénomènes de la Vie ...

Claude Bernard

5.1 INTRODUCTION

Application programs, independent of the host language, which are to make use of SQL services are subjected to the same general process:
· preprocess (for certain languages, e.g. PL/I)
· precompile
· compile
· pre-linkage edit (for reentrant C programs)
· linkage edit
· bind
to produce an executable program.

The **precompile** phase converts embedded SQL statements in the source program to statements appropriate for the host language and produces a Data Base Request Module (DBRM) from the SQL statements; this DBRM is later used as input for the bind processor. The **compile** phase converts the (precompiled) source program into an object module. The **linkage editor** phase converts the object module into an executable load module (the **binder** has superseded the linkage editor — this binder is not concerned with the DB2 bind process). The **bind** phase takes the DBRM from the precompile phase to produce a **package** or **plan**. The package (or plan) is used to determine authorisation and access paths to the database, and is stored in the DB2 database with the specified **package-name** or **plan-name**, as appropriate. At execution-time, the program being executed requires an associated plan; if the preparation phase produced packages rather than plans, the bind processor must be used to produce a plan from these packages. Packages compensate this apparent additional work with increased flexibility. Figure 5.1 shows the general form of the preparation required for a DB2 program. Note that there are two ways of producing a plan: either package or DBRMLIB member input. Because a plan created from packages does not actually include the packages but only references, a rebind of such plans is not required when the constituent packages change. Table 5.1 contains a brief description of the principal files; certain files (e.g. list files, work files, libraries) are omitted to avoid introducing unnecessary detail into the table.

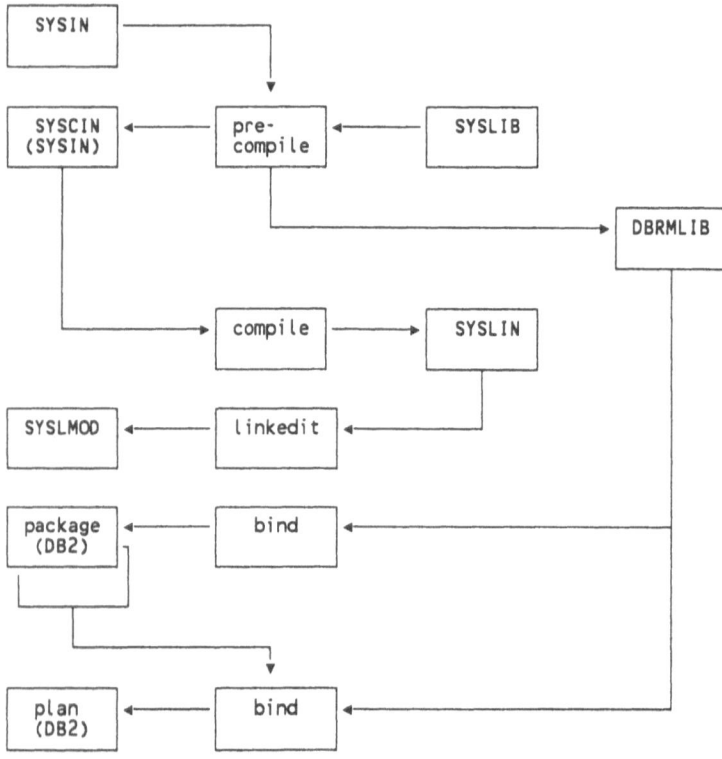

Figure 5.1 - Data flow during program preparation

Programs may be prepared for operation in the DB2 environment using either JCL batch procedures, the ISPF DB2I (DB2 Interactive) application or DSNH command. The DB2I interface has the advantage that the user is prompted for the necessary input. However, the experienced user will probably prefer to modify the standard procedures to satisfy his requirements; batch jobs avoid blockage of the terminal while the foreground job is running. DB2I is briefly described in section 5.3 and fully explained in Chapter 6; DSNH is also described in Chapter 6.

5.2 JCL PROCEDURES

IBM supplies JCL procedures for the preparation of programs written in the supported host languages; the procedures are listed in Table 5.2. The DD name for the input dataset is always SYSIN. The standard procedures do not perform a bind. Table 5.3 shows the step names for the various host languages.
Note: The standard procedures may have been modified at your site.

Table 5.1 - Principal files used during program preparation

Precompile:

SYSIN	I	source input
SYSLIB	I	library input (using SQL INCLUDE)
SYSCIN	O	precompiled source input (=compiler input)
DBRMLIB	O	database request information (DB2 access information)

Compile:

| SYSIN | I | precompiler output |
| SYSLIN | O | object module (=linkage editor input) |

Linkage editor:

| SYSLIN | I | object module (=compiler output) |
| SYSLMOD | O | load (executable) module |

Bind:

| DBRMLIB | I | database request information from precompiler |

I = input, O = output

Table 5.2 - DB2 program preparation JCL procedures

language	procedure	input step name
Assembler F	DSNHASM	PC
Assembler H High Level Assembler	DSNHASMH	PC
C	DSNHC	PC
COBOL	DSNHCOB	PC
VS COBOL II COBOL/370	DSNHCOB2	PC
PL/I	DSNHPLI	PPLI

Table 5.3 - DB2 program preparation JCL procedure step names

step\language	Assembler	C	COBOL	PL/I
preprocess	-	-	-	PPLI
precompile	PC	PC	PC	PC
compile	ASM	C	COB	PLI
pre-linkedit	-	PLKED	-	-
linkedit	LKED	LKED	LKED	LKED

Table 5.4 - Preparation step parameters

procedure\step	PC	compile	LKED
DSNHASM	HOST(ASM)	OBJECT,NODECK	XREF
DSNHASMH	HOST(ASM)	OBJECT,NODECK	XREF
DSNHC 1)	HOST(C)	RENT	MAP
DSNHCOB	HOST(COBOL)	-	XREF
DSNHCOB2	HOST(COB2)	-	XREF
DSNHPLI 2)	HOST(PLI)	OBJECT,NODECK	XREF

1) C programs have an additional pre-linkedit step (stepname: PLKED) before the actual linkage edit step.

2) PL/I programs have an additional preprocessor step (stepname: PPLI) before the DB2 precompiler step; this step has the following parameter:

          MACRO,NOSYNTAX,NODECK,NOINSOURCE

Syntax:
```
►►——// EXEC ┬─ DSNHASM──┐
            ├─ DSNHASMH─┤ ┌─,MEM=─┬─membername─┐
            ├─ DSNHC────┤ └───────┴─TEMPNAME───┘
            ├─ DSNHCOB──┤
            ├─ DSNHCOB2─┤
            └─ DSNHPLI──┘
```

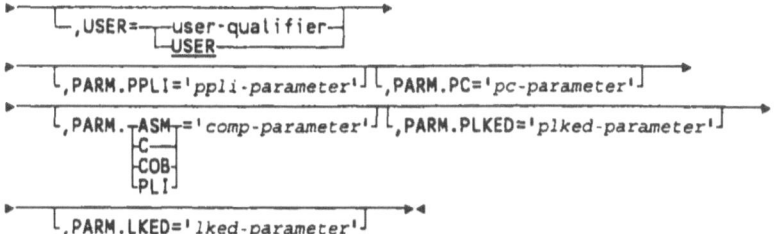

The first parameter after the EXEC keyword specifies the name of the procedure to be invoked:

DSNHASM   Assembler F
DSNHASMH   Assembler H, High Level Assembler
DSNHC   C language
DSNHCOB   COBOL
DSNHCOB2   COBOL II, COBOL/370
DSNHPLI   PL/I.

MEM = member-name

member-name specifies the member name to be assigned in the following libraries:

·   DBRM library
·   load-module library.

Default: TEMPNAME.

USER = user-qualifier

user-qualifier specifies the first qualifier to be used to form the dataset names of the following libraries:

·   source library
·   DBRM library
·   load-module library

for which following library names are generated:

user-qualifier.SRCLIB.DATA
user-qualifier.DBRMLIB.DATA
user-qualifier.RUNLIB.LOAD.

Default: USER.

The parameters for the individual steps are described in the following sections.

5.2.1 PL/I Preprocessor

The PL/I preprocessor is invoked for the DSNHPLI procedure. Refer to the appropriate manual for the description of the allowable parameters for **ppli-parameter**; DB2 itself does not require any special parameters to be specified. See Table 5.4 for the standard parameters.

5.2.2 DB2 Precompiler

The DB2 precompiler performs two functions on the SQL statements:
- they are converted into the appropriate host language statements (e.g. calls);
- they are converted into a DBRM entry, which is later used by the bind processor to define the logical access parameters to the database.

pc-parameter:

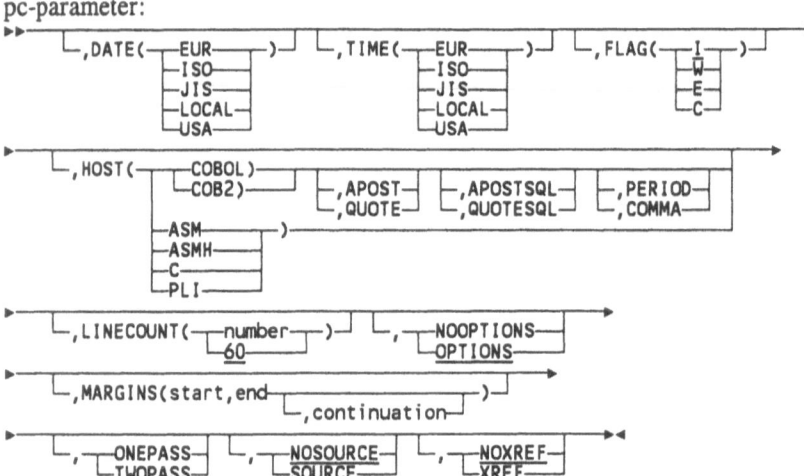

DATE(date)
The form to be used for the date representation. **Date** is one of the following:
(EUR) - IBM European format: dd.mm.yy
(ISO) - ISO format: yyyy-mm-dd
(JIS) - Japanese Industrial Standard format: yyyy-mm-dd
(LOCAL) - Site-defined format
(USA) - IBM USA format: mm/dd/yy

TIME(time)
The representation of times. **Time** is one of the following:
(EUR) - IBM European format: hh.mm.ss
(ISO) - ISO format: hh.mm.ss
(JIS) - Japanese Industrial Standard format: hh:mm:ss
(LOCAL) - Site-defined format
(USA) - IBM USA format: hh:mm [AM | PM]

FLAG(flag)
specifies the level of errors to be displayed. **Flag** is one of the following:
Default: FLAG(I)
(I) - Informational. All errors are displayed
(W) - Warning, error and completion messages
(E) - Error and completion messages
(C) - Only completion messages.

HOST(language)

> The host language.
> Default: the implicit language from the procedure name, e.g. DSNHPLI sets
> HOST(PLI). Language may be one of the following:
> **(ASM)** - Assembler F
> **(ASMH)** -Assembler H, High Level Assembler
> **(C)** - C language
> **(COBOL)** - COBOL
> **(COB2)** - COBOL II, COBOL/370
> **(FORTRAN)** - FORTRAN
> **(PLI)** - PL/I.

APOST

> An apostrophe (') is to be used as string delimiter in COBOL host language
> statements.

QUOTE

> A quote (") is to be used as string delimiter in COBOL host language
> statements.

APOSTSQL

> An apostrophe (') is to be used as string delimiter for SQL statements in
> COBOL programs.

QUOTESQL

> A quote (") is to be used as string delimiter for SQL statements in COBOL
> programs.

PERIOD

> A period (.) is to be used to separate the integral and non-integral part in
> decimal and floating-pointer literals. This parameter is only valid for COBOL
> programs.

COMMA

> A comma (,) is to be used to separate the integral and non-integral part in
> decimal and floating-pointer literals. This parameter is only valid for COBOL
> programs, cf. DECIMAL POINT IS COMMA.

LINECOUNT(number)

> **number** specifies the maximum number of lines to be printed on each page
> of the output listing.
> Default: 60.

OPTIONS

> The precompiler options are to be listed.
> Default: OPTIONS.

NOOPTIONS

> The precompiler options are not to be listed.

MARGINS(start,end[,continuation])
The margins of the source program; the default values are host language dependent. Table 5.5 shows the default values.
start - starting column.
end - ending column.
continuation - continuation column; this parameter is only used for Assembler programs.

ONEPASS
The precompiler is to use one pass to process the source statements; this means that the declaration of host variables must precede their reference.
Default for PL/I and C.
Forced for COBOL and COB2.

TWOPASS
The precompiler is to use two passes to process the source statements.
Default for Assembler.
Invalid for COBOL.

SOURCE
The source program is to be listed.

NOSOURCE
The source program is not to be listed.
Default: NOSOURCE.

XREF
A cross-reference of symbolic names used in the source program is to be listed; SQL names are listed within quotes (e.g. "PERS").

NOXREF
No cross-reference of symbolic names used in the source program is to be listed.
Default: NOXREF.

Note: For those parameters specified without default (e.g. DATE), the default defined for the installation is used.

Table 5.5 - Default margin values

language	start	end	continuation
C	1	72	-
COBOL	8	72	-
PL/I	2	72	-
Assembler	1	72	16

5.2.3 Compile

The appropriate compiler is invoked using the precompiled statements as input. Refer to the appropriate manual for the description of the allowable parameters for **comp-parameter**; DB2 itself does not require any special parameters to be specified. Table 5.4 shows the standard parameters.

5.2.4 Pre-linkedit

The pre-linker is required for programs written in the C language which are to be reentrant. Refer to the appropriate manual for the description of the allowable parameters for **plked-parameter**; DB2 itself does not require any special parameters to be specified. Table 5.4 shows the standard parameters.

5.2.5 Linkedit

The linkage editor (or binder) is invoked to produce an executable load module. Programs which are to access DB2 databases must include the necessary interface module. Three separate interfaces are available:
·   DSNALI for programs using CAF, see section 6.5
·   DSNCLI for CICS programs
·   DSNELI for all other programs.

Refer to the appropriate manual for the description of the allowable parameters for **lked-parameter**; DB2 itself does not require any special parameters to be specified. Table 5.4 shows the standard parameters.

Tip
In many cases DSNALI instead of DSNELI can be used, even when the CAF calling sequence is not adhered to, however, this does not always function correctly and may fail in the worst possible manner, i.e. it will appear to work properly.

5.2.6 Bind

The bind process stores the DBRM produced by the precompiler in the DB2 database. The bind may be invoked either interactively using DB2I or the DSNH command, or as a job with TSO executed in batch. Section 6.3.1 contains a full description of the BIND subcommand.

Tip
Because the standard IBM procedures do not include the bind process, it may be advantageous for the installation to extend these procedures to invoke the bind using TSO batch; sample JCL statements follow.

```
//TSOBATCH EXEC PGM=IKJEFT01,DYNAMNBR=20
//STEPLIB  DD   DSN=db2-library-dsname,DISP=SHR
//DBRMLIB  DD   DSN=dbrmlib-dsname,DISP=SHR
//SYSTSPRT DD   SYSOUT=*
//SYSTSIN  DD   *
   DSN
     BIND PLAN(plan-name) MEMBER(dbrm-member-name)
   END
```

dbrmlib-dsname

The dataset name of the library containing the DBRM created by the precompiler. This dataset name could also have been specified in the LIBRARY parameter for the BIND subcommand.

plan-name

The name with which the application plan is to be stored in the database.

dbrm-member-name

The name of the DBRM created by the precompiler.

Note: The **plan-name** and the **dbrm-member-name** may be the same, but need not be. A plan may also be comprised of more than one DBRM.

5.3 EXAMPLE

```
//        EXEC DSNHPLI,MEM=ALPHA,USER=BETA,
//             PARM.PC='SOURCE'
//PPLI.SYSIN DD   DSN=GAMMA.DB2.PGM(DELTA),DISP=SHR
```

Prepare the PL/I program contained as member DELTA in the dataset GAMMA.DB2.PGM as DB2 program (the source statements are to be listed by the precompiler); the prepared program is to be stored as member ALPHA in the DBRM library BETA.DBRMLIB.DATA and load-module library BETA.RUNLIB.LOAD.

5.4 DB2I (DB2 INTERACTIVE)

The DB2I primary menu enables those functions necessary for the preparation of a program to run in the DB2 environment, and for its later execution, to be selected. DB2I (described in Chapter 6) offers the following functions:
· SPUFI - process SQL statements
· DCLGEN - generate source language declarations
· prepare a DB2 application program to run (preprocess, precompile, compile, linkage edit and bind), and also optionally run the program;
· invoke DB2 precompiler
· bind, rebind, or free application plans
· run an SQL program
· issue DB2 commands
· invoke DB2 utilities.

6

DB2 Program Invocation

*The reason why the hairs stand on end, the eyes water, the throat is constricted,
the skin crawls and a shiver runs down the spine when one writes or reads a true
poem is that a true poem is necessarily an invocation of the White Goddess, or
Muse, the Mother of All Living, the ancient power of fright and lust-the female
spider or the queen bee whose embrace is death.*

The White Goddess
Robert Graves

6.1 INTRODUCTION

A DB2 program can invoked in one of two ways:
· within the DB2 environment;
· independent of DB2, but the program must connect to a DB2 subsystem.

In each case the program must have been prepared for execution as a DB2 program
using the procedures described in Chapter 5 or in this chapter. The DB2
environment itself can exist in either dialogue (TSO) or batch mode, and is invoked
using DB2 commands.

6.2 COMMANDS PERTAINING TO DB2

There are two classes of commands concerning the DB2 operational environment:
- administrative commands (e.g. START DATABASE);
- TSO commands to invoke a DB2 command processor (e.g. DSN).

This book describes only those TSO commands of interest to the application developer:
- DSN Invoke a DB2 session.
- DSNH Prepare a program in foreground.

A full description of all the DB2 commands is contained in the IBM manual: DB2 Command and Utility Reference).

6.2.1 DSN - Invoke DB2 Session

The DB2 environment is created by the TSO DSN command. The DSN command has several subcommands, e.g. the RUN subcommand used to invoke a DB2 program

Syntax:

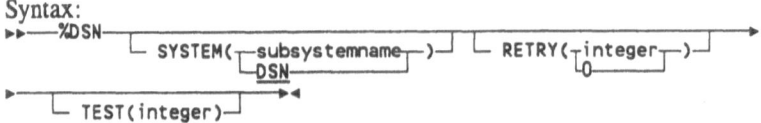

SYSTEM(subsystemname)
> The **subsystemname** specifies the name of the DB2 subsystem.
> Default: DSN.

RETRY(integer)
> The **integer** specifies the number of times an attempt to connect the DB2 subsystem is to be made. These attempts take place at 30 second intervals.
> Default: 0 (maximum 120).

TEST
> The trace facility is to be started.

Example:
```
DSN SYSTEM(DSNT)
   RUN PROGRAM(DBCB) PLAN(PDBCB)
END
```
Create a connection to the DSNT DB2 subsystem. Within this DB2 environment, invoke the DB2 program DBCB with plan PDBCB. *Note*: REXX commands must be written in quotes.

6.2.2 DSNH - Prepare Program in Foreground

The DSNH command procedure prepares a program for execution in the DB2 environment. DSNH is also invoked by DB2I for the various phases (precompilation, compilation, linkage-edit, bind, etc.). This command is included only for completeness (see the IBM manual: DB2 Command and Utility Reference for a description of the parameters).

Syntax:
```
►►──%DSNH INPUT(datasetname)────────────────►◄
                            ▲           ┐
                            └ parameter ┘
```

Example:
```
%DSNH INPUT('''TSOUS01.COBOL.PGMLIB(DBCB8)''')
```

This is equivalent to:
```
%DSNH INPUT(TSOUS01.COBOL.PGMLIB(DBCB8)) SUFFIX(NO)
```

6.3 DB2 SUBCOMMANDS

DB2 subcommands are issued either within the DB2 environment or in dialogue via DB2I (DB2 Interactive). The use of DB2I is described in Section 6.4.

This book describes only those DB2 subcommands of interest to the application developer:

· BIND PACKAGE   Build an application package.
· BIND PLAN   Build an application plan.
· DCLGEN   Generate a table declaration.
· END   Terminate DB2 session.
· FREE   Free an application plan.
· REBIND   Rebind an application plan.
· RUN   Invoke a DB2 program.
· SPUFI   Invoke SPUFI.

A full description of all the DB2 subcommands is contained in the IBM manual: DB2 Command and Utility Reference.

6.3.1 BIND PACKAGE - Build an Application Package

The application package contains the information necessary to process the SQL requests contained in the program (module). The BIND PLAN command binds one or more packages to form a plan, which is used at run-time for the database access. Alternatively, the BIND PLAN command can bind one or more DBRMs directly to form a plan.

BIND requires that TSO and DB2 be available (either dialogue or batch). Chapter 9 (Transactions) contains information concerning the significance of the ISOLATION, ACQUIRE and RELEASE parameters.

Note: The user must have been granted authorisation to perform the bind operation. The database administrator gives a user authority with the SQL GRANT. The user may have been given authority to sub-delegate his authorisations.

Syntax:

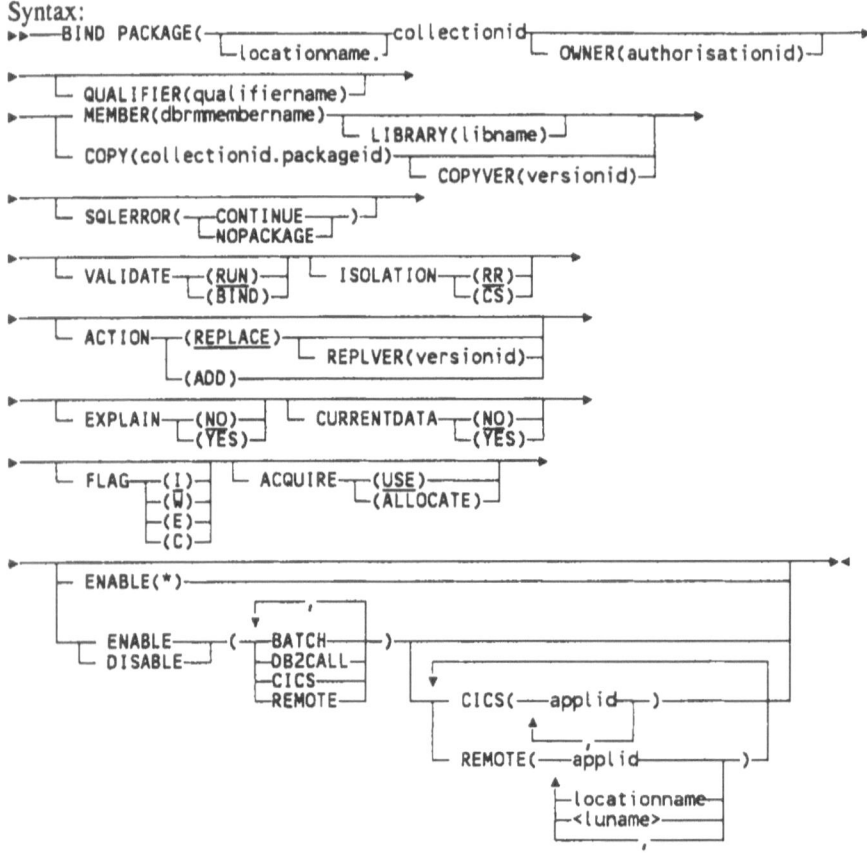

PACKAGE(locationname.collectionid)

> The **collectionid** specifies the name of the collection where the package is to be stored.
>
> The optional **locationname** specifies the location where the package is to be bound. If omitted, the plans are stored in the SYSIBM.SYSPLAN system catalogue.
>
> Default: The plan is unnamed and error checking is performed, but no plan is stored in the database.

MEMBER(dbrmmembername)

> The **dbrmmembername** specifies the names of database request modules (DBRMs) which are to be used to produce the application plan. The LIBRARY parameter identifies the library containing the DBRMs.

LIBRARY(dbrmlibraryname)

The **dbrmlibraryname** specifies the dataset name of the library containing the DBRMs.

Default: The libraries defined by the DBRMLIB DD statement.

ACTION

Specify whether the application plan may be added or replaced.

(REPLACE) - The application plan may replace an application having the same name. This is the default.

RETAIN - The bind and execute authorisations for the replaced application plan are to be retained.

Note: The default is not RETAIN, which means that any existing authorisations are lost.

(ADD) - The application plan is not to replace an application having the same name.

VALIDATE

Specify when validity checks are to be performed.

(RUN) - The validity checks are performed at execution time. This is the default.

(BIND) - The validity checks are performed during the bind processing.

ISOLATION

Specify the isolation characteristics of the application plan.

(RR) - Repeatable Read. Database values read or changed by a program using this application plan cannot be changed until the program either terminates or performs a commit. This is the default.

(CS) - Cursor Stability. Database values read by programs using this application plan are protected only while the particular row is being processed. Database values changed by a program using this application plan are protected only until the program either terminates or performs a commit.

FLAG

Specify the level of errors that are to be displayed.

(I) - Informational. All errors are displayed. This is the default.

(W) - Warning, error and completion messages.

(E) - Error and completion messages.

(C) - Completion messages only.

ACQUIRE

The ACQUIRE keyword specifies when resources are to be acquired.

(USE) - The table spaces are opened and locks are acquired only when the program using the application plan first uses them. This is the default.

(ALLOCATE) - The table spaces are opened and locks are acquired when the program allocates the application plan.

RELEASE

The RELEASE keyword specifies when resources are to be released.

(COMMIT) - The resources are released each time a commit is issued. This is
the default.
(DEALLOCATE) - The resources are released when the program terminates.

Note: If ACQUIRE(ALLOCATE) is specified, RELEASE(DEALLOCATE) must be used.

EXPLAIN

The EXPLAIN keyword specifies whether information on processing of the
SQL statements is to be provided. This information is described in Section
8.2.12.
(NO) - No information is to be provided. This is the default.
(YES) - Explain information is to be placed in the creator's
userid.PLAN_TABLE table; this table must exist when the application plan is
used.

Example:
    BIND PLAN(ALPHA) MEMBER(BETA) ACTION(ADD)
The DBRM member BETA is used to create the application plan ALPHA; the application
plan will not replace an application plan having the same name.

6.3.2 BIND PLAN - Build an Application Plan

Every program (executable module produced by the linkage editor) running in the
DB2 environment requires an application plan. The application plan contains
information necessary to process the SQL requests contained in the program. The
BIND PLAN subcommand takes either the DBRM (or DBRMs) generated by the DB2
precompiler or packages produced by the BIND PACKAGE subcommand to produce the
application plan, which it stores in the database. BIND requires that TSO and DB2 be
available (either dialogue or batch). Chapter 9 (Transactions) contains information
concerning the significance of the ISOLATION, ACQUIRE and RELEASE parameters.

Note: The user must have been granted authorisation to perform the bind operation.
The database administrator gives a user authority with the SQL GRANT. The user may
have been given authority to sub-delegate his authorisations.

Syntax:

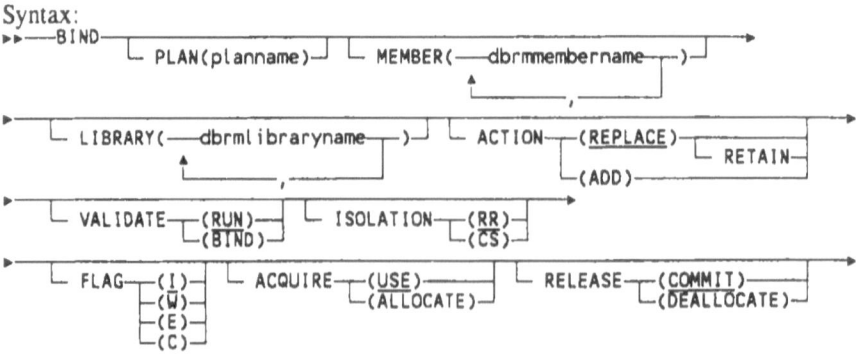

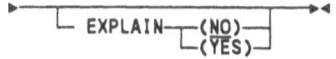

PLAN(planname)

The **planname** specifies the name with which the application plan is to be stored in the database; plans are stored in the SYSIBM.SYSPLAN system catalogue.
Default: The plan is unnamed and error checking is performed, but no plan is stored in the database.

MEMBER(dbrmmembername)

The **dbrmmembername** specifies the names of database request modules (DBRMs) which are to be used to produce the application plan. The LIBRARY parameter identifies the library containing the DBRMs.

LIBRARY(dbrmlibraryname)

The **dbrmlibraryname** specifies the dataset name of the library containing the DBRMs.
Default: The libraries defined by the DBRMLIB DD statement.

ACTION

Specify whether the application plan may be added or replaced.
(REPLACE) - The application plan may replace an application having the same name. This is the default.
RETAIN - The bind and execute authorisations for the replaced application plan are to be retained.
Note: The default is not RETAIN, which means that any existing authorisations are lost.
(ADD) - The application plan is not to replace an application having the same name.

VALIDATE

Specify when validity checks are to be performed.
(RUN) - The validity checks are performed at execution time. This is the default.
(BIND) - The validity checks are performed during the bind processing.

ISOLATION

Specify the isolation characteristics of the application plan.
(RR) - Repeatable Read. Database values read or changed by a program using this application plan cannot be changed until the program either terminates or performs a commit. This is the default.
(CS) - Cursor Stability. Database values read by programs using this application plan are protected only while the particular row is being processed. Database values changed by a program using this application plan are protected only until the program either terminates or performs a commit.

FLAG

Specify the level of errors that are to be displayed.
(I) - Informational. All errors are displayed. This is the default.
(W) - Warning, error and completion messages.
(E) - Error and completion messages.
(C) - Completion messages only.

ACQUIRE

The ACQUIRE keyword specifies when resources are to be acquired.
(USE) - The table spaces are opened and locks are acquired only when the program using the application plan first uses them. This is the default.
(ALLOCATE) - The table spaces are opened and locks are acquired when the program allocates the application plan.

RELEASE

The RELEASE keyword specifies when resources are to be released.
(COMMIT) - The resources are released each time a commit is issued. This is the default.
(DEALLOCATE) - The resources are released when the program terminates.

Note: If ACQUIRE(ALLOCATE) is specified, RELEASE(DEALLOCATE) must be used.

EXPLAIN

The EXPLAIN keyword specifies whether information on processing of the SQL statements is to be provided. This information is described in Section 8.2.12.
(NO) - No information is to be provided. This is the default.
(YES) - Explain information is to be placed in the creator's userid.PLAN_TABLE table; this table must exist when the application plan is used.

Example:
```
BIND PLAN(ALPHA) MEMBER(BETA) ACTION(ADD)
```
The DBRM member BETA is used to create the application plan ALPHA; the application plan will not replace an application plan having the same name.

6.3.3 DCLGEN - Table Declaration Generator

The DCLGEN subcommand creates the declaration for a table or view using information from the database. A COBOL or PL/I program can use this declaration with the EXEC SQL DECLARE TABLE statement.

Syntax:

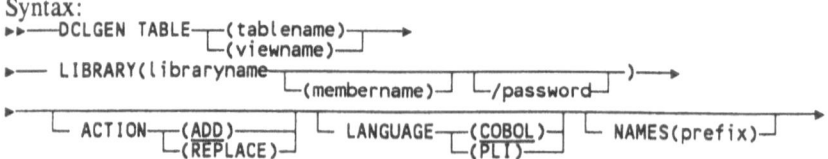

```
►───────┬─────────────────────────┬──┬──────┬───┬───────┬──────────────►◄
        └ STRUCTURE(structurename)─┘  ├ APOST┤   └ LABEL─┬─(NO)──┐
                                      └ QUOTE┘           └─(YES)─┘
```

tablename
>The name of the table for which the declaration is to be generated.

viewname
>The name of the view for which the declaration is to be generated.

LIBRARY(libraryname(membername)/password)
>**Libraryname** is the name of the dataset which is to contain the declaration. The dataset may be either partitioned (library) or sequential, and must exist. For a dataset which is not fully qualified, the following dataset name is generated:
>
>>'user-prefix.**libraryname.language**'
>
>**Language** is the default language as defined in the DB2I defaults panel. **Membername** is the member name with which the declaration is stored in the library. **Membername** must be specified for a partitioned dataset and may not be specified for a sequential dataset.

ACTION
>The ACTION keyword specifies whether the declaration may be added or replaced.
>
>(REPLACE) - The declaration may replace an entry (dataset or member) having the same name.
>
>(ADD) - The declaration is not to replace an entry having the same name. This is the default.

LANGUAGE
>The LANGUAGE keyword specifies the language for which the declaration is to be used. A separate declaration must be made for each language which is going to use it.
>
>IBM default: LANGUAGE(COBOL), although this may be altered to an installation default.
>
>(COBOL) - The target language is COBOL
>
>(PLI) - The target language is PL/I.

NAMES(prefix)
>**Prefix** is the alphanumeric prefix which is to be used for the generation of the table column names. Each generated name has the form: **prefix.n** (where n = 1, 2, etc.)

prefix:

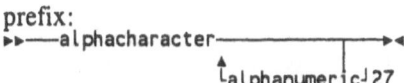

```
►►──alphacharacter────────────┬──►◄
                              ▲
                   └alphanumeric┘27
```

Example:
>NAMES(ALPHA)

Generate the names: ALPHA1, ALPHA2, etc.

STRUCTURE(structurename)
    Structurename is the name of the generated structure.
    Default: DCLtable-name or DCLview-name, as appropriate.

structurename:
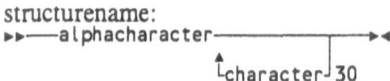

APOST
    The apostrophe (') is used as host language string delimiter; SQL uses the quotation mark (") as its string delimiter.
    Default for PL/I.

QUOTE
    The quotation mark (") is used as host language string delimiter; SQL uses the apostrophe (') as its string delimiter.
    Default for COBOL.

LABEL
    The LABEL keyword specifies whether column labels are to be placed as comments in the generated declaration.
    (NO) - No column labels are to be used. This is the default.
    (YES) - Column labels are to be used.

Example:
```
    DCLGEN TABLE (PERS) LIBRARY(ALPHA(BETA)) LANGUAGE(PLI) NAMES(U_)
```
This subcommand generates the PL/I declarations for the database table PERS as member BETA in the userid.ALPHA.PLI library, the generated column names are to have "U_" as prefix. The resulting declaration follows.

```
/***********************************************************************/
/* DCLGEN TABLE(PERS)                                                 */
/*        LIBRARY(TSOUS01.ALPHA.PLI(BETA))                            */
/*        ACTION(ADD)                                                 */
/*        LANGUAGE(PLI)                                               */
/*        NAMES(U_)                                                   */
/*        APOST                                                       */
/* ... IS THE DCLGEN COMMAND THAT MADE THE FOLLOWING STATEMENTS       */
/***********************************************************************/
EXEC SQL DECLARE PERS TABLE
             ( PNO                        DECIMAL(4,0) NOT NULL,
               PNAME                      VARCHAR(24)
             ) ;
/***********************************************************************/
/* PLI DECLARATION FOR TABLE PERS                                     */
/***********************************************************************/
DCL 1 DCLPERS,
      5 U_1        DEC FIXED(4,0),   /* PNO                           */
      5 U_2        CHAR(24) VAR;     /* PNAME                         */
/***********************************************************************/
/* THE NUMBER OF COLUMNS DESCRIBED BY THIS DECLARATION IS 2           */
/***********************************************************************/
```

6.3.4 END - Terminate DB2 Session

The END subcommand terminates the DB2 session.

Syntax:
▶▶——END——▶◀

6.3.5 FREE - Free Application Plan

The FREE subcommand is used to free (delete) application plans from the database.

Syntax:

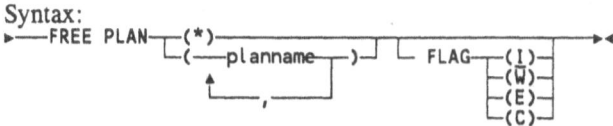

PLAN

>   The PLAN keyword specifies which application plans are to be freed.
>   **(planname)** - The name of an application plan as stored in the database.
>   (*) - All application plans for which the person invoking this subcommand
>   has the bind privilege.

FLAG

>   The level of errors to be displayed.
>   (I) - Informational. All errors are displayed. This is the default.
>   (W) - Warning, error and completion messages.
>   (E) - Error and completion messages.
>   (C) - Completion (termination) messages only.

Example:
```
FREE PLAN(ALPHA,BETA) FLAG(E)
```
The two application plans ALPHA and BETA are freed; only errors are to be displayed.

Example:
```
FREE PLAN(*)
```
All user's application plans will be freed. All messages will be displayed.

6.3.6 REBIND - Rebind Application Plan

The REBIND subcommand is used to update existing application plans when changes
have been made to the database which effect the plan; a new bind for the
application plan must be performed if changes have been made to the program
using it. Chapter 9 (Transactions) contains information concerning the significance
of the ISOLATION, ACQUIRE and RELEASE parameters.

Tip

Perform a rebind if system tables affecting the database tables associated with this
plan have been changed. This can result in significant performance improvements.
Note: An automatic rebind is performed if an index affecting the plan is deleted.

Syntax:

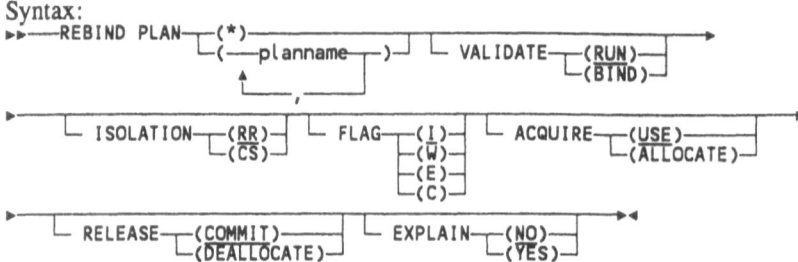

PLAN

The PLAN keyword specifies which application plans are to be rebound.

(planname) - specifies the name of the application plan as stored in the database.

(*) - All application plans for which the person invoking this subcommand has the bind privilege.

VALIDATE

The VALIDATE keyword specifies when validity checks are to be performed.

(RUN) - The validity checks are performed at execution time. This is the default.

(BIND) - The validity checks are performed during the bind processing.

ISOLATION

The ISOLATION keyword specifies the isolation characteristics of the application plan.

(RR) - Repeatable Read. Database values read or changed by a program using this application plan cannot be changed until the program either terminates or performs a commit. This is the default.

(CS) - Cursor Stability. Database values read by programs using this application plan are protected only while the particular row is being processed. Database values changed by a program using this application plan are protected only until the program either terminates or performs a commit.

FLAG

The level of errors that are to be displayed.

(I) - Informational. All errors are displayed. This is the default.

(W) - Warning, error and completion messages.

(E) - Error and completion messages.

(C) - Completion messages only.

ACQUIRE

The ACQUIRE keyword specifies when resources are to be acquired.

(USE) - The table spaces are opened and locks are acquired only when the program using the application plan first uses them. This is the default.

(ALLOCATE) - The table spaces are opened and locks are acquired when the program allocates the application plan.

RELEASE

The RELEASE keyword specifies when resources are to be released.
(COMMIT) - The resources are released each time a commit is issued. This is the default.
(DEALLOCATE) - The resources are released when the program terminates.

Note: If ACQUIRE(ALLOCATE) is specified, RELEASE(DEALLOCATE) must be used.

EXPLAIN

The EXPLAIN keyword specifies whether information how the SQL statements are processed is to be provided. This information is described in Section 8.1.12.
(NO) - No explanatory information is to be provided. This is the default.
(YES) - Explanatory information is to be placed in the creator's userid.PLAN_TABLE table; this table must exist when the application plan is used.

Example:
    REBIND PLAN(ALPHA,BETA)
A REBIND is to be made for the two application plans ALPHA and BETA.

6.3.7 RUN - Invoke DB2 Program

The RUN subcommand is used to invoke a program to run in the DB2 environment.

Syntax:

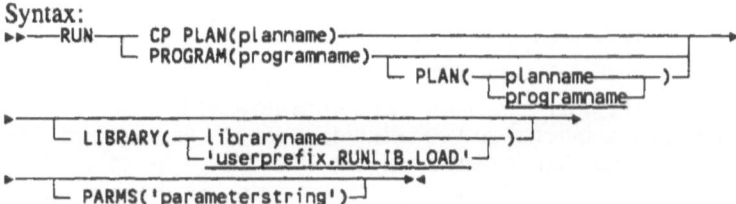

CP

The subcommand is to be initiated as a command processor; the prompt ENTER TSO COMMAND is issued. This parameter is useful in interactive debugging, see Chapter 10.

PLAN(planname)

Planname specifies the name of the program's application plan.

PROGRAM(programname)

Programname specifies the name of the program to be executed.

LIBRARY(libraryname)

Libraryname specifies the name of the library from which the program is to be fetched.
Default: The user's RUNLIB.LOAD.

PARMS(parameterstring)
>   **Parameterstring** specifies the parameters to be passed to the program.
>   Apostrophes contained in the parameter list are specified as paired
>   apostrophes.
>
>   Note: COBOL and PL/I may have two sets of parameters:
>   ·   Parameters for the run-time facility.
>   ·   Parameters for the program itself.
>   These two sets of parameters are separated by a virgule (/).

Example:
```
RUN PROGRAM(ARDB2A) PLAN(ARDB2AP) LIB('TSOUS01.RUNLIB.LOAD')
PARMS(COUNT/P1)
```
Invoke the program ARDB2A with plan ARDB2AP from 'TSOUS01.RUNLIB.LOAD'; set the
PL/I run-time COUNT option and pass P1 as execution parameter to the program.

6.3.8 SPUFI

The SPUFI subcommand invokes the SPUFI (SQL Processor Using File Input)
dialogue. This subcommand is valid only in the ISPF environment. SPUFI is
described in Section 6.4.1.

Syntax:
```
▶▶──SPUFI──▶◀
```

6.4 DB2I (DATABASE2 INTERACTIVE)

The subcommands described in Section 6.3 can also be invoked in dialogue using
DB2I. DB2I is an interactive interface to DB2 operating in the ISPF environment. The
invocation of DB2I is installation dependent, but will usually be an ISPF/PDF
selection. Figure 6.1 shows the DB2I primary option menu; the required option
number is entered after the ===>.
    DB2I options 7 (DB2 commands) and 8 (utilities) are not discussed here as they
are not directly connected with application development.

```
                       DB2I PRIMARY OPTION MENU
===>
Select one of the following DB2 functions and press ENTER.

  1   SPUFI                  (Process SQL statements)
  2   DCLGEN                 (Generate SQL and source language declarations)
  3   PROGRAM PREPARATION    (Prepare a DB2 application program to run)
  4   PRECOMPILE             (Invoke DB2 precompiler)
  5   BIND/REBIND/FREE       (BIND, REBIND, or FREE application plans)
  6   RUN                    (RUN an SQL program)
  7   DB2 COMMANDS           (Issue DB2 commands)
  8   UTILITIES              (Invoke DB2 utilities)
  D   DB2I DEFAULTS          (Set global parameters)
  X   EXIT                   (Leave DB2I)
PRESS:  END to exit          HELP for more information
```

Figure 6.1 - DB2I primary option menu

6.4.1 Option 1 - Invoke SPUFI (SQL Processor Using File Input)

SPUFI is a means of directly invoking SQL commands contained in a dataset (file). The ISPF editor may be invoked to edit (or create) the SQL commands. The processed statements are listed in the output dataset. Figure 6.2 shows the SPUFI input panel, Figure 6.3 shows the SPUFI defaults, and Figure 6.4 shows a sample display of the processed output.

Tip
SPUFI is well suited for the testing of SQL statements and for the creation of database test data.

```
                              SPUFI
===>

Enter the input data set name:        (Can be sequential or partitioned)
  1   DATA SET NAME ... ===> DB2.CNTL(CR1)
  2   VOLUME SERIAL ... ===>            (Enter if not cataloged)
  3   DATA SET PASSWORD ===>            (Enter if password protected)

Enter the output data set name:       (Must be a sequential data set)
  4   DATA SET NAME ... ===> DB2.LIST

Specify processing options:
  5   CHANGE DEFAULTS   ===> YES       (Y/N - Display SPUFI defaults panel?)
  6   EDIT INPUT ...... ===> YES       (Y/N - Enter SQL statements?)
  7   EXECUTE ......... ===> YES       (Y/N - Execute SQL statements?)
  8   AUTOCOMMIT ...... ===> YES       (Y/N - Commit after successful run?)
  9   BROWSE OUTPUT ... ===> YES       (Y/N - Browse output data set?)

PRESS: ENTER to process    END to exit    HELP for more information
```

Figure 6.2 - SPUFI input panel

```
                    CURRENT SPUFI DEFAULTS
===>

Enter the following to control your SPUFI session:
  1   ISOLATION LEVEL   ===> RR        (RR=Repeatable Read, CS=Cursor Stability)
  2   MAX SELECT LINES  ===> 250       (Maximum number of lines to be
                                         returned from a SELECT)
Output data set characteristics:
  3   RECORD LENGTH ... ===> 4092      (LRECL=Logical record length)
  4   BLOCK SIZE ...... ===> 4096      (Size of one block)
  5   RECORD FORMAT ... ===> VB        (RECFM=F, FB, FBA, V, VB, or VBA)
  6   DEVICE TYPE ..... ===> SYSDA     (Must be DASD unit name)

Output format characteristics:
  7   MAX NUMERIC FIELD ===> 20        (Maximum width for numeric fields)
  8   MAX CHAR FIELD .. ===> 80        (Maximum width for character fields)
  9   COLUMN HEADING .. ===> NAMES     (NAMES, LABELS, ANY or BOTH)

PRESS: ENTER to proceed    END to exit    HELP for more information
```

Figure 6.3 - SPUFI Defaults input panel

```
┌─────────────────────────────────────────────────────────────────┐
│ BROWSE -- TSOUS01.DB2.LIST -------------------- LINE 00000000 COL 001 080 │
│ COMMAND ===>                                           SCROLL ===> PAGE │
│ ****************************** TOP OF DATA ****************************** │
│ --------+--------+--------+--------+--------+--------+--------+------- │
│ select * from pers                                                │
│ --------+--------+--------+--------+--------+--------+--------+------- │
│    PNO  PNAME                                                      │
│ --------+--------+--------+--------+--------+--------+--------+------- │
│  3333.  GAMMA                                                     │
│  2222.  BETA                                                      │
│  1111.  ALPHA                                                     │
│  4444.  DELTA                                                     │
│  5555.  OMEGA                                                     │
│ DSNE610I NUMBER OF ROWS DISPLAYED IS 5                            │
│ DSNE616I STATEMENT EXECUTION WAS SUCCESSFUL, SQLCODE IS 100       │
│ --------+--------+--------+--------+--------+--------+--------+------- │
│ DSNE617I COMMIT PERFORMED, SQLCODE IS 0                           │
│ DSNE616I STATEMENT EXECUTION WAS SUCCESSFUL, SQLCODE IS 0         │
│ --------+--------+--------+--------+--------+--------+--------+------- │
│ DSNE601I SQL STATEMENTS ASSUMED TO BE BETWEEN COLUMNS 1 AND 72    │
│ DSNE620I NUMBER OF SQL STATEMENTS PROCESSED IS 1                  │
│ DSNE621I NUMBER OF INPUT RECORDS READ IS 1                        │
│ DSNE622I NUMBER OF OUTPUT RECORDS WRITTEN IS 20                   │
│ **************************** BOTTOM OF DATA **************************** │
└─────────────────────────────────────────────────────────────────┘
```

Figure 6.4 - Sample SPUFI output

(input) DATA SET NAME

The name of the input dataset; this dataset may be either sequential or partitioned.

VOLUME SERIAL

is required if the dataset is not catalogued.

DATA SET PASSWORD

is required to specify the password of a password-protected dataset.

(output) DATA SET NAME

The name of the output dataset which is to contain the SPUFI output; this dataset is allocated (using the SPUFI defaults) if it does not exist.

CHANGE DEFAULTS

specifies whether the SPUFI defaults are to be changed. See Figure 6.3 for a description of the SPUFI defaults.

EDIT INPUT

specifies whether the input dataset containing the SQL statements is to be edited before being processed.

EXECUTE

specifies whether the input dataset is to be passed to the SQL processor.

AUTOCOMMIT

YES specifies that an SQL commit is to be automatically performed if all of the input statements have been successfully processed.

NO specifies that the user will be prompted on completion of the processing of the input dataset to decide whether commit or rollback is to be performed; the user may also allow this decision to be deferred until a further input dataset has been processed.

Note: A SPUFI member represents a logical transaction (see Chapter 9).

BROWSE OUTPUT

YES specifies that the output dataset is to be displayed on the completion of processing.

6.4.2 Option 2 - Invoke DCLGEN (Table Declaration Generator)

The DCLGEN function creates the declaration for a table or view using information from the database. A COBOL or PL/I program can use this declaration with the EXEC SQL DECLARE TABLE statement. Figure 6.5 shows the form of the DCLGEN input panel; the input parameters are basically those described in Section 6.3.2.

```
                           DCLGEN
===>

Enter table name for which declarations are required:
 1   SOURCE TABLE NAME ===>

Enter destination data set:            (Can be sequential or partitioned)
 2   DATA SET NAME ... ===>
 3   DATA SET PASSWORD ===>            (If password protected)

Enter options as desired:
 4   ACTION .......... ===> ADD        (ADD new or REPLACE old declaration)
 5   COLUMN LABEL .... ===> NO         (Enter YES for column label)
 6   STRUCTURE NAME .. ===>                            (Optional)
 7   FIELD NAME PREFIX ===>                            (Optional)

PRESS: ENTER to process    END to exit       HELP for more information
```

Figure 6.5 - DCLGEN input panel

6.4.3 Option 3 - Perform DB2 Program Preparation

The DB2 Program Preparation function prepares a program to run in the DB2 environment. This preparation can include all necessary steps, including execution. The DB2I Defaults panel specifies which host language is to be processed. Figure 6.6 shows the form of the DB2 Program Preparation input panel.

```
                        DB2 PROGRAM PREPARATION
===>

Enter the following:
 1  INPUT DATA SET NAME .... ===> 'TSOUS01.DB2.PGM(ARDB2A4)'
 2  DATA SET NAME QUALIFIER  ===> TEMP      (For building data set names)
 3  PREPARATION ENVIRONMENT  ===> FOREGROUND(FOREGROUND,BACKGROUND,EDITJCL)
 4  RUN TIME ENVIRONMENT ... ===> TSO       (TSO, CICS, IMS)
 5  STOP IF RETURN CODE >=   ===> 8         (Lowest terminating return code)
 6  OTHER OPTIONS ===>

Select functions:          Display panel?        Perform function?
 7  CHANGE DEFAULTS ........ ===> Y  (Y/N)     .............
 8  PL/I MACRO PHASE ....... ===> N  (Y/N)     ===> N  (Y/N)
 9  PRECOMPILE ............. ===> Y  (Y/N)     ===> Y  (Y/N)
10  CICS COMMAND TRANSLATION ....  .....       ===> N  (Y/N)
11  BIND ................... ===> Y  (Y/N)     ===> Y  (Y/N)
12  COMPILE OR ASSEMBLE .... ===> Y  (Y/N)     ===> Y  (Y/N)
13  LINK ................... ===> Y  (Y/N)     ===> Y  (Y/N)
14  RUN .................... ===> Y  (Y/N)     ===> Y  (Y/N)

PRESS:   ENTER to process        END to exit       HELP for more information
```

Figure 6.6 - DB2 Program Preparation input panel

INPUT DATA SET NAME

The name of the input dataset. If the dataset name is not specified explicitly, the user's TSO prefix and the language from the DB2I Defaults panel are added as prefix and suffix, respectively. The member name for a partitioned dataset must be specified within parentheses.
Example:
'TSOUS01.DB2.PGM(ARDB2A4)'
specifies member ARDB2A4 in the dataset 'TSOUS01.DB2.PGM'

DATA SET NAME QUALIFIER

The middle qualifier to be used for building dataset names for temporary datasets.
Example:
The name of the dataset for the generated JCL statements is **userid**.TEMP.CNTL, if the dataset name qualifier is TEMP (**userid** is the high-level qualifier, CNTL is the low-level qualifier for JCL).

PREPARATION ENVIRONMENT

The environment in which the program is to be prepared:
FOREGROUND - The preparation process is to take place immediately in TSO foreground; the terminal is blocked for the duration of the preparation.
BACKGROUND - A job to perform the preparation process is to be created and submitted to run as a batch job. The submitted job uses the job statement as defined in DB2I Defaults panel.
EDITJCL - A job to perform the preparation process is to be created and passed to the edit program. The user can modify this job and must himself submit it.

RUN TIME ENVIRONMENT

The environment in which the prepared program is to run.

STOP IF RETURN CODE
> The lowest return code from any step which will cause the program preparation to terminate:
> 4 - is used for warnings
> 8 - is used for errors (higher return codes indicate severe errors).

OTHER OPTIONS
> Any additional parameters to be passed to the DSNH command procedure.

6.4.4 Option 4 - Perform DB2 Precompile

The DB2 Precompile function invokes the DB2 precompiler. Figure 6.7 shows the form of the DB2 Precompile input panel.

```
                                   PRECOMPILE
===>

Enter precompiler data sets:
 1   INPUT DATA SET .... ===> 'TSOUS01.DB2.PGM(ARDB2A4)'
 2   INCLUDE LIBRARY ... ===>

 3   DSNAME QUALIFIER .. ===> TEMP         (For building data set names)
 4   DBRM DATA SET ..... ===>

Enter processing options as desired:
 5   WHERE TO PRECOMPILE ===> FOREGROUND (FOREGROUND,BACKGROUND, or EDITJCL)
 6   OTHER OPTIONS ..... ===>

PRESS:   ENTER to process    END to exit    HELP for more information
```

Figure 6.7 - Precompile input panel

INPUT DATA SET NAME
> The name of the input dataset. If the dataset name is not specified explicitly, the user's TSO prefix and the language from the DB2I Defaults panel are added as prefix and suffix, respectively. The member name for a partitioned dataset must be specified within parentheses.
> Example:
> 'TSOUS01.DB2.PGM(ARDB2A4)'
> specifies member ARDB2A4 in the dataset 'TSOUS01.DB2.PGM'

INCLUDE LIBRARY
> The name of the input library containing members which are to be included with the EXEC SQL INCLUDE statement. If the dataset name is not specified explicitly, the user's TSO prefix is added.

DATA SET NAME QUALIFIER
> The qualifier to be used for building dataset names for temporary datasets.

DBRM DATA SET
> The name of the library which is to contain the DBRM. If the dataset name is not specified explicitly, the user's TSO prefix and DBRM are added as prefix and suffix, respectively.

WHERE TO PRECOMPILE

The environment in which the program is to be precompiled:

FOREGROUND - The program is to be immediately precompiled in TSO foreground; the terminal is blocked for the duration of the precompilation.

BACKGROUND - A job to perform the precompilation is to be created and submitted to run as a batch job. The submitted job uses the job statement as defined in DB2I Defaults panel.

EDITJCL - A job to perform the precompilation is to be created and passed to the edit program. The user can modify this job. The user must himself submit it.

OTHER OPTIONS

Any additional parameters to be passed to the precompiler.

6.4.5 Option 5 - Perform DB2 Bind Function

The DB2 Bind function performs the specified bind operation; the sub-option determines whether a bind, rebind or free (delete) is to be made. Figure 6.8 shows the form of the DB2 Bind selection panel. Figure 6.9 shows the form of the DB2 Bind input panel; the parameters are described in Section 6.3.1. Figure 6.10 shows the form of the DB2 Rebind input panel; the parameters are described in Section 6.3.5. Figure 6.11 shows the form of the DB2 Free input panel; the parameters are described in Section 6.3.4.

```
                          BIND/REBIND/FREE
 ===>

Select one of the following and press ENTER:

  1  BIND            (Add or replace an application plan)

  2  REBIND          (Rebind existing application plan or plans)

  3  FREE            (Erase application plan or plans)

PRESS:      END to exit      HELP for more information
```

Figure 6.8 - Bind selection input panel

```
                                    BIND
===>

Enter DBRM data set name(s):
  1  LIBRARY(s)  ===> TEMP.DBRM
  2  MEMBER(s)   ===> ARDB2A4
  3  PASSWORD(s) ===>

  4  MORE DBRMS? ===> NO                          (YES to list more DBRMs)

Enter options as desired:
  5  PLAN NAME ................. ===> ARDB2A4     (Required to create a plan)
  6  ACTION ON PLAN ............ ===> REPLACE     (REPLACE or ADD)
  7  RETAIN EXECUTION AUTHORITY  ===> YES         (YES to retain user list)
  8  ISOLATION LEVEL ........... ===> RR          (RR or CS)
  9  PLAN VALIDATION TIME ...... ===> RUN         (RUN or BIND)
 10  RESOURCE ACQUISITION TIME   ===> USE         (USE or ALLOCATE)
 11  RESOURCE RELEASE TIME ..... ===> COMMIT      (COMMIT or DEALLOCATE)
 12  EXPLAIN PATH SELECTION ...  ===> NO          (NO or YES)

PRESS:  ENTER to process      END to exit      HELP for more information
```

Figure 6.9 - Bind input panel

```
                                   REBIND
===>

Enter plan name(s) to be rebound, or * for all authorized plans:
  1  ===> RUDD02    4  ===>       7  ===>        10  ===>
  2  ===>           5  ===>       8  ===>        11  ===>
  3  ===>           6  ===>       9  ===>        12  ===>

Enter options as desired:
 13  ISOLATION LEVEL .......... ===> SAME    (SAME, RR, or CS)
 14  PLAN VALIDATION TIME ..... ===> SAME    (SAME, RUN, or BIND)
 15  RESOURCE ACQUISITION TIME  ===> SAME    (SAME, ALLOCATE, or USE)
 16  RESOURCE RELEASE TIME ...  ===> SAME    (SAME, DEALLOCATE, or COMMIT)
 17  EXPLAIN PATH SELECTION ..  ===> SAME    (SAME, NO, or YES)

PRESS:    ENTER to process      END to exit      HELP for more information
```

Figure 6.10 - Rebind input panel

```
                                    FREE
===>

Enter plan name(s) to be freed or * for all authorized plans:

  1  ===>          4  ===>        7  ===>        10  ===>
  2  ===>          5  ===>        8  ===>        11  ===>
  3  ===>          6  ===>        9  ===>        12  ===>

PRESS: ENTER to process      END to exit    HELP for more information
```

Figure 6.11 - Free (bind) input panel

6.4.6 Option 6 - Run an SQL Program

The DB2I Run function executes the specified program. The program must have
been correctly prepared for execution in the DB2 environment. The execution may

take place in either foreground (under TSO) or as a batch job. Figure 6.12 shows
the form of the DB2 Run input panel.

```
                                   RUN
===>

Enter the name of the program you want to run:
 1  DATA SET NAME ===> RUNLIB(ARDB2A)
 2  PASSWORD .... ===>           (Required if data set is password protected)

Enter the following as desired:
 3  PARAMETERS .. ===>
 4  PLAN NAME ... ===>              (Required if different from program name)
 5  WHERE TO RUN  ===> FOREGROUND (FOREGROUND, BACKGROUND, or EDITJCL)

NOTE : Information for running command processors is on the HELP panel.
PRESS: ENTER to process      END to exit      HELP for information
```

Figure 6.12 - Run program input panel

DATA SET NAME
The name of the library that contains the load module to be executed. If the
dataset name is not specified explicitly, the user's TSO prefix and the
qualifier LOAD are added as prefix and suffix, respectively. The member
name must be specified within parentheses.
Example:
RUNLIB(ARDB2A4)
The member ARDB2A4 in the dataset 'userid.RUNLIB.LOAD' is to be executed.

PASSWORD
The password if the load library is password protected.

PARAMETERS
Any (EXEC) parameters to be passed to the program.

PLAN NAME
The name of the application plan for the program.
Default: The load module name.

WHERE TO RUN
The environment in which the program is to be executed:
FOREGROUND - The program is to be executed in TSO foreground; the terminal
is blocked for the duration of the execution.
BACKGROUND - A job to execute the program is to be created and submitted to
run as a batch job. The submitted job uses the job statement as defined in
DB2I Defaults panel. Note: The created job will usually need to be modified
to contain datasets required by the program.
EDITJCL - A job to execute the program is to be created and passed to the
edit program. The user can modify this job. The user must himself submit
it.

6.4.7 Option D - Set DB2I Global Default Parameters

The DB2I Defaults function is used to set global defaults to be used by DB2I. The Defaults panel may be selected either directly as function or as sub-function from DB2I Program Preparation. Figure 6.13 shows the DB2I Defaults panel.

```
                          DB2I DEFAULTS
===>

Change defaults as desired:

  1  DB2 NAME ............. ===> DB2      (Subsystem identifier)
  2  DB2 CONNECTION RETRIES ===> 0        (How many retries for DB2 connection)
  3  APPLICATION LANGUAGE   ===> PLI      (ASM, ASMH, C, COBOL, COB2, FORTRAN,
                                           PLI)
  4  LINES/PAGE OF LISTING  ===> 60       (A number from 5 to 999)
  5  MESSAGE LEVEL ........ ===> I        (Information, Warning, Error, Severe)
  6  COBOL STRING DELIMITER ===> DEFAULT  (DEFAULT, ' or ")
  7  SQL STRING DELIMITER   ===> DEFAULT  (DEFAULT, ' or ")
  8  DECIMAL POINT ........ ===> .        (. or ,)

  9  DB2I JOB STATEMENT:   (Optional if your site has a SUBMIT exit)
     ===>
     ===>
     ===>
     ===>

PRESS: ENTER to save and exit     END to exit     HELP for more information
```

Figure 6.13 - Set DB2I Defaults input panel

DB2 NAME
> The name of the DB2 subsystem

DB2 CONNECTION RETRIES
> The number of retries for DB2 connection that are to be attempted; attempts are made at 30-second intervals.

APPLICATION LANGUAGE
> The host language:
> ASM - Assembler F
> ASMH - Assembler H
> C - C language
> COBOL - VS COBOL
> COB2 - VS COBOL II
> FORT - FORTRAN
> PLI - PL/I.

LINES/PAGE OF LISTING
> The number of lines per page in the output listing.

MESSAGE LEVEL
The level at which messages are produced:
I - Informational. All errors are displayed.
W - Warning, error and completion messages.
E - Error and completion messages.
C - Only completion messages.

COBOL STRING DELIMITER
The delimiter to be used for COBOL strings.

SQL STRING DELIMITER
The delimiter to be used for SQL strings.

DECIMAL POINT
The representation form for a decimal point.

DB2I JOB STATEMENT
The Job statement to be used for submitted jobs. This statement may be
omitted if the TSO SUBMIT exit generates a Job statement. *Note*: The Job
statement, if specified, must conform to your installation standards.

6.5 INVOKE PROGRAM INDEPENDENT OF DB2 (CAF INTERFACE)

Programs can use the Call Attachment Facility (CAF) to access a DB2 database (SQL
queries) without having to be in the DB2 environment. For example, batch
programs can use the CAF to invoke the DB2 environment.

The CAF functions are contained in the DSNALI program, which must be
included during linkage editing instead of DSNELI (static linkage is required, e.g.
COBOL NODYNAM option). The CAF functions are called using the standard linkage
conventions (the high-order bit of the last parameter address must be set; in the
Assembler, the VL keyword sets this bit — high-level languages set this bit as
standard).

The DSNALI load module has three entry points:

· DSNALI   DB2 connection service requests;
· DSNHLI   SQL service requests;
· DSNHLI2 SQL service requests.

A user-written interface module can be written to make available a dynamic
interface. This interface module loads the standard DSNALI (and DSNHLI2) program
(using the LOAD macro). The normal DSNHLI entry-point must be replaced by an
entry-point (using the ENTRY Assembler statement) in the interface program. This
program entry receives calls generated by the DB2 precompiler. These calls (EXEC
SQL statements) should be passed unchanged to the standard DSNHLI2 function.

DSNALI supports the following functions:
- CONNECT   Connect the calling program (address space) to DB2 and establish the invoker as being a DB2 user.
- DISCONNECT   Disconnect the calling program (address space) from DB2.
- OPEN   Establish the current task as being a DB2 user. Perform an implicit CONNECT if necessary.
- CLOSE   Remove the current task from being a DB2 user. Perform an implicit DISCONNECT if necessary.
- TRANSLATE   Set information concerning unavailable resources into the SQLCA.

If no explicit CAF calls are made, implicit CAF calls will be performed.

Assembler syntax is shown for the CAF functions, as it is the language normally used for such applications. The lengths specified in the function specifications must be adhered to. Section 6.5.6 contains sample coding for a CAF interface program.

CAF advantages:
- The program can run even when DB2 is not available.
- The program can switch between different DB2 subsystems or plans. Because only one DB2 connection can be active at any one time, the current connection must be terminated before a new connection can be made.
- Depending on the operational environment, the program testing may be simplified.
- The program can be invoked using the normal control statements (JCL, CLIST or REXX exec); i.e. the TSO TMP (Terminal Monitor Program) is not required.

CAF disadvantages:
- The program requires additional calls to the CAF initialisation and termination functions, unless implicit calls are used.
- The CAF interface must handle exception conditions (for example, DB2 shutdown).

6.5.1 CLOSE Function

The CLOSE function removes the current task from being a DB2 user.

Syntax:
```
CALL DSNALI,(function,termoption[,retcode[,reascode]]),VL
```

function
     A 12-byte area that contains 'CLOSE'.

termoption
>   A 4-byte area that contains the termination option, which is one of the
>   following values:
>   SYNC   Commit any modified data.
>   ABRT   Roll data back to previous commit.

retcode
>   A fullword in which CAF sets the return code. This parameter is optional; if
>   not provided, the return code is placed in register 15.

reascode
>   A fullword in which CAF sets the reason code. This parameter is optional; if
>   not provided, the reason code is placed in register 0. If reason code
>   parameter is specified, the return code parameter must also be specified.

Example

```
          CALL  DSNALI,(FUNC,TERMOPT),VL

...
FUNC      DC    CL12'CLOSE'
TERMOPT   DC    CL4'SYNC'
```

This code specifies that a commit of any modified data is to be made.

6.5.2 CONNECT Function

The CONNECT function connects the calling program (address space) to DB2 and
establishes the invoker as being a DB2 user. An explicit CONNECT is optional; an
implicit CONNECT using the default DB2 subsystem name is performed by OPEN or an
SQL call, if no connection has been established previously.

Syntax:

```
    CALL DSNALI,(function,subsystemname,termecb,startecb,
        ribptr[,retcode[,reascode][,srdura]]),VL
```

function
>   A 12-byte area that contains 'CONNECT'.

subsystemname
>   A 4-byte area that contains the name of the DB2 subsystem to which the
>   connect is to be made.

termecb
>   The application's ECB (Event Control Block) which is posted should DB2
>   terminate.

startecb
>   The application's ECB which is posted when DB2 completes its start-up
>   phase.

ribptr

A pointer to a 4-byte area which is set by CAF to contain the Release Information Block (RIB). Appendix E describes the format of the RIB.

retcode

A fullword in which CAF sets the return code. This parameter is optional; if not provided, the return code is placed in register 15.

reascode

A fullword in which CAF sets the reason code. This parameter is optional; if not provided, the reason code is placed in register 0. If the reason code parameter is specified, the return code parameter must also be specified.

srdura

Concurrency option. An optional 10-byte area that contains the string 'SRDURA(CD)'. If specified, the value in the CURRENT DEGREE special register applies until DISCONNECT is made, otherwise the CURRENT DEGREE setting applies between OPEN until CLOSE.

Example:
```
CALL DSNALI,(FUNC,SUBSYST,TERMECB,STARTECB,RIBPTR),VL

...
FUNC      DC    CL12'CONNECT'
SUBSYST   DC    CL4'DSN'
TERMECB   DC    F'0'
STARTECB  DC    F'0'
RIBPTR    DS    A
```
This code specifies that a connect using DSN as name of the DB2 subsystem is to be made.

6.5.3 DISCONNECT Function

The DISCONNECT function disconnects the calling program (address space) from DB2. DISCONNECT may only be used if an explicit CONNECT has been previously issued. If no explicit DISCONNECT is performed, DB2 issues an implicit DISCONNECT when the current task terminates. If no explicit CLOSE has been performed, an implicit CLOSE with the SYNC option is performed.

Syntax:
```
CALL DSNALI,(function[,retcode[,reascode]]),VL
```

function

A 12-byte area that contains 'DISCONNECT'.

retcode

A fullword in which CAF sets the return code. This parameter is optional; if not provided, the return code is placed in register 15.

reascode
> A fullword in which CAF sets the reason code. This parameter is optional; if not provided, the reason code is placed in register 0. If reason code parameter is specified, the return code parameter must also be specified.

Example:
```
CALL DSNALI,(FUNC),VL
...
FUNC    DC    CL12'DISCONNECT'
```
This code specifies that the program is to be disconnected from the DB2 subsystem.

6.5.4 OPEN Function

The OPEN function establishes the current task as being a DB2 user. An explicit OPEN is optional; an implicit OPEN is performed by the first SQL call with the name of the DBRM used as plan name.

Syntax:
```
CALL DSNALI,(function,subsystemname,planname[,retcode[,reascode]]),VL
```

function
> A 12-byte area that contains 'OPEN'.

subsystemname
> A 4-byte area that contains the name of the DB2 subsystem to which the connect is to be made.

planname
> An 8-byte area that contains the name of the plan that is to be used by the program.

retcode
> A fullword in which CAF sets the return code. This parameter is optional; if not provided, the return code is placed in register 15.

reascode
> A fullword in which CAF sets the reason code. This parameter is optional; if not provided, the reason code is placed in register 0. If reason code parameter is specified, the return code parameter must also be specified.

Example:
```
CALL DSNALI,(FUNC,SUBSYST,PLANNAME),VL
...
FUNC       DC    CL12'OPEN'
SUBSYST    DC    CL4'DSN'
PLANNAME   DC    CL8'ALPHA'
```
This code specifies that the current task (plan ALPHA) is to be established as being a user of the DB2 subsystem DSN.

6.5.5 TRANSLATE Function

The TRANSLATE function sets information concerning unavailable resources into the SQLCA (e.g. SQLCODE, SQLERRM). TRANSLATE can only be used after the OPEN function. Appendix E contains the format of the SQLCA.

Syntax:
```
CALL DSNALI,(function,sqlca[,retcode[,reascode]]),VL
```

function
> A 12-byte area that contains 'TRANSLATE'.

sqlca
> The program's SQL Communication Area (SQLCA).

retcode
> A fullword in which CAF sets the return code. This parameter is optional; if not provided, the return code is placed in register 15.

reascode
> A fullword in which CAF sets the reason code. This parameter is optional; if not provided, the reason code is placed in register 0. If reason code parameter is specified, the return code parameter must also be specified.

Example:
```
CALL DSNALI,(FUNC,USQLCA),VL
...
FUNC     DC    CL12'TRANSLATE'
USQLCA   DS    CL136           user SQLCA
```
This code sets information into the user's SQLCA named USQLCA.

6.5.6 CAF Interface Program

The following sample CAF interface program (DB2CAF) provides dynamic connection to DB2 and basic DB2 error handling. This DB2CAF interface allows COBOL programs to use dynamic calls.

DB2CAF provides two entry points:
- DB2CAFI   Initialisation processing.
- DB2CAFT   Termination processing.

DB2CAFI invocation sequence:
```
CALL DB2CAFI,(planname[,subsystem[,errorexit]]),VL
```

planname
> An 8-byte area that contains the name of the plan that is to be used by the program.

subsystemname

A 4-byte area that contains the name of the DB2 subsystem to which the connect is to be made. If omitted, the default name DSN is used.

errorexit

An 8-byte area that contains the name of the error routine that will be dynamically invoked if a DB2 termination condition occurs. This entry is optional, if omitted, the return code value of 24 will be passed to the SQL call.

DB2CAFT invocation sequence:
```
CALL DB2CAFT,(termoption),VL
```

termoption

A 4-byte area that contains the termination option, which is one of the following values:

SYNC   Commit any modified data.

ABRT   Roll data back to previous commit.

General return codes.

The DB2CAFI routine sets a return code in register 15 (COBOL RETURN-CODE special register, etc.):

0   Successful processing.

2   DB2CAFI already invoked.

Other values indicate an error condition. For simplicity, the CHECK subroutine in DB2CAF does not perform any error processing; a practical interface should display an error message, etc. Furthermore, it may be necessary to handle exception conditions appropriately, for example, recovery processing.

The Abend 99 is issued if DSNHLI (SQL call) is called without DB2CAFI having been invoked.

Coding note: To reduce size and complexity , the sample DB2CAF program uses the BAKR and PR instructions to save and restore registers using the hardware stack; equivalent coding using conventional save-areas (SAVE and RETURN macros) could also be used.

```
        DB2CAFI CSECT
        DB2CAFI AMODE 31
        DB2CAFI RMODE ANY
        * initialise CAF processing
        * initialise addressing
                BAKR  14,0            save registers
                BASR  11,0            set base register and address mode
                USING *,11
                LA    13,SA
                LM    1,3,0(1)        load parameters
        * R1: A(planname); R2: A(subsystem); R3: A(errorexit)
                MVC   PLANNAME,0(1)   planname
                LTR   1,1             test whether 2 parameters passed
```

```
              BM    LASTPARM          no second parameter (subsystem)
              MVC   SSID,0(2)         subsystem (default: DSN)
              LTR   2,2               test whether 3 parameters passed
              BM    LASTPARM          no third parameter (errorexit)
              MVC   ERREXIT,0(3)
LASTPARM LA   15,2                    RC: CAFI already performed
* load CAF modules
              L     0,LIALI
              LTR   0,0
              BNZ   EOP               modules already loaded, avoid open
              LOAD  EP=DSNALI
              ST    0,LIALI
              LOAD  EP=DSNHLI2
              ST    0,LISQL
* IDENTIFY DSNHLI
              IDENTIFY EP=DSNHLI,ENTRY=DSNHLI
              CH    15,=H'12'
              BL    IDENTOK           allow ReturnCode < 12
              BAL   14,CHECK          check ReturnCode
* CONNECT
IDENTOK  L    15,LIALI
** CALL (15),(CONNECT,SSID,TECB,SECB,RIBPTR),VL
              BAL   1,*+24
              DC    AL4(CONNECT,SSID,TECB,SECB,RIBPTR)
              OI    *-4,X'80'         set HO-byte
              BASSM 14,15
              BAL   14,CHECK
              ICM   1,B'1111',SECB    START-ECB
              BNZ   CONNERR           CONNECT nok
              LTR   15,15             CONNECT return code
              BZ    CONNOK            CONNECT ok
CONNERR  MVC  TECB,=F'1'             set TECB invalid
              LA    15,20             RC: DB2 not started
              B     DB2ERR            terminate
* OPEN
CONNOK   L    15,LIALI
** CALL (15),(OPEN,SSID,PLANNAME),VL
              BAL   1,*+16
              DC    AL4(OPEN,SSID,PLANNAME)
              OI    *-4,X'80'         set HO-byte
              BASSM 14,15
              LTR   15,15
              BZ    EOP               ok
              BAL   14,CHECK
              MVC   TECB,=F'2'        set TECB invalid
              B     DB2ERR
* dummy check routine
CHECK        BALR  9,0
              USING *,9
              BR    14
              LTORG
              DROP  9,11
              ENTRY DB2CAFT
DB2CAFT  DS   0D
* terminate CAF processing (with close option: SYNC or ABRT)
* initialise addressing
              BAKR  14,0              save registers
              BASR  15,0              set base register and address mode
              USING *,15
```

```
          LA    13,SA
          L     1,0(1)                load parameter
* R1: A(close option)
          L     14,=A(DB2CAFT1)       continuation address
          MVC   TERMOP,=C'SYNC'       default close option: SYNC
          CLC   =C'ROLLBACK',0(1)
          BNER  14
          MVC   TERMOP,=C'ABRT'       close option: ABRT
          BR    14
          DROP  15
DB2CAFT1  BASR  11,0
          USING *,11
* CLOSE
          L     15,LIALI
          LTR   15,15
          BZ    EOP                   CAFI called without initialisation
** CALL (15),(CLOSE,TERMOP),VL
          BAL   1,*+12
          DC    AL4(CLOSE,TERMOP)
          OI    *-4,X'80'             set HO-byte
          BASSM 14,15
          LTR   15,15
          BNZ   EOP                   :error routine
          DELETE EP=DSNALI
          DELETE EP=DSNHLI2
          SR    0,0                   initialise module addresses
          ST    0,LIALI
          LA    0,ABEND99
          ST    0,LISQL
          B     EOP
          DROP  11
          ENTRY DSNHLI
DSNHLI    DS    0D
          BAKR  14,0                  save registers
          BASR  10,0                  base register and address mode
          USING *,10
          LA    13,SA
          ICM   0,B'1111',TECB        terminate ECB
          BZ    DSNHLIO               ok
* set SQLCODE
* R1: A(SQLPLIST)
          L     1,0(1)                A(SQLPLIST)
          L     1,24(1)               A(SQLCA)
          LH    15,=H'-2'
          ST    15,12(1)              set SQLCODE
          B     DB2ERR
DSNHLIO   L     15,LISQL
          BASSM 14,15
EOP       PR    ,                     program return
DB2ERR    BALR  15,0
          USING *,15
          CLI   ERREXIT,C' '
          BE    DB2ERR1               no error exit
          LOAD  EPLOC=ERREXIT
          DROP  15
          LR    15,0
          BASSM 14,15
DB2ERR1   LA    15,24
          PR    ,                     program return
```

```
ABEND99   ABEND  99                        DSNHLI not initialised
SA        DS     18A
LIALI     DS     A                         entry-point address(DSNALI)
LISQL     DC     A(ABEND99)                entry-point address(DSNHLI2)
ERREXIT   DC     CL8' '                    DB2 error exit routine (blank =
*                                          standard error exit)
CONNECT   DC     CL12'CONNECT'
OPEN      DC     CL12'OPEN'
CLOSE     DC     CL12'CLOSE'
SSID      DC     CL4'DSN'                  DB2 subsystem name (default)
PLANNAME  DC     CL8' '
TERMOP    DS     CL4
SECB      DC     F'0'                      start ECB
TECB      DC     F'0'                      terminate ECB
RIBPTR    DS     A
          END
```

6.5.6.1 Invocation Example. The following sample COBOL program illustrates the use of the DB2CAF interface program shown in Section 6.5.6.

```
IDENTIFICATION DIVISION.
PROGRAM-ID. CBDBCAF.
ENVIRONMENT DIVISION.
DATA DIVISION.
WORKING-STORAGE SECTION.
    EXEC SQL INCLUDE SQLCA END-EXEC.
01  V-SSNM         PIC X(4) VALUE 'DSNT'.
01  V-PLAN         PIC X(8) VALUE 'PDBCB'.
01  V-TERM         PIC X(4) VALUE 'SYNC'.
01  V-COUNT        PIC S9(9) COMP.
PROCEDURE DIVISION.
* connect
    CALL 'DB2CAFI' USING V-PLAN V-SSNM
    IF RETURN-CODE NOT ZERO
      DISPLAY RETURN-CODE
      GOBACK
    END-IF
* query
    EXEC SQL SELECT COUNT(*)
      INTO :V-COUNT
      FROM SYSIBM.SYSTABLES
    END-EXEC
* display result
    DISPLAY 'COUNT:' V-COUNT
* display error message if SQLCODE non-zero
    IF SQLCODE NOT EQUAL ZERO
      DISPLAY 'SQLCODE:' SQLCODE
      MOVE 'ABRT' TO V-TERM
    END-IF
* close
    CALL 'DB2CAFT' USING V-TERM
* end
    STOP RUN.
END PROGRAM CBDBCAF.
```

6.5.7 Example

The following example shows the use of the CAF interface from a COBOL program. The CAFTEST program uses five CAF services:

· Connect the program to the DB2 DSNT subsystem. For completeness, the program displays the release information from the RIB (Release Information Block).
· Open the PDBCB plan on the DB2 DSNT subsystem.
· Translate any open error conditions.
· Close the plan by performing a commit.
· Disconnect the program from the DB2 subsystem.

The sample program performs a simple query: retrieve (and display) the number of entries in the SYSIBM.SYSTABLES system catalogue table. To avoid introducing unnecessary detail, the program displays CAF return codes in decimal rather than in hexadecimal.

```
        IDENTIFICATION DIVISION.
        PROGRAM-ID. DBCBCAF.
        ENVIRONMENT DIVISION.
        DATA DIVISION.
        WORKING-STORAGE SECTION.
            EXEC SQL INCLUDE SQLCA END-EXEC.
        01  V-FUNCTION      PIC X(12).
        01  V-SSNM          PIC X(4) VALUE 'DSNT'.
        01  V-PLAN          PIC X(8) VALUE 'PDBCB'.
        01  V-TERM          PIC X(4) VALUE 'SYNC'.
        01  TERMECB         PIC 9(9) COMP VALUE 0.
        01  STARTECB        PIC 9(9) COMP VALUE 0.
        01  P-RIB           POINTER.
        01  V-COUNT         PIC S9(9) COMP.
        01  V-RETCODE       PIC 9(9) COMP VALUE 0.
        01  V-REASCODE      PIC 9(9) COMP VALUE 0.
        01  OUT-CODE        PIC S9(4) SIGN LEADING SEPARATE CHARACTER.
        LINKAGE SECTION.
        01  RIB.
          02 RIBCODE        PIC 9(4) COMP.
          02 RIBTLEN        PIC 9(4) COMP.
          02 RIBEYEC        PIC X(4).
          02 RIBCID.
            03 RIBECODE     PIC X(4).
            03 RIBPCODE     PIC X(3).
            02 RIBFCODE     PIC X(2).
            02 RIBREL       PIC X(3).

          02 RIBCPTR        POINTER.
        01  RIBRVAL         PIC X(24).
        PROCEDURE DIVISION.
        * CONNECT
            MOVE 'CONNECT' TO V-FUNCTION
            CALL 'DSNALI' USING V-FUNCTION V-SSNM TERMECB
             STARTECB P-RIB V-RETCODE V-REASCODE
            IF V-RETCODE NOT ZERO
             DISPLAY 'RTC:' V-RETCODE ' RSC:' V-REASCODE
            END-IF
            SET ADDRESS OF RIB TO P-RIB.
```

```
          DISPLAY 'VERSION:' RIBREL
          SET ADDRESS OF RIBRVAL TO RIBCPTR.
          DISPLAY 'CHANGE LEVEL:' RIBRVAL
    * OPEN
          MOVE 'OPEN' TO V-FUNCTION
          CALL 'DSNALI' USING V-FUNCTION V-SSNM V-PLAN
           V-RETCODE V-REASCODE
          IF V-RETCODE NOT ZERO
             DISPLAY 'RTC:' V-RETCODE ' RSC:' V-REASCODE
    * TRANSLATE
             MOVE 'TRANSLATE' TO V-FUNCTION
             CALL 'DSNALI' USING V-FUNCTION SQLCA
              V-RETCODE V-REASCODE
             DISPLAY 'SQLERRMC:' SQLERRMC
          END-IF
    * QUERY
          EXEC SQL SELECT COUNT(*)
           INTO :V-COUNT
           FROM SYSIBM.SYSTABLES
          END-EXEC
    * display result
          DISPLAY 'COUNT:' V-COUNT
    * display error message if SQLCODE non-zero
          IF SQLCODE NOT EQUAL ZERO
             MOVE SQLCODE TO OUT-CODE
             DISPLAY 'SQLCODE:' OUT-CODE
             MOVE 'ABRT' TO V-TERM
          END-IF
    * CLOSE
          MOVE 'CLOSE' TO V-FUNCTION
          CALL 'DSNALI' USING V-FUNCTION V-TERM
           V-RETCODE V-REASCODE
          IF V-RETCODE NOT ZERO
             DISPLAY 'RTC:' V-RETCODE ' RSC:' V-REASCODE
          END-IF
    * DISCONNECT
          MOVE 'DISCONNECT' TO V-FUNCTION
          CALL 'DSNALI' USING V-FUNCTION
           V-RETCODE V-REASCODE
          IF V-RETCODE NOT ZERO
             DISPLAY 'RTC:' V-RETCODE ' RSC:' V-REASCODE
          END-IF
    * END
           STOP RUN.
        END PROGRAM DBCBCAF.
```

7

Embedded SQL

Language is the amber in which a thousand precious and subtle thoughts have been safely embedded and preserved.

On the Study of Words
Richard Trench

7.1 INTRODUCTION

All interactive SQL statements can be used from within programs (Assembler, C, COBOL, PL/I, etc.) and are called **embedded SQL statements**. There are also a number of embedded SQL statements which may only be used in programs. Embedded SQL statements are identified by EXEC SQL and are converted by the precompiler to CALL statements or definitions appropriate for the host language. Embedded SQL statements must conform to the general syntactical rules for the host language (e.g. Assembler statements are continued by setting a non-blank character in the continuation column). Embedded SQL statements in COBOL programs must be terminated with END-EXEC.

Embedded SQL statements can use:
· literals;
· DB2 names;
· host variables (prefixed by a colon (":")).

The definition of a **host variable** must be appropriate for the form of the corresponding DB2 variable. A special form of the host variable is an **indicator variable**, which contains a negative value if the corresponding database variable is null. The allowable forms for variable declarations are shown as table in the section for each host language. The colon is in many cases optional; it is only required to distinguish host variables from like-named DB2 entries. However, it is good programming practice to always use a colon; consider the consequences of adding to a DB2 table a column having the same name as a host variable.

Each program using SQL statements must define an SQL Communication Area (SQLCA). The SQLCA contains information returned by DB2 to the invoking program, e.g. SQL return code.

There are two ways of invoking SQL statements from a program:
· statically;
· dynamically.

In both cases the program using embedded SQL statements must be processed by the appropriate DB2 precompiler prior to being compiled. The DB2 precompiler converts the embedded SQL statements into statements appropriate for the host language (see Chapter 6) and creates a DBRM, which is used by the bind processor to define the logical access to the database.

The static invocation of SQL uses fixed (static) SQL statements in the application program. These SQL statements can make use of program variables as values. Authorisations for programs using static SQL can be resolved during the precompile phase.

The dynamic invocation of SQL builds the complete SQL statement at the point of execution. Authorisations for programs using dynamic SQL are resolved at the time of execution. The flexibility of dynamic SQL statements is generally paid for by increased processing time compared with using static SQL statements.

Because the SELECT statement usually returns more than one row, a special technique is required to obtain each row of data (the SELECT INTO statement is a special form of SELECT that returns only a single row). The interface for embedded SQL statements cannot return the retrieved data in a form which can be processed as host language tables, rather the rows must be individually fetched. An internal pointer, known as the **cursor**, maintains the position of the current row in the results table.

7.2 SQL STATUS

The status of each executable SQL statement after it has been processed is returned to the invoking program. Two status areas are set:
· the return code;
· the SQLCA.

The return code contains general status as to whether the statement has been successfully processed:

0	Successful execution.
4	Warning; a positive SQLCODE has been set.
8	Error; a negative SQLCODE has been set.
12	Severe error.

The setting of the return code is language dependent:

Assembler	Register 15
C	function return value
COBOL	RETURN-CODE special register
PL/I	PLIRETV variable.

Particular status information pertaining to the SQL request is stored as the SQL return code in the SQLCODE variable of the SQLCA (SQL Communication Area):

   0   Successful execution (see following note).
 >0   Warning (including end of selection).
 <0   Error.

Note: If the SQLWARN0 field in the SQLCA is not blank, a warning condition has been set.

The DSNTIAR subroutine (see Section 7.2.1) can be used to supply the SQL message text appropriate for the SQLCODE value.

7.2.1 DSNTIAR Subroutine

The DSNTIAR subroutine supplies the SQL message text appropriate for the SQLCODE value.

Calling sequence:
```
►►──CALL DSNTIAR(sqlca,messagearea,linelength)──►◄
```

sqlca
    The field that contains the SQLCA.

messagearea
    The field which is to contain the formatted message text which applies to the value contained in the SQLCODE field of the supplied **sqlca**.

    The **messagearea** has the following format:

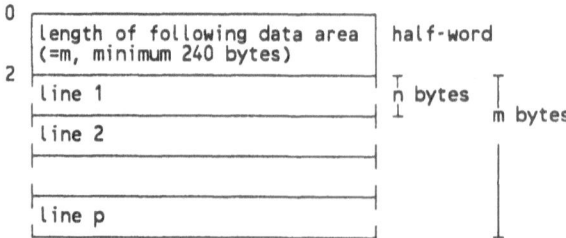

A maximum of 7 lines are returned. The end of the returned message text is signalled with a line completely filled with blanks.

linelength

   A full-word that contains the length of a message line; the minimum value
   is 72.

DSNTIAR sets one of the following return codes:

   0   Successful execution.
   4   Text to be returned is longer than the available message area, the text
        will be truncated.
   8   Error; **linelength** is less than 72.
   12   Error; **arealength** is less than 240.

Example:
```
EXEC SQL INCLUDE SQLCA;
DCL DSNTIAR ENTRY EXTERNAL OPTIONS(ASM,INTER,RETCODE);
DCL 1 MSG,
       2 MSG_LEN  FIXED BIN(15) INIT(288),
       2 MSG_TEXT CHAR(288);
DCL LRECL FIXED BIN(31,0) INIT(72);

   CALL DSNTIAR(SQLCA,MSG,LRECL);
   PUT SKIP LIST ('SQL CODE:',SQLCODE,' MESSAGE:');
   PUT SKIP LIST (SUBSTR(MSG_TEXT,1,72));
   PUT SKIP LIST (SUBSTR(MSG_TEXT,73,72));
```
This code displays the value of SQLCODE and the first two lines of message text.
Note: A comprehensive error exit should check for a variable number of text lines
delimited by a line of blanks.

7.3 PROGRAM HOST VARIABLES

Host variables used in SQL statements must satisfy certain requirements. These
requirements are host language dependent and are validated by the DB2
precompiler. The DB2 precompiler validates the form of the definitions and not
their content. Further, the precompiler does not accept all forms for definitions
which are valid for the host language. As a general rule, the form of the host
variables used by SQL statements should be as simple as possible. Tables 7.1
through 7.4 show the form of host declarations for each DB2 field type.

7.3.1 PL/I Host Variables

Table 7.1 shows the PL/I declarations.

Table 7.1 - PL/I host variable declarations

```
SMALLINT:
▶▶── DCL identifier FIXED BIN ─┬─────────┬─ ; ──▶◀
                                └  (15)  ┘

INTEGER:
▶▶── DCL identifier FIXED BIN(31) ; ──▶◀

DECIMAL(precision,scale):
▶▶── DCL identifier FIXED DEC( precision ─┬──────────────┬─);──▶◀
                                          └─,─┬─ scale ─┘
                                              └  0 ─────

FLOAT(21):
▶▶── DCL identifier FLOAT ─┬─ BIN(m) ─┬─;──▶◀
                           └─ DEC(n) ─┘
1 <= m <= 21     1 <= n <= 6

FLOAT(53):
▶▶── DCL identifier FLOAT ─┬─ BIN(m) ─┬─;──▶◀
                           └─ DEC(n) ─┘
22 <= m <= 53    7 <= n <= 16

CHAR(n):
▶▶── DCL identifier CHAR(n);──▶◀

VARCHAR(n):
▶▶── DCL identifier CHAR(n) VAR;──▶◀

DATE:
▶▶── DCL identifier CHAR(n);──▶◀
n > 9

TIME:
▶▶── DCL identifier CHAR(n);──▶◀
n > 4

TIMESTAMP:
▶▶── DCL identifier CHAR(n);──▶◀
n > 18; if n < 26 then the number of microseconds will be truncated
```

Note on Table 7.1: The PL/I declarations show the precision as a radix attribute (e.g. BIN(15)), however, the precision may just as well be specified as the type attribute (e.g. FIXED(15)); the notation was adopted to avoid unnecessary complexity in the table.

Example:
```
        DCL ALPHA CHAR(8) VARYING;.
        DCL BETA FIXED DEC(5);
```
This code defines two host variables:
```
        ALPHA [VARCHAR(8)]
        BETA  [DECIMAL(5)]
```
The corresponding DB2 attribute is contained within brackets.

7.3.2 COBOL Host Variables

Table 7.2 shows the COBOL declarations.

Table 7.2 - COBOL host variable declarations

```
SMALLINT:
▶▶──01 identifier PIC S9(n)─┬─ BINARY─────────────┬─.─▶◀
                            ├─ USAGE IS BINARY─────┤
                            ├─ COMP────────────────┤
                            └─ USAGE IS COMPUTATIONAL─┘
1 <= n <= 4

INTEGER:
▶▶──01 identifier PIC S9(n)─┬─ BINARY─────────────┬─.─▶◀
                            ├─ USAGE IS BINARY─────┤
                            ├─ COMP────────────────┤
                            └─ USAGE IS COMPUTATIONAL─┘
5 <= n <= 9

DECIMAL(precision,scale):
▶▶──01 identifier PIC S9(integer-digits)─┬────────────────────┬─▶
                                         └─V(decimal-digits)──┘
▶──┬─ COMP-3────────────────────────────┬─.─▶◀
   └─ USAGE IS─┬─ COMPUTATIONAL-3─┬──────┘
               └─ PACKED-DECIMAL──┘
integer-digits + decimal-digits = precision <= 15
decimal-digits = scale

FLOAT(21):
▶▶──01 identifier ─┬─COMP-1────────────────────┬─.─▶◀
                   └─USAGE IS COMPUTATIONAL-1──┘

FLOAT(53):
▶▶──01 identifier ─┬─COMP-2 ───────────────────┬─.─▶◀
                   └─USAGE IS COMPUTATIONAL-2──┘

CHAR(n):
▶▶──01 identifier ─┬─PIC X(n)──────────┬─.─▶◀
                   └─PICTURE IS X(n)──┘

VARCHAR(n):
▶▶──01 identifier.─▶◀
▶▶──49 identifier-1 PIC S9(4) COMP─┬────────────┬─.─▶◀
                                   └─ VALUE n──┘
▶▶──49 identifier-2 PIC X(n).─▶◀

DATE:
▶▶──01 identifier─┬─ PIC X(n)──────────┬─.─▶◀
                  └─ PICTURE IS X(n)──┘
n > 9

TIME:
▶▶──01 identifier─┬─ PIC X(n)──────────┬─.─▶◀
                  └─ PICTURE IS X(n)──┘
n > 4

TIMESTAMP:
▶▶──01 identifier─┬─ PIC X(n)──────────┬─.─▶◀
                  └─ PICTURE IS X(n)──┘
n > 18; if n < 26 then the number of microseconds will be truncated
```

Example:
```
      01  ALPHA.
         49  ALPHA-LEN  PIC S9(4) COMP VALUE 8.
         49  ALPHA-DATA PIC X(8).
      01  BETA  PIC S9(5) COMP-3.
```
This code defines two host variables:
```
      ALPHA  [VARCHAR(8)]
      BETA   [DECIMAL(5)]
```

The corresponding DB2 attribute is contained within brackets.

7.3.2.1 Nested COBOL Programs. The DB2 precompiler provides only limited support for nested COBOL programs. In particular, all SQL statements must be contained within the main (first) program. If this is not possible, some manual processing is necessary to convert the source program into a suitable form. The following method illustrates how this can be done.

1) Separate the program into its constituent parts, i.e. each nested program is a self-contained program.
2) Process each subprogram with the DB2 precompiler (DSNHPC JCL procedure). The precompiler converts EXEC SQL statements into CALL DSNHLI statements; the SQL commands are written to a DBRM member and the modified source written to an output file. If the processed subprograms are stored as copy members, they can be recombined using COPY statements (refer to be next step).
3) The modified sources are combined to recreate the original program, which the COBOL compiler processes.
4) A bind of the DBRM members is made to produce a plan.

7.3.3 Assembler Host Variables

Table 7.3 shows the Assembler declarations.

Table 7.3 - Assembler host variable declarations

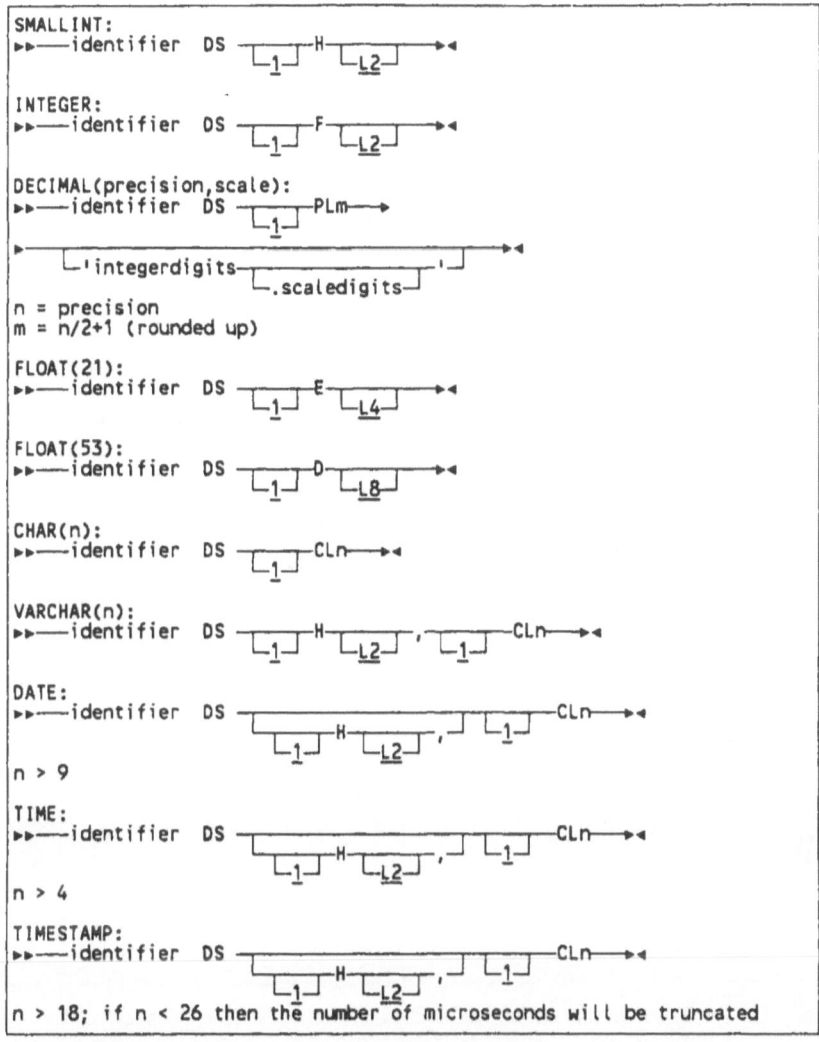

Note on Table 7.3: The Assembler declarations are shown as DS (define storage) statements, although DC (define constant) statements are also valid.

Example:
```
ALPHA     DS     H'8',CL8
BETA      DC     PL3'1234'
```

This code defines two host variables:
```
ALPHA  [VARCHAR(8)]
BETA   [DECIMAL(5)]
```
The corresponding DB2 attribute is contained within brackets.

Note: The (maximum) length of the corresponding DB2 column for BETA is 5, because a packed decimal field contains 2 digits per byte with one half-byte reserved for the sign.

7.3.4 C/370 Host Variables

Table 7.4 shows the C/370 declarations.

Table 7.4 - C/370 host variable declarations

```
SMALLINT:
▶▶──short─┬──────┬─ identifier;─▶◄
          └ int─┘

INTEGER:
▶▶──long─┬──────┬─ identifier;─▶◄
         └ int─┘

FLOAT(m):
▶▶──float identifier;─▶◄
1 <= m <= 21

FLOAT(m):
▶▶──double identifier;─▶◄
22 <= m <= 53

CHAR(1):
▶▶──char identifier;─▶◄

CHAR(n):
▶▶──char identifier[n+1];─▶◄
the last character must be \0

VARCHAR(n):
▶▶──struct {short identifier-length;─▶◄
▶▶──        char identifier-data[n];─▶◄
▶▶──        } identifier;            ─▶◄

DATE:
▶▶──char identifier[n];─▶◄
n >= 11

TIME:
▶▶──char identifier[n];─▶◄
n >= 7

TIMESTAMP:
▶▶──char identifier[n];─▶◄
n >= 20; if n < 27 then the number of microseconds will be truncated
```

Example:
```
      struct { short len;
               char data[8];
             } alpha;
      long int beta;
```
This code defines two host variables:
```
      alpha [VARCHAR(8)]
      beta  [DECIMAL(5)]
```
The corresponding DB2 attribute is contained within brackets. Lower case letters are used by convention in C to represent variable names. Note: The C language

does not support decimal host variables; decimal database values will be converted to or from the appropriate host format (refer to the preceding example).

7.4 INDICATOR VARIABLES

Indicator variables are used to indicate whether the corresponding database variable is null, i.e. the host variable associated with this database variable (data variable) contains no value. No value is not the same as a zero value (for numeric fields) or blanks (for character fields). The indicator variable has the format SMALLINT and contains (or set to contain) a negative value (usually -1; -2 indicates that the data value is null because its content is invalid) if the associated database variable is null. An indicator variable should be specified with every host variable which can be null.

The host variable name and the associated indicator variable name are specified as a pair:

```
:datavariable :indicatorvariable
```

An SQL error (-305) will be signalled, if a database value is null and no indicator variable has been defined.

Example:

```
DCL UPNAME CHAR(24) VARYING;
DCL IPNAME FIXED BIN(15);

SELECT PNAME FROM PERS INTO :UPNAME:IPNAME;
```

IPNAME contains a negative value if the database variable PNAME is null, the content of UPNAME in this case is undefined.

7.5 USE OF SQL FROM PROGRAMS

This section describes the various ways of using embedded SQL statements. The examples are based on the PERS table described in Appendix H. The Assembler program examples omit the initialisation and termination coding, as most installations have their own macros for such tasks; if this coding is required, it can be taken from the CAF example shown in Section 10.3.

Note: The program examples ignore or simplify error processing. The coding illustrates the processing techniques.

7.5.1 Static SQL

Static SQL is the simplest form of using SQL statements from within a program; the SQL statement has the same general form as for interactive SQL (except that it is preceded by EXEC SQL and terminated with EXEC-EXEC in COBOL). Values for the SQL statement can be either defined in the statement itself or contained in host variables, the host variable names are preceded by a colon (:).

Example:

The interactive SQL statement

```
DELETE FROM PERS WHERE PNO = 1234
```

can be written as the embedded SQL statement

```
EXEC SQL DELETE FROM PERS WHERE PNO = 1234;
```

using a fixed value 1234; the equivalent processing could be performed by using a host variable containing the required value, this has added flexibility when more than one value is required

```
DCL PNUM FIXED DEC(4,0);
PNUM = 1234;
EXEC SQL DELETE FROM PERS WHERE PNO = :PNUM;
```

The following program examples for static SQL perform a simple selection equivalent to the SQL query:

```
SELECT PNAME FROM PERS WHERE PNO = 2222
```

The content of PNAME is to be displayed.

Note: These example programs assume that only a single row is retrieved; an SQL error will result if more than one row satisfies the selection criterion. Section 7.5.2 describes the processing required for multiple row selection.

7.5.1.1 PL/I Static SQL Example.

```
DB2P1: PROC OPTIONS(MAIN);
DCL UPNAME CHAR(24) VARYING;
EXEC SQL INCLUDE SQLCA;
EXEC SQL SELECT PNAME
 INTO :UPNAME
 FROM PERS WHERE PNO = 2222;
/* display PNAME content */
PUT SKIP LIST (UPNAME);
END DB2P1;
```

7.5.1.2 Assembler Static SQL Example.

```
DB2A1    CSECT
   ... program initialisation
            LA    9,SQL_CA     address Communications Area
            USING SQLDSECT,9
            EXEC  SQL SELECT PNAME INTO :UPNAME FROM PERS WHERE PNO = 2222
            LH    0,UPNAME     actual length
            TPUT  UPNAME+2,(0)          display content
   ... program termination
            RETURN
            EXEC  SQL INCLUDE SQLCA    define SQL Communication Area
UPNAME   DC    HL2'24',CL24' '
SQL_WA   DS    CL(SQLDLEN)
            END
```

7.5.1.3 COBOL Static SQL Example.

```
IDENTIFICATION DIVISION.
PROGRAM-ID. DB2CB1.
ENVIRONMENT DIVISION.
DATA DIVISION.
```

```
WORKING-STORAGE SECTION.
     EXEC SQL INCLUDE SQLCA END-EXEC.
01  UPNAME.
 49  UPNAME-LEN                   PIC S9(4) COMP.
 49  UPNAME-DATA                  PIC X(24).
PROCEDURE DIVISION.
     EXEC SQL SELECT PNAME INTO :UPNAME FROM PERS WHERE PNO = 2222 END-
EXEC.
     DISPLAY UPNAME-DATA.
     STOP RUN.
```

7.5.1.4 C/370 Static SQL Example.

```
#include "stdefs.h"
#include "stdio.h"
EXEC SQL INCLUDE SQLCA;
EXEC SQL BEGIN DECLARE SECTION;
short int upno;
char upname[24];
EXEC SQL END DECLARE SECTION;
main()
{
  EXEC SQL SELECT PNO, PNAME
   INTO :upno, :upname
   FROM PERS WHERE PNO = 2222;
  printf("SQLCODE: %d %d %s\n",SQLCODE,upno,upname);
}
```

7.5.2 Static SQL SELECT with a Fixed Number of Columns and Multiple Rows

DB2 (SQL) has no direct interface to tables as supported in the host programming language. This means that SQL cannot directly return the values for more than one row to the calling program. SQL solves this by retrieving the selected rows into an internal work area and returning the individual rows. SQL uses an internal pointer called the **cursor** to maintain position to the current row.

The DECLARE statement takes the **host statement** as input and produces an internal select statement identified by **cursor**. The OPEN statement uses this select statement to access the database to initialise an internal results table; **cursor** identifies the current position in the results table. The FETCH statement retrieves the next row from the results table, SQLCODE is set to +100 when the last row has been retrieved. Static select processing is shown in Figure 7.1.

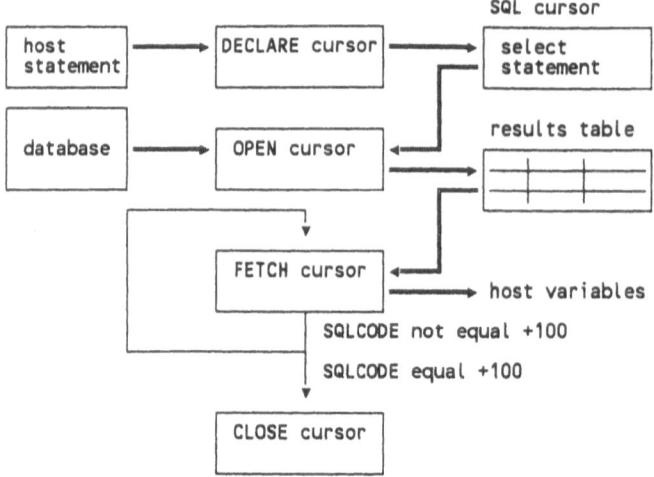

Figure 7.1 - Static select processing

The following program examples for a static SQL SELECT with a fixed number of result columns perform a full selection equivalent to the SQL query:

```
SELECT PNAME FROM PERS
```

The content of PNAME for each row satisfying the selection criterion is to be displayed.

7.5.2.1 PL/I Coding Example.

```
DB2P2: PROC OPTIONS(MAIN);
DCL UPNAME CHAR(24) VARYING;
EXEC SQL INCLUDE SQLCA;
/* define cursor */
EXEC SQL DECLARE CSR CURSOR FOR SELECT PNAME
 FROM PERS;
/* open cursor */
EXEC SQL OPEN CSR;
/* define table-end exit */
EXEC SQL WHENEVER NOT FOUND GOTO EOT;
/* fetch individual rows */
DO WHILE (SQLCODE < 100);
  EXEC SQL FETCH CSR INTO :UPNAME;
  /* display PNAME content */
  PUT SKIP LIST (UPNAME);
END;
EOT: EXEC SQL CLOSE CSR;
END DB2P2;
```

7.5.2.2 Assembler Coding Example.

```
DB2A2   CSECT
... program initialisation
        LA    9,SQL_CA     address Communications Area
        USING SQLDSECT,9
* define cursor
```

```
          DCL UPNO FIXED DECIMAL (4,0) INIT(4444);
          DCL UPNAME CHAR(10) VARYING INIT('DELTA');
          EXEC SQL INCLUDE SQLCA;
          /* prepare statement */
          EXEC SQL PREPARE STR FROM :STMT;
          /* execute statement */
          EXEC SQL EXECUTE STR USING :UPNO, :UPNAME;
          END DB2P3;
```

7.5.3.2 Assembler Dynamic SQL Example.

The Assembler program uses values defined explicitly (as literals) in the SQL statement.

```
DB2A3     CSECT
  ... program initiation
          LA      9,SQL_CA      address Communications Area
          USING SQLDSECT,9
* prepare statement
          EXEC  SQL PREPARE STR FROM :STMT
* execute statement
          EXEC  SQL EXECUTE STR
  ... program termination
          RETURN
          EXEC  SQL INCLUDE SQLCA
STMT      DC      H'80',CL80' '
          ORG     STMT+2
          DC      CL80'INSERT INTO PERS (PNO,PNAME) VALUES(4444,''DELTA'')'
SQL_CA    DS      CL(SQLDLEN)
          END
```

7.5.3.3 COBOL Dynamic SQL Example.

```
          IDENTIFICATION DIVISION.
          PROGRAM-ID. DB2CB3.
          ENVIRONMENT DIVISION.
          DATA DIVISION.
          WORKING-STORAGE SECTION.
          01  UPNAME.
            49  UPNAME-LEN              PIC  S9(4) COMP VALUE 24.
            49  UPNAME-DATA             PIC  X(24) VALUE 'DELTA'.
          01  UPNO                      PIC  S9(4) COMP VALUE 4444.
          01  STMT.
            49  STMT-LEN                PIC  S9(4) COMP VALUE 80.
            49  STMT-DATA               PIC  X(80) VALUE
                              'INSERT INTO PERS (PNO,PNAME) VALUES(?,?)'.
              EXEC SQL INCLUDE SQLCA END-EXEC.
          PROCEDURE DIVISION.
      *       prepare statement
              EXEC SQL PREPARE STR FROM :STMT END-EXEC.
      *       execute statement
              EXEC SQL EXECUTE STR USING :UPNO,:UPNAME END-EXEC.
              STOP RUN.
```

7.5.3.4 C Dynamic SQL Example.

```
          /* DB2C3 */
          #include "stdefs.h"
          #include "stdio.h"
```

```
EXEC SQL INCLUDE SQLCA;
EXEC SQL BEGIN DECLARE SECTION;
struct ( short len;
         char data[80];
       ) upname, sqlstmt;
short int upno = 4444;
EXEC SQL END DECLARE SECTION;
main()
{
  /* initialise variables */
  sqlstmt.len = 40;
  memcpy(sqlstmt.data,"insert into pers (pno,pname) values(?,?)",40);
  upname.len = 5;
  memcpy(upname.data,"DELTA",5);
  /* prepare */
  EXEC SQL PREPARE STR FROM :sqlstmt;
  printf("PREPARE SQLCODE: %d\n",SQLCODE);
  /* execute */
  EXEC SQL EXECUTE STR USING :upno,:upname;
  printf("EXECUTE SQLCODE: %d\n",SQLCODE);
}
```

7.5.4 Dynamic SQL with a Variable Number of Columns

Dynamic SQL processing with a variable number of columns (data values) requires that a SQLDA with the required number of columns entries is defined. The variable SQLN specifies the maximum number of columns (number of SQLVARN entries) contained in the SQLDA. The DESCRIBE statement uses the database to put information for the columns specified implicitly or explicitly in the **host statement** into the **host SQLDA**. The program must complete the SQLVAR entry for each column by setting the addresses of the indicator and data variables into SQLIND and SQLDATA, respectively. SQLIND requires a half-word, the size of SQLDATA is dependent on the length contained in SQLLEN. The variable SQLD specifies the actual (current) number of columns used in the SQLDA (SQLD must not be larger than SQLN). The host variable containing SQLDATA is passed to the subsequent SQL statement (the USING DESCRIPTOR keywords indicate that an SQLDA is used). There is no standard COBOL definition for the SQLDA. Figure 7.3 shows processing using the SQLDA.

As can be seen from the examples, this is by far the most complex form of SQL processing.

Note: Figure 7.3 only shows that processing particular to the SQLDA, any other processing (e.g. PREPARE) must be performed where appropriate.

Tip
A dummy SQLDA having SQLN set to 0 can be used to obtain basic information in the SQLDA for the passed SQL statement; the number of columns (data values) specified in the SQL statement is set into SQLD, although no descriptive information is returned. This information can then be used to dynamically allocate an SQLDA of the required size.

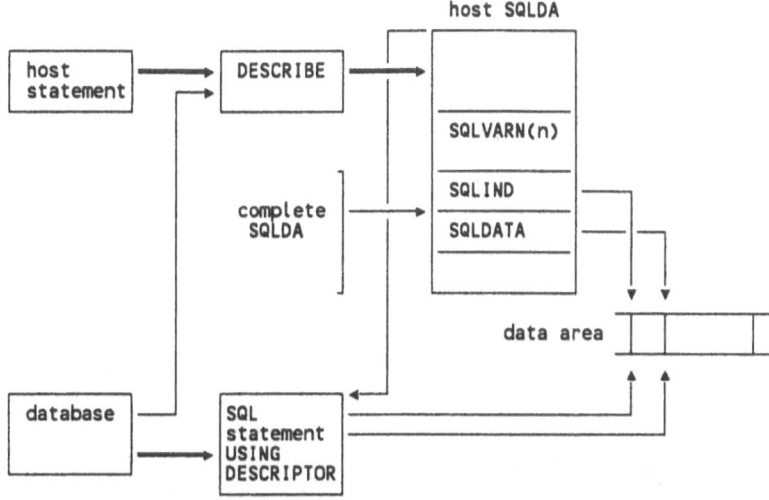

Figure 7.3 - Processing using the SQLDA

The following program examples illustrate the retrieval of a variable number of columns equivalent to the SQL query:

```
SELECT * FROM PERS
```

The content of VARCHAR fields (i.e. PNAME) for each row is to be displayed, the text *NULL* is to be displayed for null fields.

An SQLDA must be dynamically created, with one entry for each table column (the program examples assume that not more than 10 columns are present). The program examples process two types of field explicitly: VARCHAR (nulls allowed), DECIMAL; all other field types are processed as CHAR. In most cases these field types suffice (e.g. DATE and TIME fields can also be processed as character strings).

7.5.4.1 PL/I Coded Example. The PL/I program example uses controlled variables to create the SQLDA entries, another approach would be to use an array containing, say, 100 CHAR(1) elements.

```
DB2P4: PROC OPTIONS(MAIN);
/* declaration of controlled variables */
DCL 1 Y_IND FIXED BIN(15) CTL;
DCL 1 Y_VARCHAR CHAR(*) VARYING CTL;
DCL 1 Y_BIT BIT(*) CTL;
/* declaration of based variables */
DCL 1 X_IND FIXED BIN(15) BASED(XPTR);
DCL 1 X_VARCHAR CHAR(256) VARYING BASED(XPTR);
/* start of declarations */
DCL XPTR PTR;
DCL SZ FIXED BIN;
DCL STR CHAR(80) INIT('SELECT * FROM PERS');
EXEC SQL INCLUDE SQLCA;
EXEC SQL INCLUDE SQLDA;
EXEC SQL DECLARE CSR CURSOR FOR S1; /* declare cursor */
/* end of declarations */
/* start of executive code */
```

```
EXEC SQL PREPARE S1 FROM :STR;
SQLSIZE = 10; /* 10 columns, parameter for ALLOC */
ALLOC SQLDA;
SQLN = 10; /* 10 columns, maximum */
EXEC SQL DESCRIBE S1 INTO :SQLDA;
/* analyse descriptor area and acquire storage */
/* SQLD: actual no. of columns present */
DO N = 1 TO SQLD;
  ALLOC Y_IND; /* allocate indicator variable */
  SQLIND(N) = ADDR(Y_IND); /* addr of indicator variable */
  SELECT (SQLTYPE(N)); /* test internal form of data variable */
    WHEN (449) DO; /* VARCHAR */
      SZ = SQLLEN(N);  /* set maximum length */
      ALLOC Y_VARCHAR CHAR(SZ);
      SQLDATA(N) = ADDR(Y_VARCHAR);
    END;
    WHEN (484) DO; /* DECIMAL */
      /* the precision specifies the no. of decimal digits,
         two decimal digits occupy 8 bits, 4 bits are required
         for the numeric sign */
      SZ = (((SQLLEN(N)/256)+2)/2)*8; /* precision */
      ALLOC Y_BIT BIT(SZ);
      SQLDATA(N) = ADDR(Y_BIT);
    END;
    OTHERWISE DO;   /* other variable type */
      SZ = SQLLEN(N)*8; /* size in bits */
      ALLOC Y_BIT BIT(SZ);
      SQLDATA(N) = ADDR(Y_BIT);
    END;
  END;
END;
/* open cursor */
EXEC SQL OPEN CSR;
/* define table-end exit */
EXEC SQL WHENEVER NOT FOUND GOTO EOT;
/* fetch individual rows */
DO WHILE (SQLCODE = 0);
  EXEC SQL FETCH CSR USING DESCRIPTOR :SQLDA;
  IF SQLCODE = 0 THEN DO;
    /* list fields */
    DO N = 1 TO SQLD;
    XPTR = SQLIND(N); /* pointer to indicator variable */
      SELECT (SQLTYPE(N));
        WHEN (449) DO; /* VARCHAR */
          IF X_IND < 0
          THEN DO;  /* null value */
            PUT SKIP LIST ('*NULL*');
          END;
          ELSE DO;
            XPTR = SQLDATA(N); /* pointer to data */
            PUT SKIP LIST (X_VARCHAR);
          END;
        END;
        OTHERWISE; /* ignore other variable types */
      END;
    END;
  END;
END;
EOT: END DB2P4;
```

7.5.4.2 Assembler Coded Example. To simplify processing the sample
Assembler program uses static definitions for the SQLDA and the data area.

```
DB2A4      CSECT
    ... program initiation
* declare cursor
           EXEC  SQL DECLARE CSR CURSOR FOR S1
           LA    9,SQL_CA
           USING SQLDSECT,9
           LA    8,SQL_DA
           USING SQLDA,8
           LA    6,DA
* prepare
           EXEC  SQL PREPARE S1 FROM :STR
           MVC   SQLN,=H'10'           maximum no. of SQLVARN entries
* describe
           EXEC  SQL DESCRIBE S1 INTO SQL_DA
* analyse descriptor
           LH    2,SQLD               actual no. of columns
           LA    7,SQLVAR
           USING SQLVARN,7
A210       ST    6,SQLIND             A(indicator variable)
           LA    6,2(6)               L(indicator variable)
           ST    6,SQLDATA            A(data)
           LH    1,SQLLEN             logical field size
           CLC   SQLTYPE,=H'449'      VARCHAR (nulls allowed)
           BNE   A211
           STH   1,0(6)
           LA    6,2(6)
A211       CLC   SQLTYPE,=H'484'      decimal
           BNE   A212
           SR    1,1
           IC    1,SQLPRCSN           decimal precision
           LA    1,2(1)               add 2
           SRL   1,1                  field size (in bytes)
A212       AR    6,1                  update ptr
           LA    7,SQLVARN_SIZE(7)
           BCT   2,A210
* open cursor
           EXEC  SQL OPEN CSR
* define table-end exit
           EXEC  SQL WHENEVER NOT FOUND GOTO B100
A100       DS    0H
* fetch row
           EXEC  SQL FETCH CSR USING DESCRIPTOR SQL_DA
* list fields
           LH    2,SQLD               actual no. of columns
           LA    7,SQLVAR
A310       L     1,SQLIND             A(indicator variable)
           LA    3,=CL8'*NULL*'       pre-define constant
           LA    0,8
           LH    1,0(1)               indicator variable
           CH    1,=H'0'
           BL    A330                 :null data
* else display true data
           L     3,SQLDATA            A(data)
           LH    0,SQLLEN             logical field length
           CLC   SQLTYPE,=H'449'      VARCHAR?
```

```
          BNE   A320                :no
          LH    0,0(3)              actual length
          LA    3,2(3)              address of true data
A330      TPUT  (3),(0)             display
A320      LA    7,SQLVARN_SIZE(7)
          BCT   2,A310
          B     A100
B100      DS    0H
 ... program termination
STR       DC    H'80',CL80'SELECT * FROM PERS'
          LTORG
SQL_CA    DS    CL(SQLDLEN)
SQL_DA    DS    CL(10*44+16)
          ORG
DA        DS    CL100               data area
          EXEC  SQL INCLUDE SQLCA
          EXEC  SQL INCLUDE SQLDA
SQLVARN_SIZE EQU SQLVSIZ+SQLDATA-SQLVARN
          END
```

8

Embedded SQL Statements

Any general statement is like a cheque drawn on a bank. Its value depends on what is there to meet it.

ABC of Reading
Ezra Pound

8.1 INTRODUCTION

This chapter describes those SQL statements used from programs (embedded SQL statements). All SQL statements can be used from programs, although not all statements can be used interactively. This book describes only those SQL statements directly concerned with data manipulation:

8.2 STATEMENTS

This book discusses the following SQL statements:

·	BEGIN DECLARE	Start declaration of host variables.
·	CLOSE	Close cursor.
·	COMMIT	Force changes to be made to the database.
·	DECLARE CURSOR	Define cursor.
·	DECLARE STATEMENT	Define SQL statement name.
·	DECLARE TABLE	Define structure of DB2 table.
·	DELETE	Delete rows.

· DESCRIBE	Obtain information about a prepared statement.	
· END DECLARE	End declaration of host variables.	
· EXECUTE	Execute a prepared statement.	
· EXECUTE IMMEDIATE	Prepare and execute an executable SQL statement.	
· EXPLAIN	Obtain access path information.	
· FETCH	Obtain next row from results table.	
· INCLUDE	Insert code or declarations from source library.	
· INSERT	Insert rows.	
· LOCK TABLE	Set lock.	
· OPEN	Initialise results table for select.	
· PREPARE	Prepare statement for subsequent execution.	
· ROLLBACK	Revoke any pending changes.	
· SELECT INTO	Perform select to retrieve a single row.	
· UPDATE	Update rows.	
· WHENEVER	Specify processing to be performed when an SQL exception occurs (this causes a GOTO).	

The SQL reference manual should be used to obtain further information about the semantics, and for a description of the other SQL statements. A full description of the power of SQL is beyond the scope of this book. Figure 8.1 describes the general use of the statements.

statement	executable	dynamically preparable
BEGIN DECLARE	no	-
CLOSE	yes	no
COMMIT	yes	yes
DECLARE CURSOR	no	-
DECLARE STATEMENT	no	-
DECLARE TABLE	no	-
DELETE	yes	yes
DESCRIBE	yes	no
END DECLARE	no	-
EXECUTE	yes	no
EXECUTE IMMEDIATE	yes	no
EXPLAIN	yes	yes
FETCH	yes	no
INCLUDE	no	-
INSERT	yes	yes
LOCK TABLE	yes	yes
OPEN	yes	no
PREPARE	yes	no
ROLLBACK	yes	yes
SELECT INTO	yes	no
UPDATE	yes	yes
WHENEVER	no	-

Figure 8.1 - General use of SQL statements

8.2.1 BEGIN DECLARE - Start Declarations

The BEGIN DECLARE statement indicates the start of the declaration of host variables used in SQL statements. The declare statements are terminated by the END DECLARE statement. BEGIN DECLARE and END DECLARE statements are mandatory for programs written in the C language. They may be used in other programming languages, however, they will be flagged with a warning.

Syntax:
```
►►──BEGIN DECLARE SECTION──►◄
```

Example:
```
        EXEC SQL BEGIN DECLARE SECTION;
        short int upno;
        char upname[24];
        EXEC SQL END DECLARE SECTION;
```

8.2.2 CLOSE - Close Cursor

The CLOSE statement closes a cursor, this deletes the temporary table created by the OPEN CURSOR statement for the same cursor. Although all open cursors are implicitly closed on termination of the recovery unit, it is good programming practice to explicitly close a cursor with the CLOSE statement.

Syntax:
```
►►──CLOSE cursorname──►◄
```

cursor-name
        The SQL name used to identify the opened cursor.

Example:
```
        EXEC SQL DECLARE CSR CURSOR FOR SELECT PNO, PNAME FROM PERS;
        /* open cursor */
        EXEC SQL OPEN CSR;
        /* fetch individual rows */
         ...
        END;
        /* close cursor */
        EXEC SQL CLOSE CSR;
```
Close the cursor CSR associated with the "SELECT PNO, PNAME FROM PERS" selection.

8.2.3 COMMIT - Make Outstanding Database Changes Permanent

The COMMIT statement is used to complete the current unit of recovery (described in Chapter 9) and to force any changes performed during this recovery unit to be made permanent.
Note: A commit is automatically performed when the program terminates normally (i.e. does not terminate because of an abend (abnormal end)); this can have consequences when a testing environment is being used (see Chapter 10).

Syntax:
```
►►──COMMIT──┬──────┬──►◄
            └ WORK─┘
```

Example:
```
EXEC SQL UPDATE PERS
  SET PNO = 6666, PNAME = 'EPSILON'
  WHERE PNO = 5555;
EXEC SQL COMMIT;
```
Force the update of the PERS table row with PNO=5555 to be made.

8.2.4 DECLARE CURSOR - Define Cursor

The DECLARE CURSOR defines a cursor. The cursor is used for row access in a select statement which can return more than one row in the results table.

Syntax:
```
►►——DECLARE cursorname CURSOR FOR ──┬─selectstatement─┬──►◄
                                    └─statementname───┘
```

cursorname
> An SQL name used to identify the cursor; the cursor-name must be unique within the program.

selectstatement
> A select statement.

statement-name
> The SQL statement name of a select statement defined by the PREPARE statement.

Example 1:
Use a select statement for the definition of cursor CSR, which is used in the FETCH statement to retrieve rows from the results table.

```
EXEC SQL DECLARE CSR CURSOR FOR SELECT PNO, PNAME FROM PERS;
/* open cursor */
EXEC SQL OPEN CSR;
/* fetch individual rows */
DO WHILE (SQLCODE < 100);
  EXEC SQL FETCH CSR INTO :UPNO, UPNAME;
  ...
END;
```

Example 2:
Perform the same function as Example 1, but use a select statement processed by a PREPARE statement.

```
/* define cursor */
EXEC SQL DECLARE CSR CURSOR FOR S1;
/* prepare */
EXEC SQL PREPARE S1 FROM :SELSTR;
DCL SELSTR CHAR(80) VARYING INIT('SELECT PNO, PNAME FROM PERS');
/* open cursor */
EXEC SQL OPEN CSR;
/* fetch individual rows */
DO WHILE (SQLCODE < 100);
  EXEC SQL FETCH CSR INTO :UPNO, UPNAME;
  ...
END;
```

8.2.5 DECLARE STATEMENT - Define SQL Statement Name

The DECLARE statement is used to explicitly define SQL statement names. The DECLARE statement is optional, however, it is useful for documentation purposes.

Syntax:

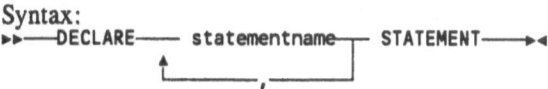

statement-name
>   The SQL statement name used in embedded SQL statements.

Example:
```
EXEC SQL DECLARE S1 STATEMENT;
EXEC SQL PREPARE S1 FROM :STRING;
```
This code specifies that S1 (used in the PREPARE statement) is an SQL statement name.

8.2.6 DECLARE TABLE - Define Table Structure

The DECLARE TABLE statement is used to explicitly define the structure of a DB2 table at precompile-time. The DECLARE TABLE statement is optional, however, it is useful for documentation purposes and for consistency validation of embedded SQL statements. Note: There is no consistency check performed against the table as it actually exists in the database; the DB2 DCLGEN command can be used obtain the definition of the table or view as it exists in the database (the INCLUDE statement is used to obtain this definition for the program).

Syntax:

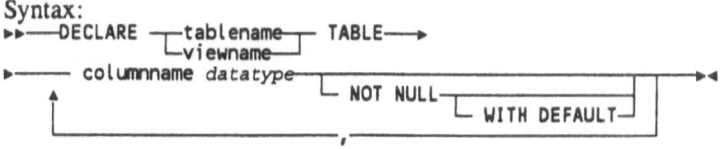

datatype:

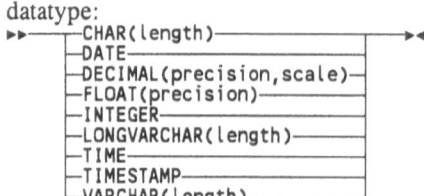

```
►►───┬─CHAR(length)──────────────┬─►◄
     ├─DATE───────────────────────┤
     ├─DECIMAL(precision,scale)───┤
     ├─FLOAT(precision)───────────┤
     ├─INTEGER────────────────────┤
     ├─LONGVARCHAR(length)────────┤
     ├─TIME───────────────────────┤
     ├─TIMESTAMP──────────────────┤
     └─VARCHAR(length)────────────┘
```

tablename

>The name of the database table.

viewname

>The name of the database view.

columnname

>The name of the column as used in embedded SQL statements. The column-
>name should, for documentation purposes, be the same as the corresponding
>column name in the database table (or view).

Example:
```
EXEC SQL DECLARE PERS TABLE
( PNO DECIMAL(4),
  PNAME VARCHAR(24) );
```
Declare the structure of the PERS table as having two columns: PNO and PNAME.

8.2.7 DELETE - Delete Rows

The DELETE statement is used to delete those rows from the table or view that
satisfy the specified selection criterion.

Syntax:

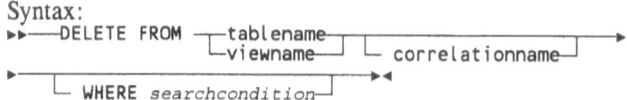

```
►►───DELETE FROM ─┬─tablename─┬─┬─────────────────────┬─►
                 └─viewname──┘ └─ correlationname─┘
►─────────────────────────────►◄
  └─ WHERE searchcondition─┘
```

tablename

>The name of the database table.

viewname

>The name of the database view.

correlationname

>The name used to refer to the previously specified **table-name** or **view-
>name**.

searchcondition

>The search condition for the rows to be deleted.

Example:
```
EXEC SQL DELETE FROM PERS WHERE PNO = 2222;
```
Delete from PERS those rows with PNO equal to 2222.

8.2.8 DESCRIBE - Obtain Information for a Prepared Statement

The DESCRIBE statement is used to obtain information about a prepared statement.

Syntax:
```
►►──DESCRIBE statementname INTO sqldescriptor─┐
                                              └ USING ──NAMES──┐      ►◄
                                                      ├LABELS─┤
                                                      ├ANY────┤
                                                      └BOTH───┘
```

statementname
> The name of an embedded SQL statement which has been prepared.

sqldescriptor
> The name of a host variable which is to contain the prepared statement. This variable maps the SQLDA (SQL Descriptor Area). Appendix E contains the definition of the SQLDA.

USING
> Specify how each variable is to be identified:

> NAMES   column name;

> LABELS   column label;

> ANY   column label (if present), otherwise column name;

> BOTH   column label and column name. Note: Two SQLVAR entries in the SQLDA are required for each column.

Example 1:
```
DCL P_STMT CHAR(80)
  INIT('SELECT * FROM PERS');
DCL 1 USER_SQLDA,
      2 USER_SQLDAID CHAR(8),
      2 USER_SQLDABC BIN FIXED(31),
      2 USER_SQLN BIN FIXED,
      2 USER_SQLD BIN FIXED,
      2 USER_SQLVAR(10),
       3 USER_SQLTYPE BIN FIXED,
       3 USER_SQLLEN BIN FIXED,
       3 USER_SQLDATA PTR,
       3 USER_SQLIND PTR,
       3 USER_SQLNAME CHAR(30) VARYING;
DCL N BIN FIXED;
EXEC SQL INCLUDE SQLCA;

USER_SQLDABC = 10*44+16;
USER_SQLN = 10; /* 10 columns */
EXEC SQL PREPARE S1 FROM :P_STMT;
EXEC SQL DESCRIBE S1 INTO :USER_SQLDA;
/* list column characteristics */
```

```
DO N = 1 TO USER_SQLD;
  PUT SKIP LIST (N,USER_SQLNAME(N),USER_SQLTYPE(N));
END;
```

This example obtains the description of the prepared statement S1 (SELECT * FROM PERS) into the user-defined SQLDA (structure USER_SQLDA), each column name and its type are subsequently listed.

Example 2:
```
DCL P_STMT CHAR(80) INIT('SELECT * FROM PERS');
EXEC SQL INCLUDE SQLCA;
EXEC SQL INCLUDE SQLDA;

EXEC SQL PREPARE S1 FROM :P_STMT;
SQLSIZE = 10; /* 10 columns */
ALLOC SQLDA;
SQLN = 10; /* 10 columns */
EXEC SQL DESCRIBE S1 INTO :SQLDA;
/* list column characteristics */
DO N = 1 TO SQLD;
  PUT SKIP LIST ('SQL:',N,SQLNAME(N),SQLTYPE(N));
END;
```

This example obtains the description of the prepared statement S1 (SELECT * FROM PERS) into the allocated SQLDA having a maximum of 10 rows, each column name and its type are subsequently listed.

8.2.9 END DECLARE - Terminate Declarations

The END DECLARE statement indicates the end of the declaration of host variables used in SQL statements. The declare statements are introduced by the BEGIN DECLARE statement. BEGIN DECLARE and END DECLARE statements are mandatory for programs written in the C language. They may be used in other programming languages, however, they will be flagged with a warning.

Syntax:
```
►►──END DECLARE SECTION──►◄
```

Example:
```
EXEC SQL BEGIN DECLARE SECTION;
short int upno;
char upname[24];
EXEC SQL END DECLARE SECTION;
```

8.2.10 EXECUTE - Execute a Prepared Statement

The EXECUTE statement is used to execute a prepared statement.

Syntax:
```
►►──EXECUTE statementname ─┬─────────────────────────────────────┬──►◄
                          └─USING ─┬─ DESCRIPTOR sqldadescriptor─┘
                                   └─ :hostvariable─┬─
                                        ▲           │
                                        └─────,─────┘
```

statementname
The name of the prepared embedded SQL statement which is to be executed.

sqldadescriptor
The name of a host variable which maps the SQLDA. The SQLDA specifies those variables which are to replace parameters (indicated by "?") in the prepared statement. The number of entries in the SQLDA and their sequence must correspond to the parameters in the prepared statement. Appendix E contains the definition of the SQLDA.

hostvariable
The name of a host variable which is to replace the corresponding parameter (indicated by "?") in the prepared statement. The number of host-variables specified and their sequence must correspond to the parameters in the prepared statement.

Example:
```
DCL 1 STMT CHAR(80) VARYING
 INIT('DELETE FROM PERS WHERE PNO=? AND PNAME=?');
EXEC SQL PREPARE STR FROM :STMT;
EXEC SQL EXECUTE STR USING :UPNO, :UPNAME;
```
Execute the string prepared as STR, which uses the two host variables: UPNO and UPNAME.

8.2.11 EXECUTE IMMEDIATE - Prepare and Execute a Statement

The EXECUTE IMMEDIATE statement prepares and executes an executable SQL statement. This statement exists only temporarily and is subsequently deleted. The EXECUTE IMMEDIATE statement is functionally equivalent to a PREPARE and EXECUTE statement pair. EXECUTE IMMEDIATE cannot be used to prepare a select statement.

Tip
It is more efficient to perform one PREPARE and to EXECUTE it repeatedly, rather than to perform repeated EXECUTE IMMEDIATES.

Syntax:
```
►►──EXECUTE IMMEDIATE ──┬─stringexpression─┬──►◄
                        └─:hostvariable────┘
```

stringexpression
A PL/I expression which yields the string forming the SQL statement to be executed.

hostvariable
The name of a host variable containing the SQL statement to be executed. For all host languages other than PL/I, this variable must have the VARCHAR attribute.

Example:
```
DCL EX_STRING VARCHAR(80) INIT('DELETE FROM PERS WHERE PNAME=''BETA''');
EXEC SQL EXECUTE IMMEDIATE :EX_STRING;
```
Delete those entries from the PERS table with PNAME containing BETA.

8.2.12 EXPLAIN - Obtain Processing Statistics

The EXPLAIN statement is used to obtain information pertaining to the delete, insert, select or update statement. The information is placed in the user's table with the name PLAN_TABLE. PLAN_TABLE must exist and have the structure shown in Figure 8.2.

Tip
In many cases a simple count on the number of rows to be processed will be sufficient to determine whether this number of rows is reasonable. This is especially true when selection criteria are created dynamically.

Syntax:

```
►►──EXPLAIN ──┬─PLAN─┬───────────────────────────────►
              └─ALL─┘  └─ SET QUERYNO=integer─┘
►──── FOR sqlstatement───►◄
```

PLAN or ALL
>   The keyword indicating that one or more rows is to be inserted into the PLAN_TABLE. PLAN and ALL are synonyms.

integer
>   A number which is assigned to the QUERYNO variable in PLAN_TABLE. If no explicit QUERYNO is specified, a number will be assigned automatically. This number can be used to identify the explain information.

sqlstatement
>   The statement for which the explain information is to be returned. This statement cannot be a host variable. If an explain is to be made on a statement which is prepared dynamically, the complete EXPLAIN statement must also be prepared dynamically.

Note: The RUNSTATS utility must have been used to update the table statistics in order that meaningful results are produced.

```
CREATE TABLE PLAN_TABLE
   (QUERYNO      INTEGER      NOT NULL,
    QBLOCKNO     SMALLINT     NOT NULL,
    APPLNAME     CHAR(8)      NOT NULL,
    PROGNAME     CHAR(8)      NOT NULL,
    PLANNO       SMALLINT     NOT NULL,
    METHOD       SMALLINT     NOT NULL,
    CREATOR      CHAR(8)      NOT NULL,
    TNAME        CHAR(18)     NOT NULL,
    TABNO        SMALLINT     NOT NULL,
    ACCESSTYPE   CHAR(2)      NOT NULL,
    MATCHCOLS    SMALLINT     NOT NULL,
```

```
        ACCESSCREATOR  CHAR(8)         NOT NULL,
        ACCESSNAME     CHAR(18)        NOT NULL,
        INDEXONLY      CHAR(1)         NOT NULL,
        SORTN_UNIQ     CHAR(1)         NOT NULL,
        SORTN_JOIN     CHAR(1)         NOT NULL,
        SORTN_ORDERBY  CHAR(1)         NOT NULL,
        SORTN_GROUPBY  CHAR(1)         NOT NULL,
        SORTC_UNIQ     CHAR(1)         NOT NULL,
        SORTC_JOIN     CHAR(1)         NOT NULL,
        SORTC_ORDERBY  CHAR(1)         NOT NULL,
        SORTC_GROUPBY  CHAR(1)         NOT NULL,
        TSLOCKMODE     CHAR(3)         NOT NULL,
        TIMESTAMP      CHAR(16)        NOT NULL,
        REMARKS        VARCHAR(254) NOT NULL)
    IN database-name.tablespace-name
```

Figure 8.2 - Basic PLAN_TABLE definition

Note on Figure 8.2: The database administrator must supply **database-name** and **tablespace-name**.

Basic PLAN_TABLE definition (the so-called 25-column format) can be augmented with further information: the 28-column format, the 30-column format, and the 34-column format.

28-column format:
```
        PREFETCH CHAR(1)            NOT NULL
        COLUMN_FN_EVAL CHAR(1)      NOT NULL
        MIXOPSEQ SMALLINT           NOT NULL
```

30-column format:
```
        VERSION VARCHAR(64)         NOT NULL
        COLLID CHAR(18)             NOT NULL
```

34-column format:
```
        ACCESS_DEGREE SMALLINT
        ACCESS_PGROUP_ID SMALLINT
        JOIN_DEGREE SMALLINT
        JOIN_PGROUP_ID SMALLINT
```

8.2.12.1 Principal PLAN_TABLE Attributes.

Tip
There are several third-party products that present the EXPLAIN information in a more easily understood form.

QUERYNO
A number that identifies the analysed query. The SET QUERYNO clause can be used to set the number explicitly, otherwise DB2 assigns the number.

QBLOCKNO
Nesting level.

APPLNAME
> The application plan name if BIND EXPLAIN.

PROGNAME
> The name of the program that contains the EXPLAIN statement.

PLANNO
> The sequence number of the individual steps.

METHOD
> The processing strategy:
>
> 0   First table that is accessed (PLANNO = 1)
> 1   Nested Loop Join
> 2   Merge Scan Join
> 3   Additional sort
> 4   Hybrid join.

CREATOR
> The creator of the corresponding table.

TNAME
> The table name.

TABNO
> The table numbering (the reference number in the SQL statement).

ACCESSTYPE
> The access type:
>
> I   Index access
> M   Multiple index
> N   Index scan
> R   Sequential access.
> I and M can be qualified.

MATCHCOLS
> The number of key fields used in the index scan.

ACCESSCREATOR
> The creator of the index.

ACCESSNAME
> The index name.

INDEXONLY
> Indicates whether only the index is used (Y) or data also needs to be accessed (N).

SORTN_UNIQ
Indicates whether a sort is performed to remove duplicate rows (Y).

SORTN_JOIN
Indicates whether a sort is performed to produce the new table for METHOD 2 or 4.

SORTN_ORDERBY
Indicates whether an ORDER BY clause performs a sort on the new table.

SORTN_GROUPBY
Indicates whether a GROUP BY clause performs a sort on the new table.

SORTC...
Similar to the SORTN... entries, but with regard to a composite table.

TSLOCKMODE
The lock mode of the table space or table.

IS	Intent share
IX	Intent exclusive
S	Share
SIX	Share with intent exclusive
U	Update
X	Exclusive.

PREFETCH
Indicates whether data pages are to be prefetched:

L	Prefetch through page list
S	Pure sequential prefetch.

COLUMN_FN_EVAL
Evaluation time point for an SQL column:

R	On data retrieval
S	When data items are sorted.

MIXOPSEQ
The sequence number in a multiple index operation.

VERSION
The version identifier for the package that contains the EXPLAIN statement.

COLLID
The collection identifier for the package that contains the EXPLAIN statement.

The following entries contain the value determined at bind-time. The actual execution-time value may be different.

ACCESS_DEGREE
The number of parallel input/output streams activated by the query.

JOIN_DEGREE
The number of parallel input/output streams used in joining the new composite table.

Example:
```
EXPLAIN PLAN FOR SELECT * FROM PERS
```

Return the following information:

```
QUERYNO  QBLOCKNO  APPLNAME  PROGNAME  PLANNO  METHOD
    70           1                    DSNESM68       1       0

CREATOR   TNAME                    TABNO  ACCESSTYPE
TSOUSR1   PERS                         1  R

MATCHCOLS  ACCESSCREATOR  ACCESSNAME              INDEXONLY
     0                                             N

SORTN   SORTN   SORTN     SORTN     SORTC  SORTC  SORTC     SORTC
UNIQ    JOIN    ORDERBY   GROUPBY   UNIQ   JOIN   ORDERBY   GROUPBY
N       N       N         N         N      N      N         N

TSLOCKMODE  TIMESTAMP              REMARKS
    S       19951117122120 30
```

8.2.13 FETCH - Position Cursor to Next Row

The FETCH statement positions the cursor at the next row in the results table and assigns those values to the host variables. SQLCODE (in the SQLCA) is set to +100 when the previous row retrieved was the last row in the results table; this value is also set if the results table is empty.

Syntax:

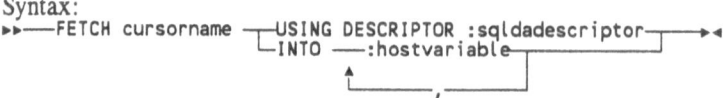

```
►►──FETCH cursorname ──┬─USING DESCRIPTOR :sqldadescriptor─┬──►◄
                       └─INTO ──:hostvariable─────────────┘
                                    ▲              │
                                    └──────,───────┘
```

cursorname
The cursor to be used for the FETCH operation and must specify a cursor defined by the DECLARE CURSOR statement.

sqldadescriptor
The name of a host variable which defines a valid SQLDA. The data from the results table replaces the data for the corresponding entry in the SQLDA. SQLWARN3 (in the SQLCA) is set to "W", if the SQLDA is not sufficiently large to contain all the data values to be returned.

hostvariable
The name of a host variable which is to contain the returned value.

Example:
```
/* declare cursor */
EXEC SQL DECLARE CSR CURSOR FOR SELECT PNO, PNAME FROM PERS;
/* open cursor */
EXEC SQL OPEN CSR;
/* fetch individual rows */
DO WHILE (SQLCODE < 100);
  EXEC SQL FETCH CSR INTO :UPNO, UPNAME;
END;
EXEC SQL CLOSE CSR;
```
Retrieve the values for each row from PERS table into the two host variables: UPNO and UPNAME.

8.2.14 INCLUDE - Include Definitions

The INCLUDE statement makes a static insertion of code or definitions into the invoking program at precompile-time. The code or definition is obtained from the source library.

Note: The INCLUDE statement must be placed at the appropriate point in the invoking program. This location depends on whether the included statements are executable and on the host language, e.g. INCLUDE SQLCA in a COBOL program must be placed in the WORKING STORAGE section.

Syntax:

SQLCA
> The description of the SQL Communications Area (SQLCA) is to be included. Appendix B contains a description of the SQLCA.

SQLDA
> The description of the SQL Descriptor Area (SQLDA) is to be included. Appendix B contains a description of the SQLDA.
> Note: No standard SQLDA definition exists for COBOL.

membername
> The name of the member containing code which is to be inserted from the source library at this point on the program.

Example:
```
EXEC SQL INCLUDE SQLCA;
```
Include the description of the SQLCA.

8.2.15 INSERT - Insert Rows

The INSERT statement inserts rows into a table or view.

Syntax:

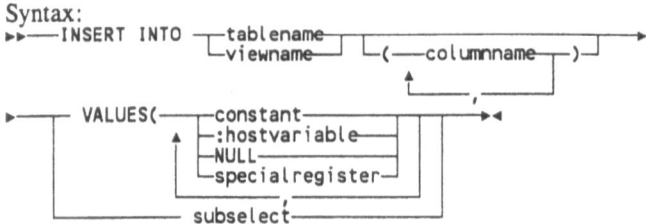

tablename
>   The name of the database table.

viewname
>   The name of the database view.

columnname
>   The name of the column as used in embedded SQL statements and must
>   correspond to a column name in the database table (or view).
>   Default: all table (or view) columns.

VALUES
>   Introduce the values for the specified columns. The number, sequence and
>   form of the specified values must correspond to the specified column
>   names.

subselect
>   The data values in the results table obtained by performing this sub-select
>   are to be used for the insertion.
>   SQLCODE is set to +100, if the results table is empty.

Example:
```
     EXEC SQL INSERT INTO PERS (PNO, PNAME) VALUES (5555,'LAMBDA');
```
Insert PNO=5555 and PNAME=LAMBDA into the PERS table.

8.2.16 LOCK TABLE - Set Lock

The LOCK TABLE statement sets a shared or exclusive, as specified, lock on a table or
table space. The lock is released when the process terminates, or issues a commit
or rollback operation; unless the associated plan was bound with
RELEASE(DEALLOCATE), in which case the table is only released when the process
terminates. Chapter 9 describes the lock process in further detail.

Syntax:

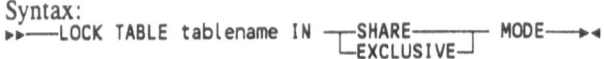

tablename
>   The name of the database table.

SHARE

> Acquire a shared lock. The shared lock prevents other processes from performing delete, insert or update processes on the table.

EXCLUSIVE

> Acquire an exclusive lock. The exclusive lock prevents other processes from accessing the table.

Example:
```
EXEC SQL LOCK TABLE PERS IN EXCLUSIVE MODE;
EXEC SQL UPDATE PERS SET PNAME = 'EPSILON' WHERE PNO = 5555;
EXEC SQL UPDATE PERS SET PNAME = 'RHO' WHERE PNO = 6666;
EXEC SQL COMMIT;
```
This example prohibits other users from accessing the PERS table during the time the two updates are being processed.

8.2.17 OPEN - Create Results Table

The OPEN statement initialises the results table for the select statement associated with the cursor. The first FETCH statement performs the select.

Syntax:

cursorname

> The name of the cursor to be opened and must specify a cursor defined by a DECLARE CURSOR statement.

USING

> Introduce the definition of the data area which is to contain the returned values. If this data area is omitted, it must be specified by the SELECT statement which returns the data values.

sqldadescriptor

> The name of a host variable which defines a valid SQLDA. The data from the results table replaces the data for the corresponding entry in the SQLDA.

hostvariable

> The name of a host variable which is to contain the returned value. The number, sequence and form of the specified host-variables must correspond to the column names specified or implied in the SELECT statement.

Example:
```
EXEC SQL DECLARE CSR CURSOR FOR SELECT PNO, PNAME FROM PERS;
/* open cursor */
EXEC SQL OPEN CSR;
/* fetch individual rows */
DO WHILE (SQLCODE < 100);
  EXEC SQL FETCH CSR INTO :UPNO, UPNAME;
  ...
END;
EXEC SQL CLOSE CSR;
```
Open the selection associated with the cursor CSR ("SELECT PNO, PNAME FROM PERS").

8.2.18 PREPARE - Prepare SQL Statement

The PREPARE statement is used to prepare an embedded SQL statement which is to be subsequently used in an EXECUTE statement.

Syntax:

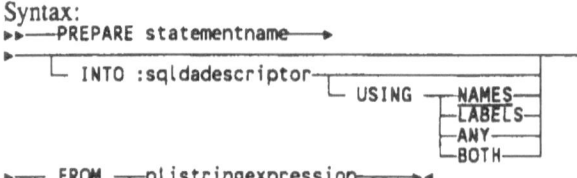

statementname
> The name of the prepared embedded SQL statement which is to be subsequently executed.

INTO
> Introduce the data area which is to contain information pertaining to the PREPARE.

sqldadescriptor
> The name of a host variable which is to contain the SQLDA.

USING
> The value that is to be assigned to each variable:
>
> NAMES   column name;
>
> LABELS   column label;
>
> ANY   column label (if present), otherwise column name;
>
> BOTH   column label and column name (two SQLVAR entries in the SQLDA are required).

FROM
> introduces the SQL statement to be prepared. The statement may contain placeholders (indicated by "?") which the EXECUTE statement replaces with the required value.

plistringexpression
    A PL/I expression which yields a string.

hostvariable
    The name of a host variable which contains the statement to be prepared.

Example:
```
DCL 1 STMT CHAR(80) VARYING
 INIT('INSERT INTO PERS (PNO,PNAME) VALUES(?,?)');
EXEC SQL PREPARE STR FROM :STMT;
EXEC SQL EXECUTE STR USING :UPNO, :UPNAME;
```
Prepare the statement contained in the STMT host variable and assign statement name STR to this prepared statement.

8.2.19 ROLLBACK - Revoke Outstanding Database Changes

The ROLLBACK statement is used to complete the current unit of recovery and to revoke any changes made to the database by this recovery unit. Chapter 9 describes **unit of recovery**.
Note: A rollback is automatically performed when the program terminates abnormally (i.e. terminates because of an abend); this can have consequences when a testing environment is being used (see Chapter 10).

Syntax:
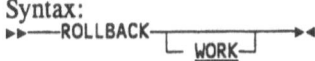

Example:
```
EXEC SQL UPDATE PERS SET PNO = 6666, PNAME = 'EPSILON' WHERE PNO = 5555;
EXEC SQL ROLLBACK;
```
Revoke the update of the PERS table row.

8.2.20 SELECT INTO - Produce Single-Row Results Table

The SELECT INTO statement uses the specified selection criteria to produce a results table having a maximum of one row. SQLCODE is set to +100 if the results table is empty. An error condition is set if more than one row would have been returned.

Syntax:
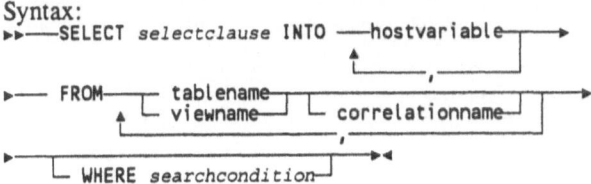

selectclause
    The select criterion.

hostvariable
> The name of a host variable which is to contain the retrieved value. An indicator should be specified for a column that can be null.

tablename
> The name of the table from which selected columns are to be retrieved.

viewname
> The name of the view from which selected columns are to be retrieved.

correlationname
> A (nick)name which may be used in the search-condition to identify the database table (or view).

searchcondition
> The select criterion.

Example:
```
DCL UPNO FIXED DECIMAL(4),
    UPNAME CHAR(24) VARYING;

EXEC SQL WHENEVER SQLERROR GOTO :SQL_ERR;
EXEC SQL SELECT PNO, PNAME INTO :UPNO, :UPNAME FROM PERS WHERE PNO=2222;
```
Select the two database fields PNO and PNAME into the two program variables UPNO and UPNAME for those database records with PNO equal to 2222.

8.2.21 UPDATE - Update Database Rows

The UPDATE statement updates those rows in a table or view which satisfy the specified search criteria. SQLERRD(3) is set to contain the number of rows updated.

Syntax - searched update:

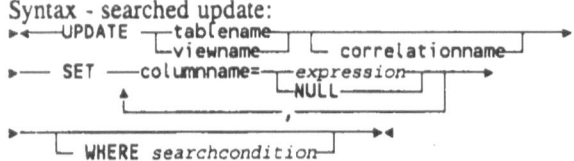

Syntax - positioned update:

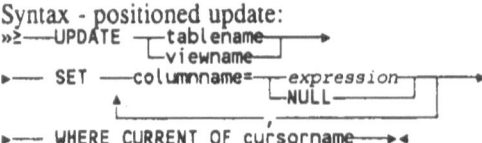

tablename
> The name of the database table.

viewname
> The name of the database view.

correlationname

A (nick)name which may be used in the search-condition to identify the database table (or view).

columnname

The name of a column in the database table (or view).

expression

The expression whose value is to be assigned to the specified column.

NULL

The column is to be set to NULL.

searchcondition

The search criteria. If no search condition is specified, all table rows are updated.

CURRENT OF

A cursor is to be used to identify the row to be updated.

cursorname

The cursor which identifies to row to be updated. **cursor-name** must specify a cursor defined in the DECLARE CURSOR statement.

Example:
```
EXEC SQL UPDATE PERS SET PNO = 6666, PNAME = 'EPSILON' WHERE PNO = 5555;
```
This example updates the PERS table row with PNO=5555 by setting PNO=6666 and PNAME=EPSILON, i.e PNO is changed from 5555 to 6666 and PNAME is set to EPSILON.

8.2.22 WHENEVER - Define Exception Processing

The WHENEVER statement specifies the processing to be performed if a subsequent SQL exception occurs. The WHENEVER remains in effect until the next WHENEVER statement is encountered.

Tip

More than one WHENEVER statement (for each error class) should only be used with caution, as the compile-time sequence, and not the execution-time sequence, determines the processing to be performed.

Syntax:

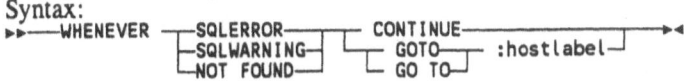

SQLERROR

The exception condition is set by a negative value of SQLCODE.

SQLWARNING

The exception condition is to be signalled when SQL issues a warning; SQLCODE is positive (but not +100) or SQLWARN0 = "W".

NOT FOUND

The exception condition is to be signalled when SQL sets the NOT FOUND condition, i.e. SQLCODE = +100.

CONTINUE

The processing is to continue at the statement following that statement which caused the exception to be signalled.
CONTINUE is the default, if no WHENEVER statement has been issued.

GOTO (or GO TO)

Control is to be passed to the statement identified by the following host-label.

hostlabel

The statement which is to receive control when the exception condition is signalled.

Example:
```
EXEC SQL WHENEVER SQLERROR GOTO :SQL_ERR;
EXEC SQL SELECT * INTO :PNO, :PNAME FROM PERS WHERE PNO=2222;
   ...
SQL_ERR: PUT SKIP LIST (SQLCODE);
RETURN(8);
```
This code causes control to be passed to the statement with label SQL_ERR if an SQL error (SQLCODE < 0) is issued.

9

Transaction Processing

A bargain is in its very essence a hostile transaction ...

Letter published in Byron's Letters and Journals

Lord Byron

9.1 INTRODUCTION

One of the major advantages of databases is non-redundant data storage. This usually means that more than one user may wish to access the same data concurrently. The processing of all possible potential conflict situations is in itself a subject for a book. This book is restricted to dealing with the DB2 (SQL) facilities for dealing with problems of concurrent access and of maintaining consistency; these two concepts are related.

9.2 SQL TRANSACTION CONCEPTS

A **transaction** (also known as **logical unit of work**) is a series of one or more SQL statements that must run as a unit. To maintain consistency, either all SQL statements in the transaction complete (i.e. the database has been updated) or all changes made by the individual SQL statements are revoked, a so-called rollback. An example of a transaction can be found in order processing: a sale involves updating the inventory record, creating a shipping entry, making an entry in the customer record, etc.; if any of these updates fails, then the database could be in an inconsistent state.

A single SQL statement is guaranteed to maintain direct database integrity during its processing. Direct database integrity means that the database remains in a consistent state while processing the statement, i.e. if not all the specified records can be processed then no records are processed, a situation which can occur if a system failure occurs during the processing.

9.3 CONSISTENCY

Consistency is related to the SQL **unit of recovery**. The unit of recovery is the interval between when SQL performs a **commit**; the end of the unit of recovery is known as a **commit point**. Within this interval the changes made to the database have not been made permanently, and may be revoked by issuing a **rollback**. The rollback revokes the changes made by that application (program) since the last commit. Commit and rollback operations can be performed either explicitly or implicitly. An **implicit commit** is made when the program terminates normally (i.e. not terminated because of an abend (abnormal end)) - this can have consequences if a testing environment is being used (see Chapter 10); an **implicit rollback** is made when the program terminates abnormally.

In our example consistency could be maintained by issuing a commit only when all the updates have completed satisfactorily. Only one unit of recovery can be active for an application at any one point of time, this means that commits cannot be nested. Figure 9.1 illustrates the processing of logical transactions.

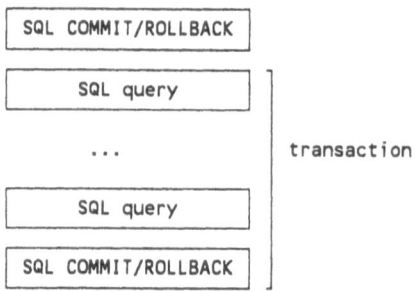

Figure 9.1 - Transaction processing

9.4 CONCURRENCY

The situation of concurrency is more complex and arises when users can modify rows being used by another user.

There are three general types of problem which can occur:

· lost update;
· uncommitted dependency;
· unrepeatable reads.

The **lost update** problem is shown in Figure 9.2. The same row (in the diagram, A) is read by both users before it is updated by each user. This means that the last user to update would override the updates made by the other user.

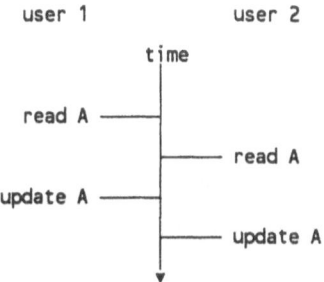

Figure 9.2 - "Lost update" problem

The **uncommitted dependency** problem is shown in Figure 9.3. The row which has been provisionally updated by user 2 is read by user 1 (and subsequently processed). At some later time user 2 revokes the changes he has made. This means that the status read by user 1 would no longer be valid.

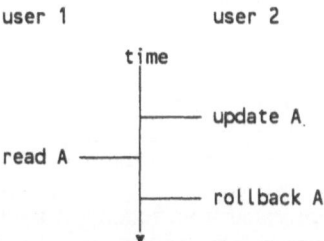

Figure 9.3 - "Uncommitted dependency" problem

The **unrepeatable reads** problem is shown in Figure 9.4. User 1 reads a row which is then subsequently updated by user 2. User 1 then re-reads the same row and, if he had retained certain data from the first read, now would find that the row is not consistent with the previous read.

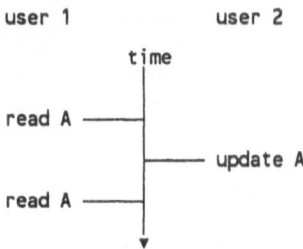

Figure 9.4 - "Unrepeatable reads" problem

The concurrency problem is usually solved by setting a **lock** during the time the logical transaction is being processed. SQL offers two explicit forms of lock:
· shared (read) - S-lock;
· exclusive (write) - X-lock.

The **shared lock** enables other users to perform read operations; the **exclusive lock** prohibits other users from accessing the locked data in any way at all. The current version of DB2 only enables locks to be set at the table level, in an unsegmented table space all tables in that table space are locked. Locks should therefore only be used when they are necessary and the locking interval should be as short as possible. Although DB2 implicitly sets the required locks, improved concurrency and resource usage may be obtained by setting locks appropriately. Locks are a complex subject that can have a profound - specialised literature should be consulted if detailed information is required.

There is a third implicit **update** lock (U-lock). The owner of a U-lock can perform read operations but not update (other users can obtain S-locks). The U-lock must be promoted to an X-lock if an update is required.

The setting of only those locks which are needed at the moment can result in another conflict situation: **deadlock**. Deadlock results when two (or more) users need a resource being held by the other user in order to be able to continue. This situation can only be rectified by one of the users releasing his resources or having his resources released for him.

The application developer can influence deadlock situations by the bind parameters he has specified. The ACQUIRE and RELEASE parameters define when resources are to be acquired and released, and, indirectly, when locks are to be set and freed. ACQUIRE(ALLOCATE) specifies that all locks required for the table spaces are set when the application plan is allocated - this avoids any possibility of deadlocks occurring, however, concurrency is adversely affected. In the worst case the application may be prevented from running if the resources cannot be obtained within a certain time interval. ACQUIRE(USE) specifies that the locks are set when they are required. Similarly, RELEASE(DEALLOCATE) releases the locks when the application plan terminates, and RELEASE(COMMIT) releases the locks when the application plan reaches the end of the unit of recovery. These settings have no effect on dynamic SQL statements. Dynamic SQL statements are processed as for ACQUIRE(USE), the locks are released at the next commit point.

DB2 uses the **timeout** mechanism to supervise deadlocks. A timeout occurs when the lock cannot be obtained within a certain time interval; this time interval is defined as a parameter during the DB2 installation.

DB2 sets **implicit locks** to counter these concurrency problems. DB2 does not allow a user to access data which has been changed but not committed by another user. If a user gets into this situation SQL will return the appropriate error code. However, in the case of unrepeatable reads, the user must specify whether re-read consistency is to be maintained; the bind ISOLATION parameter specifies either RR (Repeatable Read) or CS (Cursor Stability). Repeatable Read locks the rows until the unit of recovery is completed, whereas Cursor Stability locks only the row currently being accessed. DB2 will, if necessary, **promote** locks, as shown in Figure 9.5. DB2 Version 4 has introduced further isolation levels.

Tip
If possible use isolation level CS rather than RR. CS increases the degree of concurrency and reduces the chances of deadlock.

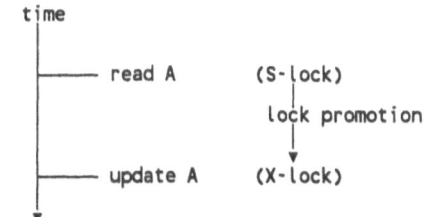

Figure 9.5 - Lock promotion

The application developer will not usually be concerned with locks, however, he must be aware of the situations which can occur and take the appropriate action. DB2 will ensure that inconsistency does not occur. However, DB2 does not guarantee that the requested operation can be performed. The success is indicated in the SQLCODE.

The SQLCODE values directly related with concurrency are:

     0   Operation successful.
  -911   Operation unsuccessful; rollback has been performed;
  -913   Operation unsuccessful; rollback has not been performed.

The unsuccessful completion of an operation will usually require that the operation is retried or some other corrective action taken.

10

Testing

The way of paradoxes is the way of truth. To test Reality we must see it on the tight-rope.

The Picture of Dorian Gray
Oscar Wilde

10.1 INTRODUCTION

All applications, DB2 or other, require to be tested. The application types described in this book (QMF, embedded SQL) require to be tested at various levels:
· SQL processing (e.g. are the correct rows retrieved);
· database application logic (e.g. are the database elements correctly processed);
· interface logic (e.g. does the application interface correctly with other components);
· general processing logic; etc.

Standard tools, of varying usefulness, are available to assist in the testing of some of these processes. These processes usually need to interact together, e.g. the data retrieved from the database with SQL is displayed using ISPF. This means that the testing of the application requires the concurrent use of these processes. Unfortunately some of the test tools are not compatible. This chapter describes how these difficulties can be overcome.

10.2 DB2 TESTING TOOLS

This section is very short, for the reason that there are not any tools for testing DB2 functions at the application level. Those DB2 testing tools available are only useful for error tracing at the system level. A standard testing facility comparable with ISPF/PDF Dialog Test is not currently available for SQL.

10.3 TESTING OF PROGRAMS USING DB2 (SQL) FACILITIES

A program which uses DB2 (SQL) facilities requires the DB2 environment. This DB2/program environment can be created in two ways:
- the program attaches DB2 dynamically (using CAF);
- the DB2 environment is invoked (using the DSN command), and the program is invoked from this environment (using the RUN subcommand).

A general cautionary note: most testing procedures involve setting breakpoints so that data areas, etc. can be examined. Such activities are relatively time consuming, and can mean that database resources (locks, etc.) are being held longer than usual.

The invocation environment in the following figures is depicted by a double-lined box.

Note: The SQL error code -927 is set if SQL statements are issued outside the DB2 environment.

10.3.1 Testing Using the CAF Interface

This method uses the natural testing environment. A dummy DSNHLI module (**CAF interface**) dynamically loads the DB2 interface. This dummy module must be initialised by the **test program**. Programs using this CAF interface must be statically linked (e.g. NODYNAM compiler option for a COBOL program). Section 6.5 describes the individual CAF functions.
   Figure 10.1 illustrates testing using the CAF interface. Figure 10.2 shows a sample CAF interface program; this program has two entry points: DB2CAFI - initialisation (load the DB2 interface, etc.), the 8-character plan name is passed as parameter; DB2CAFT - termination (delete the DB2 interface, etc.). The sample CAF interface program is coded using 24-bit addressing to avoid introducing unnecessary complexity in showing the mechanics involved. Figure 10.3 shows PL/I statements used to call this CAF interface.

Note: The application plan name specified in the CAF interface is the plan name for the test program.

Tip
Do not simply replace the DSNELI interface module by DSNALI without using the correct coding sequence (described in Section 6.5), as this method does not always work correctly.

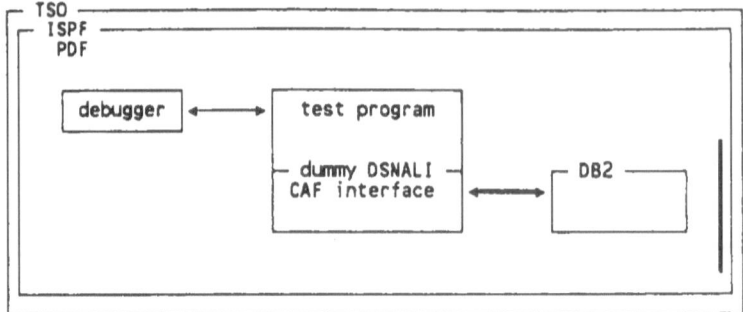

Figure 10.1 - Testing using CAF interface

```
* initialise CAF processing
DB2CAFI CSECT
* initialise addressing
        STM   14,12,12(13)          save registers
        BALR  11,0         base register
        USING *,11
        LA    15,SA         A(save-area)
        ST    13,4(15)      backward ptr
        ST    15,8(13)      forward ptr
        LR    13,15         A(new save-area)
* get parameter (plan name)
        L     1,0(1)        A(parameter)
        MVC   PLAN,0(1)     store plan name
* load interfaces
        LOAD  EP=DSNALI
        ST    0,LIALI
        LOAD  EP=DSNHLI2
        ST    0,LISQL
* CONNECT
        L     15,LIALI
        CALL  (15),(CONNECT,SSID,TECB,SECB,RIBPTR),VL
* OPEN
        L     15,LIALI
        CALL  (15),(OPEN,SSID,PLAN),VL
        B     EOP terminate routine
        DROP  11
* intercept calls generated by DB2 precompiler
        ENTRY DB2CAFT
DB2CAFT DS    0D
* terminate CAF processing
* initialise addressing
        STM   14,12,12(13)          save registers
        BALR  11,0
        USING *,11
        LA    15,SA         A(save-area)
        ST    13,4(15)      backward ptr
        ST    15,8(13)      forward ptr
        LR    13,15         A(new save-area)
* CLOSE
        L     15,LIALI
        CALL  (15),(CLOSE,TERMOP),VL
* DISCONNECT
```

```
                L     15,LIALI
                CALL  (15),(DISCONNECT),VL
       * delete modules
                DELETE EP=DSNALI
                DELETE EP=DSNHLI2
                B     EOP terminate routine
                DROP  11
                ENTRY DSNHLI
DSNHLI          DS    0D
                STM   14,12,12(13)
                BALR  10,0
                USING *,10
                LA    15,SA
                ST    13,4(15)
                ST    15,8(13)
                LR    13,15
                L     15,LISQL
                BALR  14,15
EOP             DS    0H  program end
                L     13,4(13)    restore A(old save-area)
                RETURN (14,12),RC=(15)
SA              DS    18A register save-area
LIALI           DS    A   entry-point address(DSNALI)
LISQL           DS    A   entry-point address(DSNHLI2)
CONNECT    DC         CL12'CONNECT'
OPEN       DC         CL12'OPEN'
CLOSE      DC         CL12'CLOSE'
DISCONNECT DC         CL12'DISCONNECT'
SSID       DC         CL4'DB2'
PLAN       DC         CL8' '       plan name
TERMOP     DC         CL4'SYNC'
TECB       DC         F'0'
SECB       DC         F'0'
RIBPTR     DC         A(0)
                END
```

Figure 10.2 - Sample CAF interface

```
        PCAF: PROC OPTIONS(MAIN);

        /* function definitions */
        DCL DB2CAFI ENTRY EXTERNAL OPTIONS(ASM,INTER,RETCODE);
        DCL DB2CAFT ENTRY EXTERNAL OPTIONS(ASM,INTER,RETCODE);
        /* plan name */
        DCL PLANNAME CHAR(8) INIT('ALPHA');

        /* initialise CAF interface */
        CALL DB2CAFI(PLANNAME);

            SQL (and other) processing

        /* terminate CAF interface */
        CALL DB2CAFT;
```

Figure 10.3 - Sample PL/I statements to invoke the CAF interface

10.3.2 Testing by Creating the DB2 Environment

This method requires that each environment is successively loaded from the previous environment. The TSO TEST command can be used to load the DB2 command processor. The DB2 command processor then creates the ISPF environment required for the **debugger** (e.g. COBTEST). The standard debugging environment can then be used for the **test program**. Figure 10.4 depicts the testing environment.

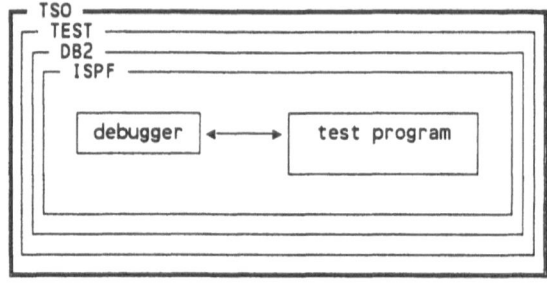

Figure 10.4 - Creation of a test environment

```
1       PROC 0
2       TEST 'DB2.TEST.DSNLOAD(DSN)' CP
3         DSN SYSTEM(DB2)
4         GO
5           RUN CP PLAN(XDB2COB1)
6           ISPSTART PGM(ISRFPR) PARM(IGZTPIN2,ISRFP10) NEWAPPL(DPA)
7         END
8       END
```

Figure 10.5 - Sample CLIST to invoke the COBTEST testing environment

Explanation of CLIST (Figure 10.5)

2   Load the DB2 interface (DSN program) as a command processor (parameter CP). The library name, in this case DB2.TEST.DSNLOAD, must be the name used in your installation.

3   Load the DSN command processor.

4   Execute the loaded DSN command processor.

5   Specify that the program having application plan XDB2COB1 is to be executed. The library does not need to be specified in the RUN statement, as the library specified in the debugger invocation panel is used. Note: The program is actually loaded only when the debugger has been invoked.

6   Invoke the debugger. Table 10.1 contains the program name (PGM parameter), the parameters (PARM parameter), and the new ISPF application identifier name (NEWAPPL parameter). Note: NEWAPPL is not required for certain debuggers.

7   Terminate the DSN command processor (DB2 environment).

8   Terminate the TEST environment, i.e. return to TSO.

Note: The ISPF/PDF environment is not created with this CLIST; this could be created by the invocation of ISPF/PDF instead of the debugging program, the debugging panel is then called from the ISPF/PDF environment.

Example
        ISPSTART PANEL(ISRƏPRIM) OPT(4.11)
This statement invokes the PL/I interactive debug.

10.3.3 Testing Using ISPF/PDF DIALOG TEST

This method can only used be used with the ISPF/PDF Dialog Test component; an intermediate CLIST or REXX exec (**command procedure**) invokes the DB2 environment and executes the **test program** from within this environment. Dialog Test functions (e.g. breakpoints) must have been previously set in order that the control is returned to **DIALOG TEST**. Figure 10.6 illustrates testing with ISPF/PDF Dialog Test. When ISPF/PDF Dialog Test is invoked the function to be invoked is a command procedure (for example, AX1 shown in Figure 10.7).

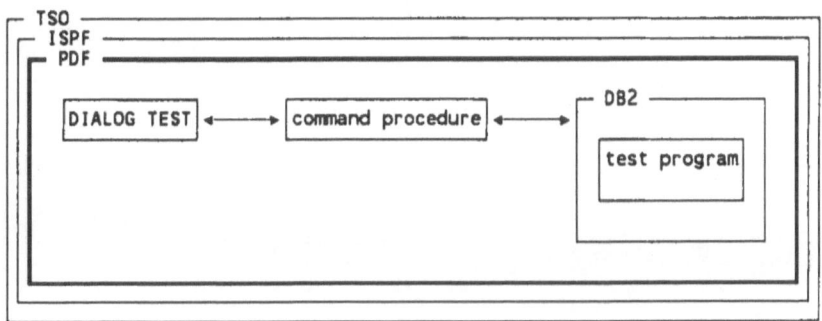

Figure 10.6 - Testing with ISPF/PDF Dialog Test

```
1       PROC 0
2       DSN
3         RUN PROGRAM(ARDB2P1) PLAN(ARDB2P1) LIBRARY('TSUSERO.TEST.LOAD')
4       END
```

Figure 10.7 - Sample invocation CLIST from ISPF/PDF Dialog Test

Explanation of CLIST (Figure 10.7)

2   Invoke the DB2 interface (DSN program).

3   Execute the program ARDB2P1 contained in library 'TSUSERO.TEST.LOAD'.

4   Terminate the DSN command processor (DB2 environment).

10.4 COMMIT/ROLLBACK IN THE TESTING ENVIRONMENT

As mentioned in Chapter 9, an implicit commit or rollback is performed when the program terminates normally or abnormally, respectively. In the testing environment the program here is the debugger and not the program being tested. The debugger will in many cases intercept the abnormal termination of the program being tested and itself terminate normally. This means that an implicit commit could be performed when it normally would not have been. The user should be aware of this phenomenon.

10.5 SUMMARY

None of these approaches is entirely satisfactory, as they all require either changes to the program or to the environment. A direct interface from the testing environment to DB2 is currently missing from the standard IBM debuggers. However, some third-party (non-IBM) products offer this feature.

11

Worked Example

Example is always more efficacious than precept.

Samuel Johnson
Rasselas

11.1 INTRODUCTION

This worked example illustrates two different approaches to writing a relatively simple DB2 application.

11.2 PROBLEM SPECIFICATION

A DB2 database is to be created for retrieval of information on computer software topics.

· Table name:

```
LIT
```

· Columns:

```
FORMNO CHAR(9)
TITLE VARCHAR(64)
TOPIC CHAR(8)
DESCR VARCHAR(240)
```

where only DESCR may contain NULL values.

A dialogue is to be created to give a display of selected documents. The first phase displays a list of topics. A selection is made on one of these topics and the list of the corresponding documents displayed in form number order (the message "** NO DESCRIPTION PRESENT **" is displayed if the DESCR field is null). A message is to be displayed should SQL return an error condition.

Two separate solutions using the QMF Callable Interface (DSQCIX) and a COBOL program using embedded SQL are to be made. ISPF Dialog Manager serves as the user interface.

Creation and initialization of the table are not strictly part of the exercise; the solutions in Section 11.2.1 and 11.2.2 are shown for completeness.

11.2.1 Create Table

SPUFI can be used to create the table; Figure 11.1 lists the SQL query to create the table. Note: Obtain **database-name** and **tablespace-name** from your database administrator.

```
CREATE TABLE LIT
 (FORMNO CHAR(9) NOT NULL,
  TITLE VARCHAR(64) NOT NULL,
  TOPIC CHAR(8) NOT NULL,
  DESCR VARCHAR(240))
 IN database-name.tablespace-name
```

Figure 11.1 - SQL statements to create LIT table

11.2.2 Insert Records into Table

SPUFI can be used to insert records into the table. A selection of DB2 and QMF documents is used as data. The data used are illustrative and do not necessarily represent the current documents. Figure 11.2 lists a sample of the SQL query to load data into the table. Figure 11.3 shows the report of the data as used in the examples. Note: Some entries have been defined without a description to show the use of indicator variables.

```
INSERT INTO LIT
VALUES ('SC26-4888','DATABASE 2 VERSION 3 ADMINISTRATION GUIDE',
        'DB2','DBA REFERENCE');
INSERT INTO LIT
VALUES ('SC26-4886','DATABASE 2 VERSION 3 GENERAL INFORMATION',
        'DB2',NULL);
```

Figure 11.2 - Sample SQL statements to insert rows into LIT table

11.2.3 Panel Displays

Two ISPF (table display) panels are used to display the found data items. Panel X11PAN1 displays the topics; a selection for the required topic is made from this display. The panel X11PAN2 displays the documents for the selected topic. Figure 11.4 shows the display of the topics using the data depicted in Figure 11.3. Figure 11.5 shows the display of the documents selected for topic DB2 using the data depicted in Figure 11.3.

```
FORMNO      TOPIC  TITLE / DESCR
---------   ---    --------------------------------------------------
GC26-4886   DB2    IBM DATABASE 2 VERSION 3 GENERAL INFORMATION
                   -
GC26-4894   DB2    DATABASE 2 VERSION 3 MASTER INDEX
                   DB2 BIBLIOGRAPHY AND KEYWORD INDEX
LY27-9603   DB2    DATABASE 2 VERSION 3 DIAGNOSIS GUIDE AND REFERENCE
                   -
SC26-3077   DB2    DATABASE 2 VERSION 3 USAGE OF DISTRIBUTED DATA MANAGEMENT
                   -
SC26-4888   DB2    DATABASE 2 VERSION 3 ADMINISTRATION GUIDE
                   DBA REFERENCE
SC26-4889   DB2    DATABASE 2 VERSION 3 APPLICATION PROGRAMMING AND SQL GUIDE
                   PROGRAMMER REFERENCE
SC26-4890   DB2    DATABASE 2 VERSION 3 SQL REFERENCE
                   -
SC26-4891   DB2    DATABASE 2 VERSION 3 COMMAND AND UTILITY REFERENCE
                   -
SC26-4892   DB2    DATABASE 2 VERSION 3 MESSAGES AND CODES
                   -
SX26-3801   DB2    DATABASE 2 VERSION 3 REFERENCE SUMMARY
                   "POCKET" REFERENCE

SC26-4713   QMF    QUERY MANAGEMENT FACILITY GENERAL INFORMATION
                   -
SC26-4714   QMF    QUERY MANAGEMENT FACILITY LEARNERS GUIDE
                   BEGINNERS GUIDE TO QMF
SC26-4715   QMF    QUERY MANAGEMENT FACILITY ADVANCED USERS GUIDE
                   MORE ADVANCED USES OF QMF (INCLUDING INTERFACING)
SC26-4716   QMF    QUERY MANAGEMENT FACILITY REFERENCE
                   ESSENTIAL QMF MANUAL
SC26-4717   QMF    QUERY MANAGEMENT FACILITY QUERY-BY-EXAMPLE GUIDE AND
REFERENCE
                   -
SC26-4722   QMF    QUERY MANAGEMENT FACILITY APPLICATION DEVELOPMENT GUIDE
                   QMF REFERENCE FOR USE WITH OTHER PROGRAMMING LANGUAGES
SC26-4834   QMF    QUERY MANAGEMENT FACILITY MESSAGES AND CODES
                   -
SX26-3783   QMF    QUERY MANAGEMENT FACILITY REFERENCE SUMMARY
                   "POCKET" REFERENCE
```

Figure 11.3 - Report showing content of LIT table

```
pan1---------------------- Topic selection ----------------- ROW 1 OF 2
COMMAND ===>                                        SCROLL ===> 0010

s = select
    Topic
s   DB2
    QMF
****************************** BOTTOM OF DATA ******************************
```

Figure 11.4 - Display of topics using panel X11PAN1

```
pan2---------------------- Document display --------------- ROW 1 OF 6
COMMAND ===>                                      SCROLL ===> 0010

Topic:DB2
GC26-4886  DB2   IBM DATABASE 2 VERSION 3 GENERAL INFORMATION
             ** NO DESCRIPTION PRESENT **
GC26-4894 DATABASE 2 VERSION 3 MASTER INDEX
          DB2 BIBLIOGRAPHY AND KEYWORD INDEX
LY27-9603 DATABASE 2 VERSION 3 DIAGNOSIS GUIDE AND REFERENCE
          ** NO DESCRIPTION PRESENT **
SC26-3077 DATABASE 2 VERSION 3 USAGE OF DISTRIBUTED DATA MANAGEMENT
          ** NO DESCRIPTION PRESENT **
SC26-4888 DATABASE 2 VERSION 3 ADMINISTRATION GUIDE
          DBA REFERENCE
SC26-4889 DATABASE 2 VERSION 3 APPLICATION PROGRAMMING AND SQL GUIDE
          PROGRAMMER REFERENCE
SC26-4890 DATABASE 2 VERSION 3 SQL REFERENCE
          ** NO DESCRIPTION PRESENT **
SC26-4891 DATABASE 2 VERSION 3 COMMAND AND UTILITY REFERENCE
          ** NO DESCRIPTION PRESENT **
SC26-4892 DATABASE 2 VERSION 3 MESSAGES AND CODES
          ** NO DESCRIPTION PRESENT **
SX26-3801 DATABASE 2 VERSION 3 REFERENCE SUMMARY
          "POCKET" REFERENCE
***************************** BOTTOM OF DATA  *****************************
```

Figure 11.5 - Display of documents using panel X11PAN2

11.2.4 Panel Definitions

The two ISPF panels used to display the data items are shown in Figure 11.6 and Figure 11.7.

```
- X11PAN1 -
)ATTR
# TYPE(OUTPUT) CAPS(ON)
  TYPE(INPUT) CAPS(ON)
)BODY
%pan1---------------------- Topic selection ----------------------------
%COMMAND ===>_ZCMD                              +SCROLL ===>_SAMT+
%
%s = select
+   Topic
)MODEL
  Z+#TOPIC   +
)INIT
.ZVARS='OP'
IF (&SAMT = ' ') &SAMT = 'HALF'
)PROC
)END
```

Figure 11.6 - Definition of panel X11PAN1

```
┌─ X11PAN2 ────────────────────────────────────────────────────────────┐
│ )ATTR                                                                  │
│ # TYPE(OUTPUT) CAPS(ON)                                                │
│ )BODY                                                                  │
│ %pan2--------------------- Document display ------------------------   │
│ %COMMAND ===> _ZCMD                                  +SCROLL ===>_SAMT+ │
│ %                                                                      │
│ +Topic:&TOPIC                                                          │
│ )MODEL                                                                 │
│ #FORMNO    #TITLE                                                      │
│            #DESCR                                                      │
│ )INIT                                                                  │
│ IF (&SAMT = '') &SAMT = 'HALF'                                         │
│ )END                                                                   │
└────────────────────────────────────────────────────────────────────┘
```

Figure 11.7 - Definition of panel X11PAN2

11.3 QMF SOLUTION

X11EX Processing exec:
```
 1      /* REXX - QMF Callable Interface */
 2      ADDRESS TSO
 3      CALL MSG 'OFF'
 4      uid = SYSVAR('SYSUID')
 5      fn = "TEMP.DATA";
 6      "DELETE" fn
 7      "ALLOC F(DSQPNLE) DSN('QMF.TEST.DSQPNLE') SHR REUS"
 8      "ALLOC F(DSQDEBUG) DUMMY REUS"
 9      "ALLOC F(DSQPRINT) SP(15,2) TR UNIT(WKSP)
        RECFM(V B) LRECL(300) BLKSIZE(23404) DSORG(PS)"
10      "ALLOC F(ADMGGMAP) DSN('QMF.TEST.DSQMAPE') SHR REUS"

11      CALL DSQCIX "START",
        "(DSQSDBUG=ALL,DSQSMODE=B,DSQSSUBS=DB2T"
12      IF RESULT > 0 THEN CALL DSQ_ERROR
13      CALL DSQCIX "RUN QUERY X11QT"
        IF RESULT > 0 THEN CALL DSQ_ERROR
14      CALL DSQCIX "EXPORT DATA TO '"uid".TEMP.DATA'",
                    "(CONFIRM=NO DATAFORMAT=IXF"
        IF RESULT > 0 THEN CALL DSQ_ERROR
15      CALL maketab1
16      ADDRESS ISPEXEC "TBDISPL TEMP1 PANEL(X11PAN1)"
17      IF RC > 0 | op <> 'S' THEN EXIT
        "DELETE" fn

18      CALL DSQCIX "SET GLOBAL(PT='''"topic"'''"
        IF RESULT > 0 THEN CALL DSQ_ERROR
        CALL DSQCIX "RUN QUERY X11Q2"
        IF RESULT > 0 THEN CALL DSQ_ERROR
        CALL DSQCIX "EXPORT DATA TO '"uid".TEMP.DATA'",
                    "(CONFIRM=NO DATAFORMAT=IXF"
        IF RESULT > 0 THEN CALL DSQ_ERROR
19      CALL maketab2
        ADDRESS ISPEXEC "TBDISPL TEMP2 PANEL(X11PAN2)"
20      CALL DSQCIX "EXIT"
21      EXIT

22      DSQ_ERROR:
        SAY 'DSQCIX error'
        SAY RESULT dsq_message_id dsq_message_text
        EXIT

23      maketab1:
```

```
            "ALLOC F(QMFOUT) DA("fn") SHR REUS"
            ADDRESS ISPEXEC
            "TBCREATE TEMP1 NAMES(TOPIC) NOWRITE REPLACE"
            ADDRESS TSO "EXECIO * DISKR QMFOUT (STEM r. FINIS"
            IF RC = 0 THEN DO i = 1 TO r.0
              PARSE VAR r.i rectype 2 . 8 topic
              IF rectype = 'D' THEN "TBADD TEMP1"
            END
            "TBTOP TEMP1"
            RETURN

24     maketab2:
            "ALLOC F(QMFOUT) DA("fn") SHR REUS"
            ADDRESS ISPEXEC
            "TBCREATE TEMP2 NAMES(FORMNO,TITLE,DESCR) NOWRITE REPLACE"
            ADDRESS TSO "EXECIO * DISKR QMFOUT (STEM r. FINIS"
            ix = 6
            j = 0
            IF RC = 0 THEN DO i = 1 TO r.0
              PARSE VAR r.i rectype 2 .
              IF rectype = 'C' THEN DO
                j = j+1
                PARSE VAR r.i . 38 size.j 44 .
              END
              IF rectype = 'D' THEN DO
                n1 = 8+size.1
                n2.1 = n1+2
                n2.2 = n2.1+2
                n2.3 = n2.2+size.2
                n3.1 = n2.3+2
                n3.2 = n3.1+2
                n3.3 = n3.2+size.2
                PARSE VAR r.i . 8 formno =(n1) ,
                      ltitle =(n2.1) ltitle =(n2.2) title =(n2.3) ,
                      ldescr =(n3.1) ldescr =(n3.2) descr =(n3.3) .
                title = SUBSTR(title,1,C2D(ltitle))
                IF ldescr = 'ffff'X
                  THEN descr = '** NO DESCRIPTION PRESENT **'
                  ELSE descr = SUBSTR(descr,1,C2D(ldescr))
                "TBADD TEMP2"
              END
            END
            "TBTOP TEMP2"
            RETURN
```

Figure 11.8 shows the two QMF two queries: X11Q1 and X11Q2. The REXX exec X11EX performs the report processing. Figure 11.9 shows the function diagram using QMF.

```
┌ X11Q1 ───────────────────────────┐
│ SELECT DISTINCT TOPIC FROM LIT    │
└───────────────────────────────────┘

┌ X11Q2 ──────────────────────────────────────────────────────────────┐
│ SELECT FORMNO,TITLE,DESCR FROM LIT WHERE TOPIC=&PT ORDER BY FORMNO    │
└──────────────────────────────────────────────────────────────────────┘
```

Figure 11.8 - QMF queries

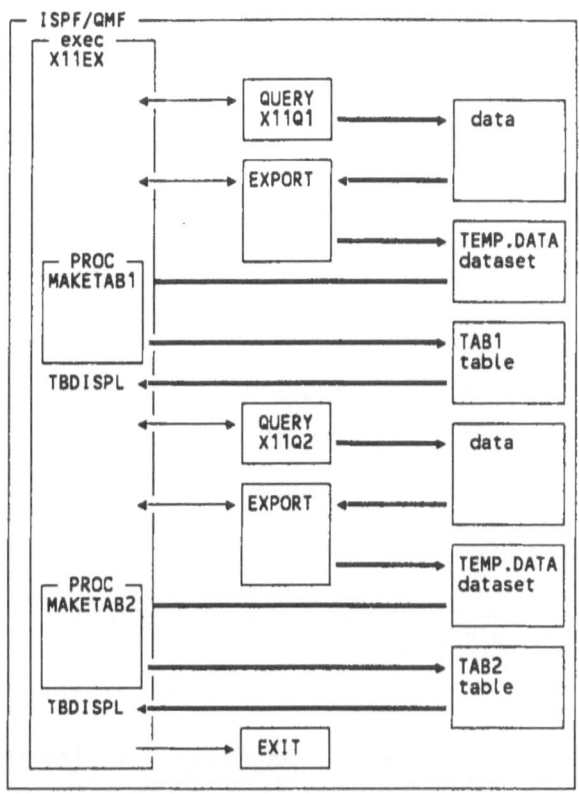

─── data flow
◄── control

Figure 11.9 - QMF functional solution

Explanation of X11EX exec:

1   Header to identify a REXX exec. A REXX exec must have a comment
     containing the word REXX to distinguish it from a CLIST.

2   Set TSO as the current environment. All commands are passed to the current
     environment. Note: Because TSO is the default environment, this statement
     is not strictly necessary.

3   Suppress the display of messages.

4   Obtain the current userid.

5   Specify the dataset name to be used for the output dataset into which QMF
     exports data.

6   Precautionary delete of the output dataset.

7   Allocate the QMF panel library; this dataset must be present even if it is not
     used, for example, QMF invoked in background. The appropriate
     installation dataset name must be used.

8   Allocate the debug dataset; an allocation must be present, although the dataset may be set to DUMMY.

9   Allocate the QMF print dataset.

10   Allocate the GDDM panel library; this dataset must be present even if it is not used.

11   Initiate the QMF Callable Interface. The DSQSMODE=B parameter specifies that QMF is to run in background (batch.); i.e. no panels are to be displayed. The DSQSSUBS=DSNT parameter specifies the DB2 subsystem (here DSNT).

12   Call the internal DSQ_ERROR routine if the QMF Callable Interface returns an error condition (RESULT > 0).

13   Run the X11Q1 query. This query must have been previously stored in QMF.

14   Export the query results. The CONFIRM=NO parameter avoids prompting in various conditions, for example, if the dataset will be overwritten. The IXF data format is most suitable for manipulation.

15   Call the internal MAKETAB1 routine to create an ISPF table from the exported data.

16   Use the ISPF TBDISPL service to display the formatted query results (a selectable list of the unique topics).

17   Check whether a line from the table display has been selected (RC = 0 and OP = 's').

18   Pass the selected topic as global parameter to QMF. The subsequent X11Q2 query uses the parameter PT. Note the use of triple apostrophes for character literals.

19   Call the internal MAKETAB2 routine to create an ISPF table from the exported data. Use the ISPF TBDISPL service to display the formatted query results (a list of the literature for the specified topic). Note: A new dataset must be used, as the attributes for the previous dataset may not necessarily be compatible.

20   Terminate the QMF Callable Interface.

21   Terminate the REXX exec.

22   The DSQ_ERROR routine displays QMF debugging information and terminates processing.

23   The MAKETAB1 routine reads the exported data file and extracts the data records to create ISPF table entries.

24   The MAKETAB2 routine reads the exported data file and extracts the column and data records to create ISPF table entries. The column records specify the lengths of the data entries.

11.4 PROGRAM SOLUTION

Figure 11.10 shows the function diagram using a program. Figure 11.11 shows the COBOL program: X11COB. A detailed explanation of the processing involved follows the program code.

In the interests of improved diagnostics, the INCLUDE LITDCL SQL statement is used to include the table declaration. If the table declaration is present, the DB2 preprocessor can perform certain consistency checks on the SQL statements, which otherwise would be validated at bind-time or run-time. Table declarations can be either hand-coded or generated with the DCLGEN command processor (SPUFI provides an interface to the DCLGEN command processor); DCLGEN generates the table declaration from the DB2 entries.

This particular example shows a potential problem with generated table declarations. TITLE (one of the table columns) is a reserved COBOL word which would cause a compilation error. The solution is to specify an explicit prefix that DCLGEN uses for the generated table field names.

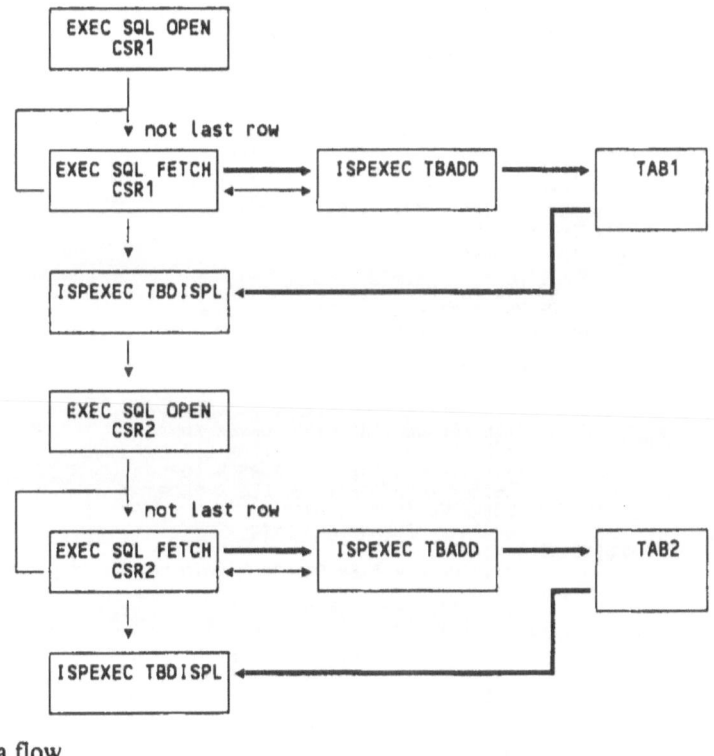

━━ data flow
◄━━ control

Figure 11.10 - Program functional solution

x11COB program code

```
        IDENTIFICATION DIVISION.
        PROGRAM-ID. X11COB.
        DATA DIVISION.
        WORKING-STORAGE SECTION.
1               EXEC SQL INCLUDE SQLCA END-EXEC.
        * DB2 host variables
2       01 UFORMNO    PIC X(9).
        01 UTOPIC     PIC X(8).
        01 UTITLE.
        49 UTITLE-L PIC S9(4) BINARY.
        49 UTITLE-D PIC X(256).
        01 VTITLE     PIC X(256).
        01 UDESCR.
        49 UDESCR-L PIC S9(4) BINARY.
        49 UDESCR-D PIC X(256).
        01 VDESCR     PIC X(256).
        01 IDESCR     PIC S9(4) BINARY.
        * ISPF variables
        01 VL         PIC S9(9) BINARY.
        01 OP         PIC X(1).
        * ISPF variable names
        01 V-OP       PIC X(8) VALUE 'OP'.
        01 V-TOPIC    PIC X(8) VALUE 'TOPIC'.
        01 V-FORMNO   PIC X(8) VALUE 'FORMNO'.
        01 V-DESCR    PIC X(8) VALUE 'DESCR'.
        01 V-TITLE    PIC X(8) VALUE 'TITLE'.
        * ISPF object names
        01 V-TAB1     PIC X(8) VALUE 'TAB1'.
        01 V-TAB2     PIC X(8) VALUE 'TAB2'.
        01 V-X11PAN1  PIC X(8) VALUE 'X11PAN1'.
        01 V-X11PAN2  PIC X(8) VALUE 'X11PAN2'.
        * ISPF keywords
        01 V-CHAR     PIC X(8) VALUE 'CHAR'.
        01 V-VDEFINE  PIC X(8) VALUE 'VDEFINE'.
        01 V-VREPLACE PIC X(8) VALUE 'VREPLACE'.
        01 V-TBADD    PIC X(8) VALUE 'TBADD'.
        01 V-TBTOP    PIC X(8) VALUE 'TBTOP'.
        01 V-TBDISPL  PIC X(8) VALUE 'TBDISPL'.
        * DSNTIAR message area
        01 MSG.
                02 MSG-LEN PIC S9(4) BINARY VALUE 288.
                02 MSG-TEXT PIC X(288).
        01 LRECL PIC S9(9) BINARY VALUE 72.
        *
        01 D-SQLCODE PIC S9(4) SIGN LEADING.
        *
3               EXEC SQL INCLUDE LITDCL END-EXEC.
4               EXEC SQL DECLARE CSR1 CURSOR FOR
                SELECT DISTINCT TOPIC FROM LIT END-EXEC.
        EXEC SQL DECLARE CSR2 CURSOR FOR
                SELECT FORMNO, TITLE, DESCR FROM LIT
                WHERE TOPIC = :UTOPIC
                ORDER BY FORMNO END-EXEC.
        PROCEDURE DIVISION.
6               EXEC SQL WHENEVER SQLERROR GOTO SQL-ERROR END-EXEC.
        * ISPF definitions
7               CALL 'ISPLINK' USING BY CONTENT 'TBCREATE'
                'TAB1 ' '(TOPIC)' ' ' 'NOWRITE' 'REPLACE'
8               CALL 'ISPLINK' USING BY CONTENT 'TBCREATE'
                'TAB2 ' ' ' '(FORMNO,TITLE,DESCR)' 'NOWRITE'
                'REPLACE'
                MOVE 1 TO VL
                CALL 'ISPLINK'
                USING V-VDEFINE V-OP OP V-CHAR VL
                MOVE 8 TO VL
                CALL 'ISPLINK'
                USING V-VDEFINE V-TOPIC UTOPIC V-CHAR VL
                MOVE 9 TO VL
                CALL 'ISPLINK'
```

```
                              USING V-VDEFINE V-FORMNO UFORMNO V-CHAR VL
                    * get TOPIC list
      9                       EXEC SQL OPEN CSR1 END-EXEC
                    * fetch individual rows
     10                       PERFORM TEST AFTER UNTIL SQLCODE = 100
                                EXEC SQL FETCH CSR1 INTO :UTOPIC END-EXEC
                                IF SQLCODE = 0 THEN
     11                           CALL 'ISPLINK' USING V-TBADD V-TAB1
                                END-IF
                              END-PERFORM
                    * position at table top
                              CALL 'ISPLINK' USING BY CONTENT 'TBTOP' 'TAB1 '
                    * display
     12                       CALL 'ISPLINK' USING V-TBDISPL V-TAB1 V-X11PAN1
     13                       IF RETURN-CODE < 8 THEN PERFORM
                    * retrieve documents for selected topic
     14                         EXEC SQL OPEN CSR2 END-EXEC
                    * fetch individual rows
     15                         PERFORM TEST BEFORE UNTIL SQLCODE = 100
                                  EXEC SQL FETCH CSR2 INTO :UFORMNO, :UTITLE,
                                  :UDESCR:IDESCR END-EXEC
     16                           IF SQLCODE = 0 THEN PERFORM
                                    MOVE UTITLE-L TO VL
                                    CALL 'ISPLINK' USING
                                    V-VREPLACE V-TITLE VL UTITLE-D
     17                             IF IDESCR = -1 THEN
                                      MOVE '** no description present **'
                                      TO UDESCR-D
                                      MOVE 28 TO UDESCR-L
                                    END-IF
                                    MOVE UDESCR-L TO VL
                                    CALL 'ISPLINK' USING V-VREPLACE V-DESCR VL
                                    UDESCR-D
                                    CALL 'ISPLINK' USING V-TBADD V-TAB2
                                  END-PERFORM
                                END-IF
                              END-PERFORM
                              CALL 'ISPLINK' USING V-TBTOP V-TAB2
                              CALL 'ISPLINK' USING V-TBDISPL V-TAB2
                              V-X11PAN2
                            END-PERFORM
                          END-IF
     18                   STOP RUN.
     19         SQL-ERROR.
                    * SQL error exit
                            MOVE SQLCODE TO D-SQLCODE
     20                     DISPLAY 'SQL error - SQLCODE:' D-SQLCODE
                            CALL 'DSNTIAR' USING SQLCA MSG LRECL
     21                     DISPLAY 'SQL MESSAGE:'
     22                     DISPLAY MSG-TEXT(1:72)
     23                     DISPLAY MSG-TEXT(73:72)
                            GOBACK.
               END PROGRAM X11COB.
```

Figure 11.11 - Program X11COB

Explanation of program X11COB:

1   Declaration of SQLCA (SQL Communication Area).

2   Declaration of the host variables which are used as database variables.
     IDESCR is declared as an indicator variable; i.e. will contain -1 if the
     corresponding database value (UDESCR) has no value. UTITLE and UDESCR are
     varying length character variables.

3   Include the table declaration. This statement is not strictly necessary, but it enables the DB2 preprocessor to perform certain validity checks.

4   Declaration of SQL selection criterion (SELECT DISTINCT TOPIC FROM LIT); the database cursor CSR1 locates the current row.

5   Declaration of SQL selection criterion (SELECT FORMNO, TITLE, DESCR FROM LIT WHERE TOPIC = :UTOPIC); the database cursor CSR2 locates the current row. Note: The host variable UTOPIC contains the value of TOPIC to be selected.

6   SQL error conditions are to cause a branch to be made to the block SQL-ERROR. The WHENEVER SQLERROR statement avoids having to explicitly code to check the SQLCODE after each SQL statement.

7   Create the ISPF table TAB1 with column TOPIC; the NOWRITE parameter specifies that the table is only to exist in main-storage.

8   Create the ISPF table TAB2 with columns FORMNO, TITLE and DESCR.

9   Open SQL cursor CSR1; this prepares for the subsequent selection (FETCH).

10   Initiate the read loop; rows are read until SQLCODE +100 (end of selection) is signalled. The next row is read and its values are stored in the program variable UTOPIC which is also an ISPF variable because of the associated VDEFINE statement.

11   If the row is successfully read (SQLCODE = 0), an ISPF table row is written in TAB1.

12   Display the contents of ISPF table TAB1 using panel X11PAN1.

13   Execute the following block when a table row has been selected (RETURN-CODE = 8 indicates that the END key has been pressed to terminate panel processing).

14   Open SQL cursor CSR2.

15   Initiate the read loop; rows are read until SQLCODE +100 (end of selection) is signalled. The next row is read and its values are stored in the program variables UFORMNO, VTITLE and VDESCR; the indicator variable IDESCR is set if the database value for DESCR is null. UFORMNO is also an ISPF variable because of the associated VDEFINE statement.

16   If the row is successfully read (SQLCODE = 0), the following block is executed.

17   If the indicator variable (IDESCR) for DESCR is set, set the text "** no description present **" into the program variable VDESCR.

18   Terminate the program.

19   Introduce section for SQL error processing.

20   List the SQL error code (variable SQLCODE in the SQLCA).

21   Call the subroutine DSNTIAR to obtain the message associated with the content of SQLCODE.

22   List the first line of message text.

23   List the second line of message text. Note: In the interests of simplicity
      only the first two lines of message text are displayed, the last line of
      message text is a complete line of blanks.

11.5 SUMMARY

In this example the QMF solution is more complex than the program solution.
However, the application developer must decide what is the best solution for his
problem. QMF as an application tool is particularly appropriate when the powerful
QMF features are used; for example, report formatting. The program solution
offers improved performance (static SQL) and increased security for changes to the
database (the program (plan) and not the user is authorized to update the database).
The QMF solution will usually be easier to maintain (the REXX language is a higher
programming language) and offers easier access to the associated products (e.g.
ISPF).

Appendix A

Syntax Notation

Syntax Diagram

This book makes use of syntax diagrams to describe the syntax of expressions. Syntax diagrams are read left to right, top to bottom.

▶▶— indicates the beginning of a statement

—▶◀ indicates the end of a statement

—▶ indicates that the statement is continued

▶— indicates the continuation of the statement

· Mandatory items cannot be branched around.

Example:

· If **one** of a number of mandatory items **must** be selected, then these items appear in a vertical stack.

Example:

· Multiple options appear in a vertical stack, **one** of the specified options **may** be selected.

Example:

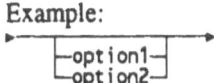

There are two forms of repetition — either one or more options of a specified group of options may be selected (any one option may be selected at most once), or one or more options of a specified group of options may be selected any number of time.

Selective repetition:

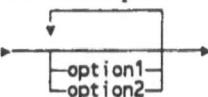

Both option1 and option2 may be selected not more than once.

Normal repetition:

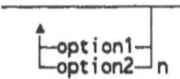

Option1 and option2 may be selected any number of times, unless n is specified, in which case n specifies the maximum number of repetitions.

If the repeat arrow contains an item, then this item is mandatory for repetitions.

Example:

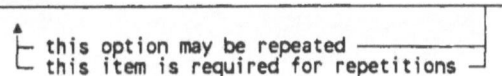

An item written in upper case must be spelled exactly as shown, an item written in lower case is replaced by a valid entry (described in the text). An underlined entry is the default value.

Example:

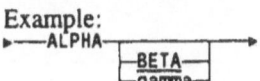

The first item is mandatory and must be ALPHA; the second item is optional, the default value is BETA.

If an item is written italicised, then this is a parameter, the definition of which follows.

Example:
►—*logicaloperator*—►

logicaloperator:

```
►►─────────────────────►◄
        ┌─AND─┐
        └─OR──┘
```

The "logicaloperator" parameter may be replaced by one of the optional values: AND or OR.

A syntax diagram is formed by combining the simple elements defined above.

Font
The sans serif font is used to depict commands, keywords or data set names.

Example:
The QMF statement TSO DELETE is a command which invokes the TSO component DELETE.

Appendix B

SQL Data Areas

SQLCA (SQL Communication Area)

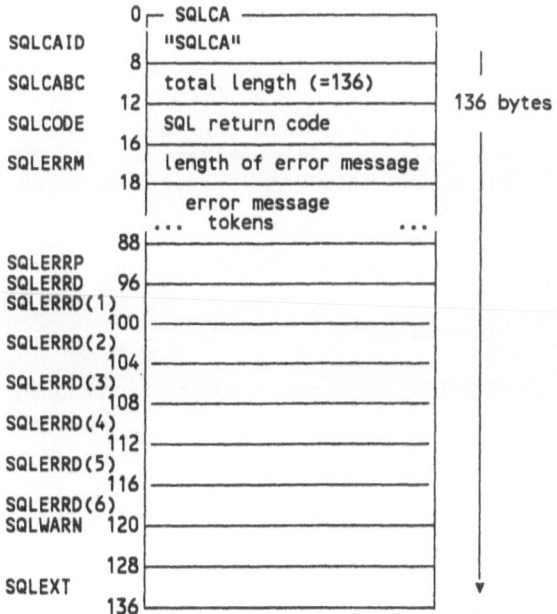

Figure B.1 - SQLCA format

Table B.1 - SQLCA fields

Field name	Data type	Description
SQLCAID	CHAR(8)	SQLCA identifier: "SQLCA"
SQLCABC	INTEGER	total length of SQLCA (136 bytes)
SQLCODE	INTEGER	SQL return code
SQLERRM	VARCHAR(70)	SQL error message tokens
SQLERRML	-	length of error message tokens
SQLERRMC	-	error message tokens (each separated by x'FF')
SQLERRP	CHAR(8)	diagnostic information
SQLERRD	-	codes set by various DB2 components
SQLERRD(1)	INTEGER	Relational Data System error code.
SQLERRD(2)	INTEGER	Data Manager error code.
SQLERRD(3)	INTEGER	number of rows affected by DELETE, INSERT or UPDATE operation
SQLERRD(4)	FLOAT *	estimate of the amount of resources required by this statement
SQLERRD(5)	INTEGER	position of syntax error in PREPARE or EXECUTE IMMEDIATE statement
SQLERRD(6)	INTEGER	Buffer Manager error code
SQLWARN	-	warning flags
SQLWARN0	CHAR(1)	blank if all the other warning flags are also blank, otherwise "W"
SQLWARN1	CHAR(1)	"W" if value assigned to a host variable has been truncated
SQLWARN2	CHAR(1)	"W" if null values have been eliminated from the search argument
SQLWARN3	CHAR(1)	"W" if the number of columns returned is larger than the number of host variables specified
SQLWARN4	CHAR(1)	"W" if DELETE or UPDATE statement does not contain a SELECT clause
SQLWARN5	CHAR(1)	"W" if the statement is invalid
SQLWARN6	CHAR(1)	"W" if a DATE or TIME value has been adjusted because it was invalid
SQLWARN7	CHAR(1)	reserved
SQLEXT	CHAR(8)	reserved

* The library definitions specify SQLERRD as being an array of 6 integer elements.

PL/I Definitions:
```
DECLARE
  1 SQLCA,
    2 SQLCAID CHAR(8),
    2 SQLCABC FIXED(31) BINARY,
    2 SQLCODE FIXED(31) BINARY,
    2 SQLERRM CHAR(70) VAR,
    2 SQLERRP CHAR(8),
    2 SQLERRD(6) FIXED(31) BINARY,
    2 SQLWARN,
      3 SQLWARN0 CHAR(1),
      3 SQLWARN1 CHAR(1),
      3 SQLWARN2 CHAR(1),
```

```
              3 SQLWARN3 CHAR(1),
              3 SQLWARN4 CHAR(1),
              3 SQLWARN5 CHAR(1),
              3 SQLWARN6 CHAR(1),
              3 SQLWARN7 CHAR(1),
            2 SQLEXT CHAR(8);
```

COBOL Definitions

```
    SQLCA.
    05 SQLCAID    PIC X(8).
    05 SQLCABC    PIC S9(9) COMP-4.
    05 SQLCODE    PIC S9(9) COMP-4.
    05 SQLERRM.
       49 SQLERRML PIC S9(4) COMP-4.
       49 SQLERRMC PIC X(70).
    05 SQLERRP    PIC X(8).
    05 SQLERRD    OCCURS 6 TIMES
                  PIC S9(9) COMP-4.
    05 SQLWARN.
       10 SQLWARN0 PIC X.
       10 SQLWARN1 PIC X.
       10 SQLWARN2 PIC X.
       10 SQLWARN3 PIC X.
       10 SQLWARN4 PIC X.
       10 SQLWARN5 PIC X.
       10 SQLWARN6 PIC X.
       10 SQLWARN7 PIC X.
    05 SQLEXT     PIC X(8).
```

Assembler Definitions:

```
    SQLCA     DS    0F
    SQLCAID   DS    CL8      ID
    SQLCABC   DS    F        BYTE COUNT
    SQLCODE   DS    F        RETURN CODE
    SQLERRM   DS    H,CL70   ERR MSG PARMS
    SQLERRP   DS    CL8      IMPL-DEPENDENT
    SQLERRD   DS    6F
    SQLWARN   DS    0C       WARNING FLAGS
    SQLWARN0 DS     C'W' IF ANY
    SQLWARN1 DS     C'W' = WARNING
    SQLWARN2 DS     C'W' = WARNING
    SQLWARN3 DS     C'W' = WARNING
    SQLWARN4 DS     C'W' = WARNING
    SQLWARN5 DS     C'W' = WARNING
    SQLWARN6 DS     C'W' = WARNING
    SQLWARN7 DS     C'W' = WARNING
    SQLEXT    DS    CL8
```

C Language Definitions

```
#ifndef SQLCODE
struct sqlca
   { unsigned  char     sqlcaid[8];
              long     sqlcabc;
              long     sqlcode;
              short    sqlerrml;
     unsigned char     sqlerrmc[70];
     unsigned char     sqlerrp[8];
              long     sqlerrd[6];
     unsigned char     sqlwarn[8];
     unsigned char     sqlext[8];
         } ;
#define SQLCODE  sqlca.sqlcode
#define SQLWARN0 sqlca.sqlwarn[0]
#define SQLWARN1 sqlca.sqlwarn[1]
#define SQLWARN2 sqlca.sqlwarn[2]
#define SQLWARN3 sqlca.sqlwarn[3]
#define SQLWARN4 sqlca.sqlwarn[4]
#define SQLWARN5 sqlca.sqlwarn[5]
#define SQLWARN6 sqlca.sqlwarn[6]
#define SQLWARN7 sqlca.sqlwarn[7]
#endif
struct sqlca sqlca;
```

SQLDA (SQL Descriptor Area)

The SQLDA contains data required for the embedded SQL DESCRIBE statement. The EXECUTE, FETCH, OPEN and PREPARE embedded SQL statements may also make use of the SQLDA. A sample SQLDA is shown in Figure B.3.

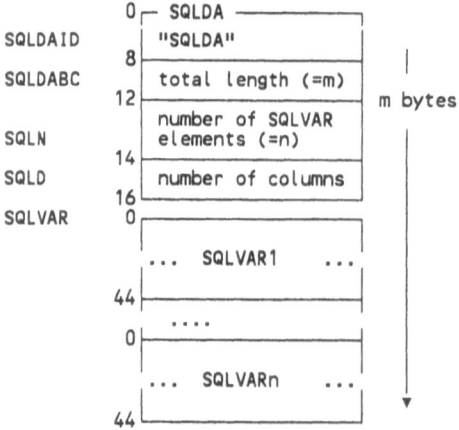

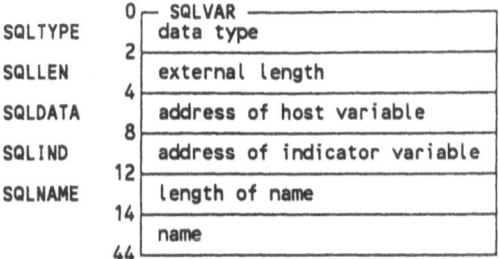

Figure B.2 - SQLDA format

Table B.2 - SQLDA fields

Field name	Data type	Description
SQLDAID	CHAR(8)	SQLDA identifier "SQLDA"
SQLDABC	INTEGER	total length of SQLDA
SQLN	SMALLINT	maximum number SQLVAR entries
SQLD	SMALLINT	current number of columns (SQLVAR entries)

SQLVAR describes each column:

Field name	Data type	Description
SQLTYPE	SMALLINT	data type (see Table B.3)
SQLLEN	SMALLINT	external length of data item
SQLDATA	pointer	address of host variable
SQLIND	pointer	address of indicator variable; a half-word containing a negative value (usually -1) if the host variable is null
SQLNAME	VARCHAR(30)	name or label

Table B.3 - Data type codes

SQLTYPE	data type
384/385	DATE fixed-length character string representation of a date
388/389	TIME fixed-length character string representation of a time
392/393	TIMESTAMP fixed-length character string representation of a timestamp
448/449	VARCHAR varying-length character string
452/453	CHAR fixed-length character string
456/457	LONG VARCHAR varying-length long character string
460/461	VARCHAR varying-length character string terminated with the C-language null character
464/465	VARGRAPHIC * varying-length graphic string
468/469	GRAPHIC * fixed-length graphic string
472/473	LONG VARGRAPHIC * varying-length long graphic string
480/481	FLOAT floating-point
484/485	DECIMAL packed decimal
496/497	INTEGER large binary integer
500/501	SMALLINT small binary integer
504/505	(no data type) precision in byte 1 and scale in byte 2.

* graphic means DBCS

Note on Table B.3: QMF control areas and records which store the null indicator explicitly use the same data type code (the even-numbered code) to identify both kinds of entry. The odd-numbered data type code indicates that nulls are allowed.

The standard SQLDA definitions for various host languages follow. Note: there is no standard library SQLDA definition for COBOL.

PL/I SQLDA Definition:
```
     DECLARE
       1 SQLDA BASED(SQLDAPTR),
         2 SQLDAID CHAR(8),
         2 SQLDABC FIXED(31) BINARY,
         2 SQLN    FIXED(15) BINARY,
         2 SQLD    FIXED(15) BINARY,
```

```
            2 SQLVAR(SQLSIZE REFER(SQLN)),
              3 SQLTYPE FIXED(15) BINARY,
              3 SQLLEN FIXED(15) BINARY,
              3 SQLDATA POINTER,
              3 SQLIND POINTER,
              3 SQLNAME CHAR(30) VAR;
        DECLARE SQLSIZE FIXED(15) BINARY;
        DECLARE SQLDAPTR POINTER;
```

Assembler SQLDA Definition:

```
    SQLDA    DSECT               .
    SQLDAID  DS     CL8       ID
    SQLDABC  DS     F         BYTE COUNT
    SQLN     DS     H         TOTAL VARS
    SQLD     DS     H         PERTINENT VARS
    SQLVAR   DS     0F        BEGIN VARS
    SQLVARN  DSECT  ,         NTH VARIABLE
    SQLTYPE  DS     H         TYPE CODE
    SQLLEN   DS     0H        NAME LENGTH
    SQLPRCSN DS     X         DEC PRECISION
    SQLSCALE DS     X         DEC SCALE
    SQLDATA  DS     A         ADDR OF VAR
    SQLIND   DS     A         ADDR OF IND
    SQLNAME  DS     H,CL30    DESCRIBE NAME
    SQLVSIZ  EQU    *-SQLDATA
```

C Language SQLDA Definition:

```
    #ifndef SQLDASIZE
    struct sqlda
       ( unsigned char    sqldaid[8];
                   long    sqldabc;
                   short   sqln;
                   short   sqld;
                   struct sqlvar
                                ( short   sqltype;
                                  short   sqllen;
                        unsigned char  *sqldata;
                                  short  *sqlind;
                                  struct sqlname
                                               ( short   length;
                                        unsigned char    data[30];
                                                  ) sqlname;
                                ) sqlvar[1];
                ) ;
    #define SQLDASIZE(n) \
        ( sizeof(struct sqlda) + ((n)-1) * sizeof(struct sqlvar) )
    #endif
```

Example:

The format of the SQLDA constructed for the selection:

    SELECT PNO, PNAME FROM PERS

with

    PNO   DECIMAL(4,0) and value 3333
    PNAME VARCHAR(24) and value "ALPHA"

is shown in Figure B.3.

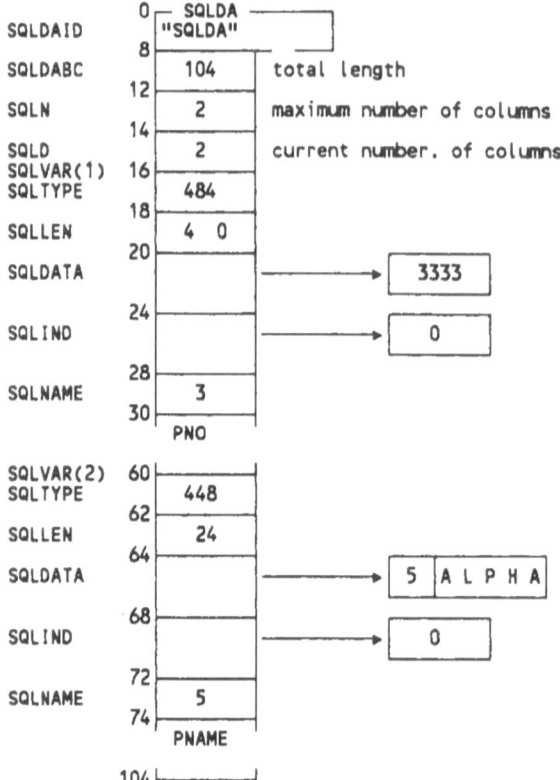

Figure B.3 - Sample SQLDA

RIB (Release Information Block)

The DSNDRIB macro produces a DSECT named RIB, whose structure is shown in Table B.4. In addition, the following code line containing the current DB2 release is generated:

```
    RIBRVAL  DC      CL3'vrm'
```

v = version
r = release
m = modification level

Table B.4 - RIB fields

field name	data type	description
RIBCODE	H	RIB identifier
RIBTLEN	H	block length
RIBEYEC	CL4	eye-catcher "RIB"
RIBCID RIBECODE RIBPCODE RIBFCODE RIBREL	- CL4 CL3 CL2 3CL1	component identifier environment code (5740)) program number product code (XYR)) feature code release identifier: version, release, modification level
RIBCPTR RIBCNUMB	A HL1	address of RIBCINFO (change level information array) number of elements in RIBCINFO
	XL3 XL16	reserved reserved

Appendix C

Glossary

abend   Word formed from **ab**normal **end**. An abend occurs when a program does not terminate normally, i.e. because an error situation has been detected. Two forms of abend may occur: system and user. A system abend is detected by the operating system (e.g. program exception, system failure). A user abend is issued by the program itself, e.g. the program has determined that it cannot continue processing. User abends should be avoided; in most cases a program completion code can be set to indicate that processing failed.

alphabetic   The set of characters containing the lower and upper case letters together with the three national characters: #, @ and $.

alphanumeric   The set of **alphabetic** characters together with the ten numeric digits.

application plan   Processing strategy for the embedded SQL statements; also known as **plan**. The application plan is identified by its unique **application plan name**. Every executable program that uses DB2 services requires an application plan. An application plan is formed from DBRM members or packages.

Assembler   Low-level programming language for low-level machine-dependent programming tasks.

bind   The processing performed on embedded SQL statements to produce control statements suitable for use in accessing the DB2 database.

C	Modern mid-level programming language for low-level machine-independent programming tasks (Assembler replacement).
catalog	In the DB2 sense, the collection of system tables stored in the database.
CICS	Customer Information Control System, monitor system to provide on-line transaction processing facilities for programs.
CLIST	Procedure consisting of TSO commands and subcommands and control statements. CLISTs are also known as **command procedures**.
COBOL	COmmon Business Oriented Language. High-level commercial programming language.
column	A vertical element of a table and is generally synonymous with a field in conventional data processing.
command procedure	See CLIST and REXX procedure.
commit	The action of making changes to the database permanent. See also **revoke**.
compiler	A software component which converts a source program into an object module.
CSP	Cross System Product. IBM application generator with interface to DB2 and ISPF.
cursor	In the DB2 context, an internal pointer to a row in a table.
dataset	IBM term for a file.
database	A logically related set of named data elements. Database systems isolate users from the physical data storage.
DATABASE2	IBM relational data base, usually known as DB2.
DBMS	Database Management System. A program to control the use of a database.
DB2	DATABASE2. IBM relational data base.
DBCS	Double-Byte Character Set. A set of pairs of characters used to represent characters in Far-East languages (Chinese, Japanese, Korean, etc.). Also known as **graphic data** in DB2.
DBRM	Data Base Request Module. Each program using SQL services requires a DBRM to describe the logical access. The DBRM is produced by the DB2 precompiler and is used as input to the Bind processor. The bound DBRM is stored in the database.
DCLGEN	Declarations generator. Creates program declarations for the elements in a DB2 table or view.
DD	Data Definition. The JCL statement used to assign the physical data (dataset, printer output class, etc.) to the logical dataset defined in the program. The **ddname** links the logical dataset to the JCL DD statement.
Dialog Manager	ISPF component which administers dialogue facilities. Dialog Manager is usually synonymous with ISPF.

dialogue   Man-machine interaction using a terminal directly attached to computer. Various levels of program systems (application program, terminal monitor program, etc.) control the dialogue.

DSORG   Dataset organisation. The organisation of information in a dataset.

dynamic SQL   The creation of SQL statements at run-time. This means that authorisations and processing strategies must also be made at run-time.

embedded SQL   See ESQL.

ESQL   Embedded SQL. The SQL statements used in a program.

exec   Lowercase. A synonym for a REXX procedure.

EXEC   Uppercase. Execute program of procedure. The JCL statement used to invoke a program or JCL procedure.

file   A collection of data (= dataset). Also with regard to TSO it is equivalent to the JCL DD statement, **filename** is then equivalent to the **ddname**.

FORTRAN   FORmula TRANslation. High-level scientific programming language.

GDDM   Graphic Data Display Manager. IBM product consisting of basic subroutines for processing and displaying graphic data. Note: Graphic data here does not imply DBCS data.

GDF   Graphics Data File. GDDM data format which contains processed graphs.

graphic data   See DBCS.

half-word   A signed binary number which occupies 2 bytes. This is the same internal representation as a DB2 SMALLINT variable.

help environment   Sub-environment used to provide on-line assistance.

help panel   Panel which is used for display or data entry within the help environment.

host language   A programming language which can use embedded SQL statements, i.e. a language for which a DB2 precompiler exists. The following host languages are currently supported: Assembler, C, COBOL, FORTRAN, PL/I.

host variable   A variable contained in a program and used as DB2 data element.

IBM   International Business Machines Corporation, supplier of DB2, CICS, ISPF, MVS, QMF, etc. licensed products.

ICU   Interactive Chart Utility. A user-friendly dialogue interface to PGF for the processing of business (presentation) graphics.

IMS   Information Management System. IBM hierarchical database system.

indicator variable A host variable used to indicate whether the associated data value actually contains data or is null. The **indicator variable**

	is set to contain a negative value (usually -1), if the host value is null.
interactive SQL	SQL statements directly invoked (e.g. using DB2I or QMF).
ISPEXEC	ISPF component which provides dialogue services for CLISTs and REXX procedures.
ISPF	Interactive System Productivity Facility, IBM programming system to provide dialogue facilities. ISPF requires TSO. ISPF is required by QMF and SPUFI.
ISPLINK	ISPF component which provides dialogue services for programs.
ISPSTART	ISPF component which invokes the ISPF environment.
JCL	Job Control Language. The statements used to control the processing of a batch job. The principal JCL statements are: DD and EXEC.
library	A partitioned dataset.
Linkage Editor	IBM program to combine one or more object modules into a load module.
load module	Machine-readable Linkage Editor output in a form suitable for loading into virtual storage for execution.
locking	The means of stopping other users from accessing (read lock) or changing data (write lock), and is used to maintain data integrity.
LRECL	Logical record length. The number of characters forming a record.
member	Independent part of a partitioned dataset. A member can be directly accessed and processed as if it were a sequential dataset.
MVS	Multiple Virtual Systems operating system.
null	For DB2, a special value indicating that this particular element (row-column) does not actually contain a value, it is not the same as 0 (for a numeric field) or blank (for a character field). See indicator variable.
object module	machine-readable compiler output.
package	A non-executable plan that is associated with a program.
panel	Form with which data is to be displayed on a display terminal.
partitioned dataset	A data set comprising of members. Each member can be accessed directly by means of its (member) name.
PDF	Program Development Facility, IBM dialogue utility package to assist the programmer in program development. PDF is an ISPF application.
PGF	Presentation Graphics Feature. Library of routines using GDDM to create presentation (business) graphics. ICU is a dialogue interface to PGF.

PL/I   Modern high-level programming language combining many of the features of COBOL and FORTRAN.

precompilation The action of converting embedded SQL statements to statements which can be processed by the host language. The precompiler also produces a DBRM entry from the SQL statements.

profile pool   The pool of dialogue variables belonging to a particular application. The profile pool is retained across ISPF/TSO sessions.

QBE   Query-By-Example. QMF component which simplifies the creation of ad-hoc queries.

QMF   Query Management Facility. End-user interface to DB2.

query   General term for an SQL statement.

revoke   The action of ignoring those changes made to the database since the last **commit**.

REXX   Restructured Extended Executor. REXX is a high-level programming language functionally similar to CLIST. REXX is more powerful than the CLIST language and has largely superseded it.

row   A horizontal element of a table and is generally synonymous with a record in conventional data processing.

SAA   Systems Application Architecture. SAA is an IBM concept designed to provide a standard interface to the user (application developer).

session   The dialogue environment for the current user. TSO is the lowest level session.

shared pool   The pool of dialogue variables belonging to the current ISPF session.

source program Input to a compiler. A source program constitutes the "computer instructions" produced by the programmer. Source programs can exist in a number of levels of detail. **Low-level** languages (e.g. Assembler) require that the programmer has an intimate knowledge of the machine instructions available on the computer on which his program will run. **High-level** languages (e.g. PL/I) remove much of this burden from the programmer and enable him to be more concerned with the procedure required to solve his program; such languages are often referred to as **procedure oriented** languages. So called **4th generation** languages (CLISTs offer certain features) are **problem oriented**. Modern high-level languages offer structuring facilities.

SPUFI   SQL Processor Using File Input. A TSO/ISPF program which can be used to process SQL statements. It is generally used to test SQL statements, perform simple DB2 administrative

	test SQL statements, perform simple DB2 administrative functions and to load limited amounts of data into DB2 tables. SPUFI, as its name implies, takes its input from datasets.
SQL	Structured Query Language. The statements used to access a DB2 database.
SQLCA	SQL Communication Area. A system area used by SQL to pass information concerning the execution of an SQL statement back to the program. Its most important field is SQLCODE, which indicates the status of the most recently executed SQL statement.
SQLDA	SQL Descriptor Area. A program area used by SQL to obtain (or return) information pertaining to the columns of the specified SQL statement, e.g. column type, column length.
static SQL	The creation of SQL statements at the time of writing the program.
system table	A database table used for internal administrative purposes, e.g. the system table SYSIBM.SYSTABLES contains an entry for each table (and view) stored in the database. Each system table name is qualified by SYSIBM.
table	In the database sense, a two-dimensional array of elements stored in or retrieved from the database.
table space	The physical (disk) storage area used to contain one or more tables.
transaction	Generally synonymous with a query.
TSO	Time Sharing Option, programming system to provide users with on-line access to computing system. TSO is now a standard MVS component.
unit of recovery	The interval between two commits or revokes.
unit of work	Transaction.
userid	The unique code for the user when he logs onto the TSO system. Also used by SQL for authorisation purposes.
view	In the database sense, a subset of one or more database tables.
word	A signed binary number which occupies 4 bytes. This is the same internal representation as a DB2 INTEGER variable.

Index

```
        } upname;
EXEC SQL END DECLARE SECTION;
char upname_data[25];
main()
{
  /* define cursor */
  EXEC SQL
   DECLARE CSR CURSOR FOR
   SELECT PNO, PNAME
   FROM PERS;
  /* open cursor */
  EXEC SQL OPEN CSR;
  /* fetch individual rows */
  do {
        EXEC SQL FETCH CSR
         INTO :upno, :upname;
        /* clear target to X'00' */
        memset(upname_data,0x00,25);
        /* move actual length */
        memcpy(upname_data,upname.data,upname.len);
        printf("SQLCODE: %d %d %s\n",SQLCODE,upno,upname_data);
    } while (SQLCODE < 100);
  EXEC SQL CLOSE CSR;
}
```

7.5.3 Dynamic SQL

Sections 7.5.1 and 7.5.2 described the use of static embedded SQL. Dynamic embedded SQL builds the SQL statement at execution-time. The PREPARE statement takes the **host statement** as input and produces an internal SQL statement identified by its **statement** name. The EXECUTE statement processes this statement. The function of the PREPARE statement and the EXECUTE statement can be combined in a single EXECUTE IMMEDIATE statement. Figure 7.2 illustrates the processing involved.

The PREPARE statement can use ? as placeholder that is replaced by the value of the corresponding host variable specified in the EXECUTE statement.

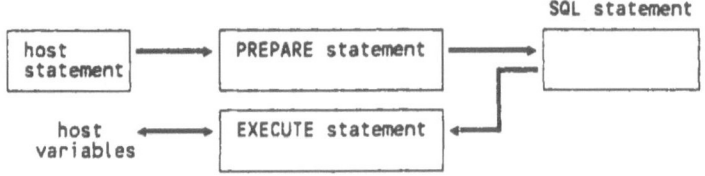

Figure 7.2 - Dynamic SQL processing

The following program examples for dynamic SQL are equivalent to the SQL query:
```
INSERT INTO PERS (PNO,PNAME) VALUES(4444,'DELTA')
```

7.5.3.1 PL/I Dynamic SQL Example.
The PL/I program uses values defined as host variables.

```
DB2P3: PROC OPTIONS(MAIN);
DCL STMT CHAR(80) VARYING
 INIT('INSERT INTO PERS (PNO,PNAME) VALUES(?,?)');
```

```
          EXEC  SQL DECLARE CSR CURSOR FOR SELECT PNAME FROM PERS
* open cursor
          EXEC  SQL OPEN CSR
* define table-end exit
          EXEC  SQL WHENEVER NOT FOUND GOTO B100
A100      DS    0H
* fetch next row
          EXEC  SQL FETCH CSR INTO :UPNAME
* list PNAME content
          LH    0,UPNAME     actual length
          TPUT  UPNAME+2,(0)          display PNAME content
          B     A100         loop
B100      EXEC  SQL CLOSE CSR
 ... program termination
          RETURN
UPNAME    DC    HL2'24',CL24' '
SQL_CA    DS    CL(SQLDLEN)
          EXEC  SQL INCLUDE SQLCA   define Communications Area
          END
```

7.5.2.3 COBOL Coding Example.

```
IDENTIFICATION DIVISION.
PROGRAM-ID. DB2CB2.
ENVIRONMENT DIVISION.
DATA DIVISION.
WORKING-STORAGE SECTION.
01 UPNAME.
   49 UPNAME-LEN             PIC  S9(4) COMP.
   49 UPNAME-DATA            PIC  X(24).
01 UPNO                      PIC  S9(4) COMP-3.
   EXEC SQL INCLUDE SQLCA END-EXEC.
PROCEDURE DIVISION.
*      define cursor
       EXEC SQL DECLARE CSR CURSOR
        FOR SELECT PNO, PNAME FROM PERS
       END-EXEC
*      open cursor
       EXEC SQL OPEN CSR END-EXEC
*      fetch individual rows
       PERFORM WITH TEST AFTER UNTIL SQLCODE = 100
           MOVE SPACES TO UPNAME-DATA
           EXEC SQL FETCH CSR INTO :UPNO, :UPNAME END-EXEC
           IF SQLCODE EQUAL 0 THEN DISPLAY UPNAME-DATA UPNO END-IF
       END-PERFORM
       EXEC SQL CLOSE CSR END-EXEC
       STOP RUN.
```

7.5.2.4 C/370 Coding Example.

```
/* db2c2 */
#include "stdefs.h"
#include "stdio.h"
EXEC SQL INCLUDE SQLCA;
EXEC SQL BEGIN DECLARE SECTION;
short int upno;
struct { short len;
         char data[24];
```